Mindfulness and Social Work

Also Available from Lyceum Books, Inc.

Mindfulness and Social Work

Steven F. Hick
Carleton University

BOOKS, INC.

Chicago, Illinois

© Lyceum Books, Inc., 2009
Published by LYCEUM BOOKS, INC.
5758 S. Blackstone Ave.
Chicago, Illinois 60637
773 + 643-1903 (Fax)
773 + 643-1902 (Phone)
lyceum@lyceumbooks.com
http://www.lyceumbooks.com

10 9   15 16

ISBN 978-1-933478-60-9

Library of Congress Cataloging-in-Publication Data

Hick, Steven F.
   Mindfulness and social work / Steven Hick.
      p.   cm.
   ISBN 978-1-933478-60-9
   1. Social service.   2. Social service—Practice.   3. Social case work.   I. Title.
   HV40.H58   2009
   361—dc22

                                              2008050678

Contents

About the Editor

Steven F. Hick, PhD, is associate professor at the School of Social Work, Carleton University, in Ottawa, Canada. He is a writer, teacher, human rights advocate, and researcher. He teaches in the area of mindfulness, human rights practice, social worker formation, and community development. He offers MBSR courses and social worker training in interpersonal mindfulness. He is co-founder of War Child Canada, an organization that educates Canadian youths about war and helps children in war zones. He is widely published in peer-reviewed journals and is the author of *Mindfulness and the Therapeutic Relationship* (2008), *Social Work in Canada* (2nd ed., 2005), *Social Work: A Critical Turn* (2005), *Social Welfare in Canada: Understanding Income Security* (2nd ed., 2007), *Advocacy, Activism, and the Internet* (2002), *Children's Rights and the Internet* (2001), and *Human Rights and the Internet* (2000).

Exercises and Figures

Exercises

Figures

Preface

There is widespread and growing interest in mindfulness within the social work profession. All helping professions, including psychology and medicine, are using mindfulness, but in many ways social work has engaged with it in unique ways. There are a range of books that detail mindfulness-based interventions, and one (Hick & Bien, 2008) that examines mindfulness and the therapeutic relationship. This is the first book on the topic of mindfulness with a specific social work focus. As we know, social work is much more than a profession doing individual and group therapy. Social workers, unlike other helping professions, practice at the community and policy levels as well. A generalist or structural practitioner might endeavor to practice at all three levels. This book therefore aims to explore how mindfulness might prove useful for social workers in relation to professional self (the inner dimension), client interventions (micro-practice), and community work (micro- and mezzo-practice).

The book presents a model for the use of mindfulness in social work practice and provides detailed discussion of how it can be incorporated into practice with individuals, families, groups, and communities. The exercises in the book can be used by workers themselves or with clients.

The first three chapters of the book lay the foundation for the exploration of applications of mindfulness within the professional practice of social work. While we admittedly only scratch the surface, these chapters should leave readers with a sense of what mindfulness is, how to go about practicing it, and a few theoretical, spiritual, and ethical considerations.

How mindfulness might affect the professional social worker is the topic of chapters 4 through 7. These chapters examine how the cultivation of mindfulness within social workers themselves might shift practice, influence client-workers relationships, or provide a means for self-care. This comprehensive coverage is warranted, as research has linked mindfulness with positive helping relationships, and further research has found that the helping relationship has more impact on outcomes than intervention techniques (Hick & Bien, 2008).

The next three chapters delve into mindfulness interventions. Much has been written and researched in this area and can be read elsewhere, but these chapters touch upon intervention with children, families, and immigrants in new ways. Finally, chapters 11, 12, and 13 explore mindfulness and community work. The authors of these chapters illustrate the importance of continuously connecting the personal and the political, not only in our analysis but also in our approach to our work. Fighting for justice and mobilizing communities is passionate and personal work, and these chapters provide new guidance not offered elsewhere.

Social work is a unique profession, and consequently it is engaging with mindfulness practice in new ways. Up until this point, most of my work within the field of mindfulness has been with psychologists and health workers. They are mostly concerned with mindfulness-based interventions that address specific disorders. There is some recent recognition that mindfulness has potential in the area of therapeutic relationships. My most recent edited collection, entitled *Mindfulness and the Therapeutic Relationship* (Hick & Bien, 2008), explores this. In addition to mindfulness-based interventions, social workers are interested in how mindfulness might affect them personally and socially. When I put out the call for chapters, I was pleasantly surprised (though not extremely surprised) to find three chapters on mindfulness and community work. In the end, it seems that social workers understand that serving others and changing the world is all about love. As bell hooks (2006) puts it, "The practice of love is the most powerful antidote to the politics of domination."

References

Hick, S. F., & Bien, T. (2008). *Mindfulness and the therapeutic relationship*. New York: Guilford Press.

hooks, b. (2006, July). Toward a worldwide culture of love. *Shambhala Sun.* Retrieved January 26, 2009, from http://www.shambhalasun.com/index .php?option = com_content&task = view&id = 2940&Itemid = 0

Acknowledgments

First, I have to recognize the crucial help freely given by Sarah Todd and Liora Birnbaum in reviewing chapters while I recovered from a concussion. Their help greatly improved the chapters they reviewed. Central to crafting a book on mindfulness is one's personal mindfulness meditation practice. Regarding this, I have been helped by many friends in the Ottawa area, especially Lynette Monteiro and Frank Musten. I am profoundly grateful to all of them. I would especially like to express my appreciation to all my meditation teachers over the years, who are too numerous to list. I would like to offer a special thanks to several teachers who have had a profound impact on my practice and commitment to mindfulness—Thich Nhat Hanh, Rebecca Bradshaw, Florence Meleo-Meyer, and Gregory Kramer. At Carleton University, my colleagues have been supportive and at the same time have challenged me to look deeply. Carleton University was the first to offer a mindfulness and social work course, and it has become a favorite of students'. I am deeply grateful to all my mindfulness-based stress reduction students for their support and insightful questions and reflections. Finally, a warm thank you to my wife, Vaida, and my children, Kristina and Justin, for always being supportive as I wandered off on yet another seven-day or ten-day mindfulness retreat.

CHAPTER ONE

Mindfulness and Social Work: Paying Attention to Ourselves, Our Clients, and Society

Steven F. Hick

What is mindfulness? What are its foundations, and how can it help social workers in their practice? Mindfulness is an orientation to our everyday experiences that can be cultivated by means of various exercises and practices. By opening up in a particular way to their internal and external experiences, social workers and clients are better able to understand what is happening to them in both a psychological and sociological sense. With this understanding, people are better able to see the variety of ways in which they can respond. Habitual reactions are more easily avoided, and inner peace and balance are developed. Social workers are increasingly using aspects of mindfulness in three ways: (1) as a means of self-care, looking inward, and cultivating mindfulness within themselves; (2) directly in their practice as an intervention within micro-practice (direct intervention with individuals, families, and groups) and in mezzo- and macro-practice (community work and policy); and (3) as a means to positively affect the helping or therapeutic relationship between social worker and client.

I came across mindfulness during my recovery from two major concussions. This story is detailed in a journal article in *Reflections: Narratives of Professional Helping* (Hick, 2008b). It took over a year to recover the first time, and three months the second time. I discovered that mindfulness had the potential to positively affect my healing. But it did not end there—the benefits of being mindful started to show them-selves in unexpected ways in my life and my social work practice, and I began to experience more clarity of thought, balance, and peace of mind. Once convinced that this was helping at the personal level, I began to see how it might be integrated into my teaching, clinical work, and community work. It has profoundly and radically changed my social work practice and the way that I live in the world. In fact, I had become disillusioned with direct practice and entered the policy field, but mindfulness has provided me with a new way to enter into relation-ships with clients that feels real, helpful, and empowering.

It is important to understand that although mindfulness often involves meditation, it is not all about introspection. Meditation is often misunderstood as a kind of narcissistic or hedonistic activity focused on the self. It actually has more to do with how we live in society. Self-awareness is central, but within a context of understanding yourself before you can effectively help others. Ultimately, the consequence may be recognition that there is really no-self[1]—that we are all intercon-nected. This can greatly affect how we respond to clients and to injus-tice in society. What we practice while meditating is merely practice for living and acting in the world. Meditation allows us to practice within a more controlled environment outside the hectic pace of living. But ultimately, we must take the practice out into the world. Mindfulness has the potential to affect social work most profoundly when it is sus-tained and integrated into our everyday work and actions. I see medi-tating as practice for my engagement with others and the world, not as some new way to relax (although this may be a byproduct) or to disen-gage from the world.

We will explore a variety of theoretical, practice-oriented, and process-oriented definitions of mindfulness that have emerged in the literature. Untangling the multiplicity of definitions is challenging. Mindfulness, however, is embodied and experiential, making objective instrumental definition difficult, if not impossible. It is tricky to under-stand conceptually and should ideally be experienced to be compre-hended. It is a journey that is cultivated through sustained practice rather than absorbed from a book—although books can help. So while this book may be helpful for formulating mindfulness and its uses for social work, ultimately you may need to sit quietly and breathe and perhaps engage in some of the exercises in this book.

---

1. The notion of no-self is complex and unique to Buddhism and many mindfulness practices. In order to experience no-self, one has first to fully know oneself. This is most often revealed with sustained meditation practice. For example, with sustained meditation, one sees that the *knowing* of an experience or thought is not personal; it doesn't have an identity, nor is it enduring.

Why Mindfulness Now?

Oprah Winfrey has produced the SoulSeries webcast, a ten-part Internet series of talks and meditations with Eckhart Tolle. Although Tolle does not use the word *mindfulness*, he is essentially talking about the same thing—how to live in the present moment, as he puts it. Upwards of 10 million people have logged on to hear Tolle and to meditate with him. This illustrates an astonishing attraction to his message and the work of mindfulness. Perhaps this is filling a spiritual void that has been left as Westerners increasingly abandon their traditional religions, or perhaps people are seeking new ways to heal and grow outside of religion. Whatever the cause, the interest is expanding rapidly.

Mindfulness, with its emphasis on awareness of the present moment, is central to models of well-being within virtually all spiritual traditions, but it can be practiced in a secular context and does not require the support of a religion. The first uses of the term *mindfulness* in the English language appeared in English translations of texts written by Siddhartha Gautama, whom we call the Buddha. "Mindfulness" is the English translation of the Pali word *sati*. Pali is the language that was used by the Buddha 2,600 years ago. Usage of the term evolved, and in the recent past it has become associated with a type of meditation, although not all mindfulness practices involve meditation (see, for example, acceptance and commitment therapy and dialectical behavior therapy later in this chapter). All this is to say that Buddhism is not the only tradition to incorporate meditation or mindfulness into its practices. All spiritual traditions have some form of meditation on or contemplation of the present moment as part of their way of life. Furthermore, mindfulness does not require devotion to any spiritual or religious tradition. It can be practiced in an entirely secular context. This makes it extremely accessible to most social workers and clients. But before introducing the practices, it would be wise for the worker to understand the client's spiritual traditions or practices, if any.

In the last twenty-five years, Western practitioners from a variety of fields have engaged in mindfulness as a healing modality (Segal, Williams, & Teasdale, 2002), for practitioner training (Hick, 2008a), for self-care (Schure, Christopher, & Christopher, 2008), and for social change (Hick & Furlotte, 2009a). Hick and Bien (2008) have explored ways in which cultivating mindfulness within practitioners themselves might be helpful in enhancing the therapeutic relationship. It has been found to be useful in addressing a wide variety of illnesses and difficulties, as well as social conditions within larger society (Hick & Furlotte, 2009a). In the past decade, there has been a large increase in the number of studies on the efficacy of mindfulness interventions for addressing various illnesses and difficulties, which are reviewed later in this chapter.

In addition, this chapter reviews how researchers in the field are reflecting on what is actually being measured, and asking questions such as, What are the components or mechanisms of action underlying mindfulness, and how do mindfulness interventions actually work? This has led several researchers to work on developing an operational definition of mindfulness, and some have developed measurement scales, all of which are discussed in this chapter. Social workers are increasingly integrating mindfulness into their practice, often in creative ways. The chapter ends with an examination of this, a review of the social work literature, and a suggested model for social workers using mindfulness in their practice.

Mindfulness: It's Not What You Think

Mindfulness is purposefully paying attention to the present moment with an attitude of openness, nonjudgment, and acceptance. This definition contains the core element of mindfulness. First, this definition posits that practice occurs on purpose. In other words, one must set the intention and be motivated to cultivate it. Secondly, the definition states that mindfulness is about paying attention to the present moment. The idea here is threefold. First, by paying attention to the present moment, we are truly alive for the moments that comprise our lives. Second, we jump out of autopilot, where we are half here and half lost in thought. This autopilot mode has been associated with inclinations toward depression, anxiety, and other negative states. When we are not paying attention, it is easier for us to unconsciously slip into rumination or some other negative mind state. Third, we are less likely to miss input signals from our bodies, which may be warnings of worse things to come. The body is an excellent early warning system but is largely ignored. Finally, there are preliminary research findings showing how mindfulness can contribute to empowerment and consciousness raising, which can lead to both personal and societal change (Hick & Furlotte, 2009b). The attitudes of openness, nonjudgment, and acceptance are other important elements of the definition. Here the message is that we must be open to, accept, and step into what is happening in the present moment before we can change it. This includes our inner and external experiences. This is not passive resignation, but rather acceptance of that which is uncontrollable or lack of resistance to that which is already happening. From this stance we are in alignment with life and better able to face difficulties with more balance and options.

A variety of researchers have outlined the definitional parameters of mindfulness. This has been done for the purposes of specifying the construct for measurement purposes. While the definitions are some-what different, they contain core similarities. Shapiro, Carlson, Astin, and Freedman (2006) posit three components (axioms) of mindfulness:

1. "On purpose" or intention,
2. "Paying attention" or attention,
3. "In a particular way" or attitude (mindfulness qualities). (p. 375)

They propose a model of the mechanisms of mindfulness whereby intentionally attending with openness and nonjudgmentalness leads to a significant shift in perspective, which they term "reperceiving." Reperceiving refers to a fundamental shift in perspective—an ability to disidentify from the contents of consciousness (i.e., thoughts) and view one's moment-by-moment experience with greater clarity and objectiv-ity (Shapiro et al., 2006). It is similar to the cognitive therapy concept of decentering.

Mark Lau and his team at the Centre for Addiction and Mental Health in Toronto describe mindfulness as a "nonelaborative, nonjudg-mental, present-centered form of awareness in which each thought, feeling, or sensation that arises in the attentional field is acknowledged and accepted as it is" (Lau et al., 2006). They introduce the notion of non-elaboration to indicate that it is not thinking about what arises, but rather noticing, bringing awareness, and letting go. Similarly, Baer, Smith, Hopkins, Krietemeyer, and Toney (2006) examine five facets of mindfulness: (1) observing, (2) describing, (3) acting with awareness, (4) nonjudging of inner experience, and (5) non-reactivity to inner experi-ence. Their notion of non-reactivity is similar to the idea of non-elaboration. In a similar attempt to operationalize mindfulness, Bishop et al. (2004) summarize all this nicely with their conception of mindful-ness as comprising two main components. The first is metacognitive skills, which involve sustained self-regulated attention, attention switching, and the inhibition of elaborative processing. The second component refers to one's orientation to the experience. This includes the maintenance of an attitude of curiosity, acceptance of one's experi-ence, and an openness to observing what comes up in the field of awareness.

Advocates of acceptance and commitment therapy define mindful-ness from the point of view of relational frame theory, a behavioral account of human language and cognition (see Hayes, Barnes-Holmes, & Roche, 2001, for a full description). Mindfulness according to this perspective aims to increase psychological flexibility or the con-scious ability to completely contact the present moment and the reac-tions it produces and change behavior in the situation in the service of chosen values (Fletcher & Hayes, 2005). Acceptance and commitment therapy is fostered by six processes: defusion, acceptance, contact with the present moment, self-as-context, values, and committed action.

Mindfulness and Mindlessness: Langer's Definition

Ellen Langer, professor of Psychology at Harvard University, draws out new categories in the formulation of mindfulness. The definitions used within therapeutic or wellness domains normally do not include these formulations. Instead, these definitions would be considered elaboration or thinking *about* experience. In addition, Langer (1989) adds a twist by looking at the social ramifications of paying attention. Her research has shown how being mindful can lead to the creation of new categories of thinking and innovative solutions to problems. Langer (1997) has defined the construct of mindfulness as consisting of five components: openness to novelty, alertness to distinction, sensitivity to differing contexts, implicit awareness of multiple perspectives, and an orientation to the present. Her view of mindfulness as a process of drawing novel distinctions is unique (Langer & Moldoveanu, 2000). In her research on mindful learning, she has found that the process of drawing novel distinctions can lead to four consequences: (1) greater sensitivity to one's environment, (2) more openness to new information, (3) the creation of new categories for structuring perception, and (4) enhanced awareness of multiple perspectives in problem solving (Langer & Moldoveanu, 2000). She explains that mindfulness is not just about paying attention to the present moment. It is about making a conscious effort to be in the moment and not to ignore the environment.

In her book entitled *Mindfulness*, Langer (1989) discusses the negative consequences of mindlessness. She finds that people may rely too rigidly on fixed categories and distinctions that limit their thinking and can also lead to stereotyping and to mislabeling. Thinking in terms of categories can be helpful in a world where we have so many choices and so much information to deal with on a daily basis, but the categories can often limit our thinking and our options.

This may be of particular concern when one is changing something, for example, working toward building a better world. If we follow Langer's reasoning, perhaps the categories used to think about the economy and society preempt any attempts to change it by limiting our options. Langer (1989) explores the dangers of "zoning out," not thinking, or not paying attention. She finds that people who are in this mental state do not shift perspectives or weigh their options. This can certainly be a problem when new situations arise, but often it is a way for people to conserve mental energy for times when it is truly needed. Performing routine tasks using automatic actions can make tasks faster. For instance, touch typists often slow down if they start looking at the keys. The problem with acting without paying attention to what you are doing, according to Langer, is that you risk relying on routine or old mental patterns of thinking. She found that people need to be able to recognize when they are on autopilot and decide when they need to really focus.

Langer's formulation emphasizes cognitive action on the perceived internal and external stimuli. Such cognitive action involves the creation of new categories and the seeking of multiple perspectives for problem solving. This adds a new dimension to the other definitions. The others emphasize nonjudgmental awareness of what is happening, to which Langer adds cognitive action. Langer does not provide any guidance on how someone can go about cultivating mindfulness and avoiding mindlessness, and to date no social workers have taken up her definition of mindfulness to inform their work. But in reading Langer, one is struck by the potential appropriateness of her orientation for social workers, particularly those involved in policy, advocacy, and community work. This may be a useful area for future research.

Mindfulness: Shifting from "Doing" Mode to "Being" Mode

The textual displays of mindfulness provide ideas about what mindfulness is, but they are just guideposts pointing in a direction. Mindfulness cannot be truly captured in language. It cannot capture what must really be experienced in order to be understood. This is perhaps why virtually all mindfulness interventions insist that practitioners have their own daily mindfulness practice before they consider using mindfulness with clients, and that they practice for a period of time—often two years or more—before doing so.

It is often said that mindfulness is a shift from "doing" mode to "being" mode. This is not intellectual perception, but rather perception with the whole being. As human beings we are more like "human doings," keeping ourselves busy with endless activities and tasks. This often operates to distract us from our lives. Doing mode involves a lot of thinking about the future or the past, not being fully in the present. We spend most of our time half lost in thought, dwelling on the past, or fantasizing about the future. But don't take my word for it—you should verify this for yourself. Next time you are in the shower or brushing your teeth or driving a car, see how much of the time you are present with the activity and how much you are not. All in all, we might say that we are not really all that present for our lives. And to make things worse, much of this thinking is conceptual, using various categories and labels to order the thoughts into "good" and "bad" experiences. This can lead to a grasping for what the mind labels good and a resistance to the bad. This grasping and resistance can lead to unease and even intense anguish. Mindfulness is about not minding what happens—a kind of inner non-resistance to what happens. This does not mean that we no longer take action to bring about change in our lives or society. On the contrary, when our being is aligned with the present moment, our actions become empowered by an often untapped intelligence—what Eckhart Tolle calls "the intelligence of Life itself" (2005, p. 199).

Being mode accepts what is happening in the present moment and involves directly experiencing the present without asking ourselves, "Is it good?" or "Is it bad?" Meditation can be an activity that is character-ized by a being mode. But this is not always the case. We can get too caught up in relaxing and doing meditation right. Meditation then becomes driven by a doing mode rather than a being mode. This is where mindfulness comes in. It is nonjudgmental moment-to-moment awareness. In short, it is dwelling in the being mode with acceptance. To stay in the being mode, we need to hold it lightly. As soon as we grasp or strive for a being mode state of mind, it will vanish. Even if the mind is active, we are merely aware of active mind. We are not trying to blank out or suppress thoughts. By continuously being aware of and attending to the emergent nature of phenomena as they arise in con-sciousness, we can begin to recognize the nature of attachments made to these phenomena as they arise. These attachments give them sig-nificance. As we will see, this basic realization can have profound impacts on our relationship to difficulties in our lives—for us as social workers and for clients.

Mindfulness generally involves meditation, which one can do sitting on a chair or on a cushion on the floor, standing or lying down, in movement, or during any number of daily activities. Meditation is an activity that sounds easy—sit and follow your breath, as in exercise 1.2— but it can present difficulties. It takes patience, energy, and determina-tion. Meditation is useful because it cultivates a capacity for paying attention. It allows us to develop this capacity in a controlled environ-ment with less sensory stimulation than is normally present in our daily lives. Once it is cultivated in this environment, it can more easily be transferred to our everyday lives. One begins meditation training by simplifying and narrowing one's focus of attention, for example, on the breath or parts of the body. By intentionally observing something like the breath, a feature of life that is almost always taken for granted, one begins to train the mind in mindfulness. By simply feeling the sensa-tions of the breath entering and leaving the body, one can practice being in the present moment. It sounds like a simple exercise, but trying it reveals how difficult it actually is to do. The mind will wander off, thinking about this or that—what happened yesterday or planning the afternoon. This is entirely normal and not any indication that meditation might not be for you. In fact, noticing that the mind has wandered is a moment of mindfulness. While guiding people in meditation, I often instruct people to congratulate themselves for having noticed the wandering mind and then to gently bring their awareness back to the breath.

Mindfulness does not end with the cultivation of concentration or the focusing of our attention on a particular object, such as the breath. It goes on with practices intended to cultivate insight or deep seeing. *Insight* refers to a clear awareness of what is happening as it happens. This is perhaps what most distinguishes mindfulness meditation from meditation techniques that involve only concentrating on an object and settling the mind down until the mental activity of ordinary waking consciousness is transcended. An example is transcendental meditation (TM), a trademarked form of meditation introduced in 1958 by Maharishi Mahesh Yogi. The result of TM is a sense of rapture and calm. In mindfulness meditation, concentration is merely the precursor to the cultivation of awareness or tuning into your emotional states, moods, thoughts, and physical sensations.

Different forms of meditation, body awareness work, and hypnosis have influenced social work practice for many decades. The influence of mindfulness is more recent. Some are referring to mindfulness and its tremendous impact on psychology as the third wave in Western psychology (Hayes, 2004; Hayes, Follette, & Linehan, 2004). The first wave was behavior therapy, primarily in the 1960s, followed by cognitive therapy, which developed in the 1970s. Third-wave interventions include mindfulness training or practices directed toward the development of particular qualities such as awareness, acceptance, compassion, and openness to new experience. The influence within social work is similar.

Clinical Benefits of Being Mindful

Studies of clinical interventions using mindfulness have shown a wide variety of benefits, as explained in the next section. Furthermore, neuroscience studies have indicated positive changes to the brain and the body's immune function after even brief meditation experience. Several benefits have been identified in the literature.

- Clear awareness of thoughts and emotions
- Ability to relate in new ways to pain and difficulties

- Ability to experience/transform or defuse emotional distress
- Space where creative solutions can arise
- Development of self-awareness and positive self-image
- Greater sense of well-being and ease in the world
- Ability to respond to stress more effectively
- Ability to make choices with greater clarity and awareness

As one reads about the potential benefits of mindfulness, it is crucial to remember that mindfulness is a non-striving activity. If one tries too hard to attain some special state, often the opposite occurs. This happens because when the special state does not occur, which is inevitably the case, judgment and self-criticism kick in. The judging mind is tight and tense, which is the opposite of the effect desired. Relaxation is often a byproduct of mindfulness, but in my experience, if it is set up as a goal at the outset, it will be elusive. This presents an interesting paradox for social work practitioners offering mindfulness interventions. Most often, people come to social workers with expectations and the desire for results. Within a mindfulness approach, these expectations may have to be placed to the side, at least in the beginning phases. Clients are usually told in the first session to put aside their goals and let go or let things be and rest in awareness, observing the mind, body, and the world unfolding in the present moment. *Letting go* refers to the ability to relinquish involvement in self-perpetuating cognitive routines—freeing oneself from the attachment and aversion that drive us.

While much of the research on mindfulness involves clinical trials of various mindfulness interventions (see next section), there is a rapidly emerging body of research on brain function and mindfulness meditation. Davidson, Kabat-Zinn, Schumacher, Rosenkranz, Muller, Santorelli, et al. (2003) found an increase in brain function and increased immune activity with twenty-five participants in mindfulness-based stress reduction (MBSR). The participants' pre- and post-MBSR electroencephalography showed increased left anterior activation, which is associated with increased positive emotion, compared to a control group. The MBSR group also showed an increased immune capability when given an influenza vaccine. In another study, using functional MRI scans of the brain, Jha, Krompinger, and Baime (2007) found that mindfulness meditation can improve attention-related responses by enhancing the ability to orient attention (limiting attention to a subset of inputs) and to alert (maintaining an alert state of preparedness). They found enhanced functioning of the bilateral dorsal frontoparietal system (orienting) and the ventral frontoparietal system (alerting). Such studies begin to show how mindfulness meditation can directly change our brains (called neuroplasticity) and bodies.

Mindfulness Applications

Mindfulness has been used in a wide variety of clinical and therapeutic contexts. It is being used in group settings in programs such as MBSR programs (Kabat-Zinn, 1990). To a more limited degree, mindfulness is being used in individual interventions and in community applications. In their overview of mindfulness-based interventions, Salmon, Santorelli, and Kabat-Zinn (1998) documented 240 programs. Baer (2003, 2006) and Praissman (2008) provide reviews of mindfulness-based interventions.

Most often it is a requirement for a social worker offering mindfulness interventions in any format to have adopted the practice for him- or herself (Segal, Teasdale, Williams, & Gemar, 2002). Kabat-Zinn (2003) maintains that practitioners need to recognize the distinctive qualities of mindfulness as a meditative process and that mindfulness is not simply a technique to be handed on to others. To date, there is no research to substantiate this claim.

Now being offered in over 250 medical centers in the United States, MBSR is the most widely used mindfulness intervention. MBSR has been shown to be effective with chronic pain (Kabat-Zinn, 1984, 1990; Kabat-Zinn, Lipworth, Burney, & Sellers, 1987), stress (Shapiro, Schwartz, & Bonner, 1998), caregiver stress (Minor, Carlson, Mackenzie, Zernicke, & Jones, 2006), disordered eating (Kristeller & Hallett, 1999), psoriasis (Kabat-Zinn et al., 1998), cancer (Monti et al., 2006; Speca, Carlson, Goodey, & Angen, 2000), and suicidal behavior (Linehan, Armstrong, Suarez, Allmon, & Heard, 1991; Williams, Duggan, Crane, & Fennell, 2006).

A meta-analysis of studies testing the clinical effectiveness of MBSR found a significant effect size of $d = 0.5$ (Grossman, Schmidt, Niemann, & Walach, 2004). Within these interventions, mindfulness has a twofold aim: first, to gain insight into how automatic and habitual patterns of over-identification and cognitive reactivity to sensations, thoughts, and emotions increase stress and emotional distress, and second, to reduce the vulnerability of these mind states, thereby producing lasting improvements in emotional well-being (Lau et al., 2006).

MBSR consists of eight weekly two- to three-hour classes and one daylong class. It includes formal guided instruction in mindfulness meditation and mindful body movement practices. In addition, it includes exercises to enhance awareness in everyday life; daily assignments lasting from forty-five minutes to an hour, which are largely meditations; and methods for improving communication. The program emphasizes being present with sensations within the body, and then expanding this to emotions and thoughts and then ultimately to communication and life in general. MBSR aims to help people develop an ongoing meditation practice.

Building on MBSR, mindfulness-based cognitive therapy (MBCT) was developed as a treatment approach to reduce relapse and recurrence of depression (Segal, Williams, et al., 2002). Two controlled clinical trials found that MBCT can reduce the likelihood of relapse by 40 percent to 50 percent in people who have suffered three or more previous episodes of depression (Kenny & Williams, 2007; Ma & Teasdale, 2004; Teasdale, Segal, Williams, Ridgeway, Soulsby, & Lau, 2000). MBCT combines several elements of cognitive therapy techniques such as education on the role of negative thoughts, and how rumination, avoidance, suppression, and struggling with unhelpful cognitions and emotions can perpetuate distress rather than resolve it (Williams et al., 2006). MBCT does, however, differ substantially from cognitive therapy. It focuses on the acceptance of thoughts as thoughts rather than strategies to change the content of thinking. Instead of teaching participants how to replace negative thoughts with positive thoughts, MBCT focuses on teaching people to notice the effects of negative thoughts and how to change their relationships to them. Recently research has been exploring how MBCT can be used with people who display suicidal behavior (Williams et al., 2006).

Other well-known programs include dialectical behavior therapy and acceptance and commitment therapy. Dialectical behavior therapy (DBT) integrates behavior therapy with mindfulness practices; it was originally developed to treat people diagnosed with borderline personality disorder (Linehan, 1993). DBT is wider in scope than other mindfulness interventions, including a range of behavioral and cognitive strategies designed to help individuals change their behaviors, emotions, and thoughts. Robins and Chapman (2004), in their review of DBT studies, showed strong empirical support for its efficacy. Huss and Baer (2007) explore the potential utility of integrating MBCT with DBT for a range of problems. DBT is expanding beyond its original intended target population for conditions such as depression and anxiety (Marra, 2004) and is showing some promising results.

The last mindfulness-based intervention that will be reviewed here is acceptance and commitment therapy, or ACT (Hayes, Strosahl, & Wilson, 1999). Like MBSR, ACT takes a wellness approach and is not targeted at a particular illness or disorder. ACT aims to alter the potentially harmful effects of unwanted thoughts and feelings by modifying the psychological contexts in which they are experienced. This emphasis on function and context is based on the behavior-analytic philosophy of functional contextualism (Biglan & Hayes, 1996) and relational frame theory (Hayes et al., 2001). According to Hayes (2005), ACT is designed to help people change the way they approach their problems. It uses techniques within three categories: mindfulness, acceptance, and values-based living. In addition to the mindfulness practices that other interventions use, ACT guides participants through various exercises that cultivate active forms of acceptance or embracing the moment as it is (for example, see exercise 1.2). Hayes points out that this is a difficult idea to grasp, as it is not nihilistic self-defeatism or indifference to pain and suffering. Other exercises explore participants' values, life goals, and strategies for effective action.

The practices contained in mindfulness-based interventions include a variety of exercises and meditations. MBSR and MBCT emphasize formal guided meditations combined with informal mindful-living exercises. ACT and DBT emphasize nonmeditation-based activities and exercises. For example, ACT uses different exercises that focus on noticing, observing, letting go, and accepting that are not meditation based. For example, one ACT exercise called Leaves in a Stream helps clients detach from the language of thoughts. In it clients are asked to close their eyes and imagine leaves floating down a stream. Clients are guided in noticing their thoughts as they arise, imagining placing each thought on a leaf, and watching it float away. This nonjudgmental approach to thoughts enables people to tap into acceptance. Similarly, DBT aims to develop skills that are focused on observing, describing, participating, taking a nonjudgmental stance, and focusing, largely without any of the meditation practice of MBSR or MBCT. See exercise 1.1 for an example of a DBT exercise. This exercise is intended to assist you in desensitizing yourself to intense emotions. Desensitization is the process of engaging with an emotion to reduce the fear associated with it.

Social workers are offering a variety of mindfulness-based group interventions in a range of contexts, from hospitals to community health clinics and private practice. In addition, social workers are experimenting with combining various aspects of the interventions for specific populations and integrating particular aspects into individual and family practice.

While social workers are using all the therapies described above, they are also engaging with mindfulness in unique ways, due in part to the uniqueness of the profession. Social workers are often more likely than other helping professionals to be providing services to the severely disadvantaged in society. Another distinct feature of social work is its historical and current focus on considering the person in his or her context or environment. This generally involves more consideration of economic and social structures. As you will see in the review of the mindfulness and social work literature, social workers are engaging with ideas around mindfulness in unique ways. For example, social workers, more so than other serving professions, are considering the role of mindfulness in helping caregivers and people who care for chronically ill family members (Minor et al., 2006). In this context social workers

---

EXERCISE 1.1

Mindfulness of Painful Emotions

1. Feel the emotion. Take a moment to get in touch with the emotion. Don't choose an emotion that is too overwhelming when you first do this exercise. Now, imagine the emotion as a wave in the ocean. It comes toward you, like a wave coming toward the shore, and then recedes. Follow the flow of the waves as they rise to a peak and then recede and finally break.
2. Next, imagine that you are on a warm beach, the sun warming your face and a cool breeze blowing on your face. Imagine that the emotion is a wave on the ocean and the cool breeze blowing on your face makes the emotion a little lighter and less intense.
3. Imagine yourself at the beach, where the water is so blue that you can see the crystal-white water as the waves come toward the shore—flowing, rising, and then receding and breaking.
4. Imagine that the emotion is intense, but only when you look at it from a distance—as you would look at the ocean from a distance. As you get closer, just as the waves become less intense as they reach the shore, so too do your emotions. Imagining that the sun warms your body and the cool breeze cools your face; observe the emotion as small and less intense.
5. Go back and forth between the image of the ocean, which allows you to feel comfortable and steady, and the emotion, which makes you feel tense and afraid. As you go back and forth, notice the breath as you inhale and exhale. Feel the rhythmic flow of the breath.
6. Notice the flow of the breath in and out and the waves flowing toward and away from the shore. Paying close attention to the emotion, notice how you can increase and decrease its intensity—how it can flow in and out like the waves of the ocean.
7. Notice how you can influence your feelings as you pay attention to it in this way. Notice how going back and forth between the comforting experience of being on the beach and the mindfulness of an emotion changes your experience of the emotion.

Source: Adapted from Marra, T. (2004). *The dialectical behavior therapy workbook for overcoming depression and anxiety*. Oakland, CA: New Harbinger.

---

are considering the ways in which mindfulness can contribute to mental health rather than discussing it in terms of treatment for a mental disorder defined by the *Diagnostic and Statistical Manual of Mental Disorders*. Other distinctive engagements with mindfulness include examination of mindfulness and the positive transformation of professional self-concept (Birnbaum, 2005b) and the investigation of ways that mindfulness might shift forms of knowing within a critical or social justice approach to practice (Wong, 2004). The discussion of community work and mindfulness is unique and not available in any other publication, as far as I know.

Measures of Mindfulness: Objectified or Embodied?

The conceptual definitions of mindfulness are being operationalized into measures of mindfulness. These scales, developed within the discipline of psychology, are being used primarily to research the effectiveness of clinical interventions that aim to increase mindfulness in a client population. Social workers endeavoring to prove the effectiveness of mindfulness interventions are using the scales. There are nine mindfulness measures, eight of which are based on the self-reporting of particular trait-like measures, and one measures mindfulness as a state-like construct. The trait-based measures are the Five Facet Mindfulness Questionnaire (Baer et al., 2006), the Mindful Attention Awareness Scale (Brown & Ryan, 2003), the Freiburg Mindfulness Inventory (Buchheld, Grossman, & Walach, 2001), the Kentucky Inventory of Mindfulness Skills (Baer, Smith, & Allen, 2004), the Cognitive and Affective Mindfulness Scale (Feldman, Hayes, Kumar, & Greeson, 2004), the Mindfulness Questionnaire (Chadwick, Hember, Mead, Lilley, & Dagnan, 2005), the Revised Cognitive and Affective Mindfulness Scale (Feldman et al., 2006), and the Philadelphia Mindfulness Scale (Cardaciotto, Herbert, Forman, Moitra, & Farrow, 2008).

The scales tend to measure different aspects of mindfulness and take different approaches. The newest instrument, the Five Facet Mindfulness Questionnaire, resulted from factor analysis of questionnaires measuring a trait-like general tendency to be mindful in daily life. It consists of thirty-nine items assessing five facets of mindfulness: observing, describing, acting with awareness, nonjudging of inner experience, and non-reactivity to inner experience. It has become the measure of choice for researchers, replacing the Mindful Attention Awareness Scale as the standard. Brown and Ryan's (2003) Mindful Attention Awareness Scale measures attention and awareness but does not measure other important aspects of mindfulness such as compassion, nonjudgmental, openness to new experiences, insightful understanding, and non-striving. The Kentucky Inventory of Mindfulness Skills primarily measures qualities and skills taught in dialectical behavioral therapy. Lau and ten colleagues (2006) developed the Toronto Mindfulness Scale, which takes a different approach. It measures mindfulness as a state-like phenomenon (as opposed to a trait-like quality) that is induced and maintained through attention regulation. The scale is a reliable and valid measure useful in investigations of the mediating role of mindful awareness in mindfulness-based interventions (Lau et al., 2006).

Perhaps surprisingly, there is little in the way of critique of this objectified and somewhat positivist approach to developing scales that measure mindfulness. Given the obvious similarities between mindfulness and phenomenology in its approach to phenomena and consciousness, it is surprising that mindfulness researchers have not questioned the conceptualization and categorization of mindfulness into researchable hypotheses in favor, perhaps, of reflections and inquiry into the foundations of current knowledge based on lived experience.

Mindfulness seems antithetical to objectification and measurement. Since mindfulness is a state of mind that is embodied by people, it is in many ways beyond concepts. The objectification and abstract conceptualization of mindfulness is contradictory and may even be counterproductive. Can we use conceptually based positivist research methodologies to capture something that is experiential? Are the current initiatives to operationalize and objectively measure mindfulness consistent with the embodied nature of mindfulness? This is difficult to answer. Generally the attempts to define and capture mindfulness have enlivened debate and discussion at academic conferences. From my experience as a mindfulness practitioner, I see mindfulness as entirely empirical in that I do not take anything as the truth until I personally subject it to experiential testing (not experimental testing).

Perhaps mindfulness can be researched, but I imagine that it would have to make use of methods that are quite different from those commonly used in the social sciences. Such research initiatives would need to proceed from an embodied, open-ended, reflective mode. *Embodied mode* refers to reflection that brings mind and body together. *Open-ended reflection* denotes a reflection in which one is aware that the reflection itself is a form of experience that can be done mindfully. This can disrupt the habitual chain of thinking. Research in a positivist mode tends to see reflection as just *on* experience. Mindfulness-based research would see reflection as *in* the experience itself.

Mindfulness Practices: Meditation and More

Formal and informal meditation practices and nonmeditation-based exercises are currently used to cultivate mindfulness. Formal meditation involves sustained attention on a particular object (i.e., the breath) or choiceless awareness (with whatever arises). An example of this kind of meditation is exercise 1.2, called Awareness of Breathing. The breath

EXERCISE 1.2

Awareness of Breathing

1. Find a comfortable position either on the floor, on a cushion, or on a chair. If you are on a chair, place your feet flat on the floor, and hold your back straight but not rigid. Sit very still, breathing normally, in a quiet room, if that is possible.

2. Assume an attitude of nonjudging, patience, non-striving, acceptance, trust, and letting be.

3. Let go of any agenda about how things should be. Do not try to make anything in particular happen; do not even try to relax.

4. Bring awareness to your abdomen, allowing the abdomen to relax and become soft, gently letting the abdomen stay soft.

5. Direct your attention to the sensations of your breath as it comes and goes. Concentrate your awareness at the place in your body where you can feel the breath come and go most easily and naturally. For some, this is the abdomen, for others the chest, and for others the nose. Let your attention settle, and focus exactly on that place where the breath sensations are easiest for you to feel.

6. Allow the breath to breathe itself—flowing naturally—not trying to control it. This practice is about strengthening attention and awareness, not controlling the breath.

7. Let go of any thoughts about how many breaths you are taking or the next breath or the last breath—just this breath, moment by moment. If it helps you to focus, you could silently whisper to yourself, "In" on the in breath, "Out" on the out breath, and "Pause" for the spaces between breaths.

8. Let your attention settle more deeply on the variety of sensations of the breath in the body. Remain present for the entire cycle of the breath in the body. Notice the beginning of the in breath, the middle, the end, and space between.

9. Notice the changing patterns of sensations—how each breath is different. Perhaps you notice that some breaths are shallow and some deep, some strong and some weak, some rough and some smooth. Feel each breath as if you are breathing for the first time—with intense curiosity.

10. When the mind wanders, do not be surprised. Gently notice where it went. Is it on another part of the body? A thought or a series of thoughts? Perhaps worry or anxiety or planning? No matter where it goes, with patience and kindness, gently escort your attention back to the place in the body where you are concentrating on your breath sensation. Remember that recognizing that the mind is wandering is a moment of mindfulness. It is part of the training of the mind that you have undertaken.

(exercise 1.2 continued)

11. Keep your belly soft, noticing any tightness or tension in the body. Allow softening.
12. Do not try too hard. Do not even try to be a good meditator. Simply make your best effort to pay attention to the breath sensations with nonjudging. Let things be. Let distractions go.
13. Continue to open up as much as possible, allowing yourself to feel the sensations of each breath directly, as best you can.
14. Bring your awareness back to the room, wiggle your fingers, and stretch forward if you like. Gently open your eyes—notice how you are feeling, then let that feeling go. Avoid any attempts to make any single meditation session the standard for how all others must be. Let each practice session stand alone. If your mind tends to compare and to judge one session against another, just notice that and let it go. Try not to judge yourself for having judged. It is merely the habit of the judging mind. Just let it go.

is central to mindfulness. Being aware of one's breathing throughout the day as often as possible can be powerfully transformative. Conscious breathing takes attention away from thinking. It stops the mind. Try it for yourself—try breathing consciously and thinking at the same time. You will find that it is impossible. Awareness of breath forces you into the present moment and into the "being" mode.

The best way to understand formal meditation practice is to meditate. This can be done while we are sitting, lying down, moving (yoga is meditation in motion), or standing. Informal mindfulness is the application of mindful attention in everyday life. We might mindfully brush our teeth or mindfully eat a raisin, the latter being the first exercise in several mindfulness interventions. Mindful conversation and mindful walking are other informal mindfulness practices introduced in a variety of clinical and therapeutic settings. But any daily activity can be the object of informal mindfulness practice. In my mindfulness classes I engage people early on with informal practice, asking them to mindfully undertake one activity each day between classes and report on the experience. The list of activities they report is endless and includes mindfully folding laundry, brushing teeth, and sitting in the yard, paying attention to aromas.

We can look at eating as an example of how this process might operate (see exercise 1.3). Often when we eat, we simply shovel the food in our mouths, sometimes while watching TV or reading the newspaper.

EXERCISE 1.3

Mindful Eating

1. Sit quietly, taking an upright and dignified posture, noticing any sensations in your body. Perhaps you notice the sensation of the buttocks touching the chair. Notice the anticipation in your mind of the meal to come.
2. Look closely at the food on your plate, noticing the color, the smells. Perhaps you notice the steam coming off any hot items. Take a really close look at the food.
3. Slowly beginning to eat, notice your fork as it is placed into the food or perhaps noticing the knife setting through a piece of food. Perhaps you notice the texture of the food as it is cut. Notice the amount of food that you are taking. Be aware of your arm bringing the food to your mouth and how both your arm and your mouth know exactly what to do.
4. Take a mindful bite. Pay attention to the texture and taste of the food as you bite into it and chew it. Explore any sensations in the body as you taste the food.
5. Bring awareness to how the food changes as you chew. Notice when the impulse to swallow arises. Is the food fully chewed, or has the pleasurable taste sensation brought about a desire for more food *now*? If the food is very tasty, there might be a tendency to gobble the food.
6. Eat slowly mouthful by mouthful, exploring all the sensations. Treat this mindful eating as you would any other meditation practice. If your mind wanders, as it inevitably will, notice the wandering, and gently bring your attention back to eating.
7. If you find that your eating is speeding up, simply pause, putting down your utensil, closing your eyes, and gently bringing your awareness to your body sitting in the chair and the food on your plate.

We may not be aware of the actual activity of eating. In eating meditation, we eat slowly, noticing the sensations of the food in our mouths, the tastes, perhaps how the tastes and sensations change as we chew and then when we swallow. We bring into our awareness the entire process and its accompanying sensations. We might tune into the smells and visuals of the food. Engaging in mindfulness in daily living activities such as eating not only enables people to cultivate awareness; it enables people to see how being mindful can change their experience of living. Participants report that their usual experience of eating changes. It is more vivid and alive. Informal practice is the precursor to mindful living. It is meditation in action, whereby we are in touch with everything that is going on within us physically, emotionally, and mentally.

Mindfulness can also be cultivated using nonmeditation-based practices. Nonmeditation-based mindfulness exercises are used primarily in dialectical behavior therapy (Linehan, 1993) and ACT (Hayes et al., 1999). ACT consists of forty-one exercises, nine of which are of the formal or informal meditation type. ACT uses an exercise called Your Suffering Inventory, in which a person lists and ranks painful and difficult issues in his or her life. There is an ACT exercise that asks participants to get a clear picture of a yellow Jeep in their minds and then try as hard as they can not to think even one single thought of a yellow Jeep. Participants quickly learn how difficult it is to suppress thoughts. Exercise 1.4 is an example of a nonmeditation-based ACT exercise. In DBT, a variety of questionnaires, tables, and exercises are used to assist clients in regulating emotions, increasing a sense of personal identity, and

---

EXERCISE 1.4

Watching the Mind Train: Nonmeditation ACT Exercise

1. Imagine that you are at a railway bridge, looking down at three train tracks going under the bridge. Three slowly moving trains amble along, one on each of the tracks.
2. Now, picture the first train carrying the things you notice in the present moment, such as sensations and feelings—for example, sounds, body sensations, heartbeats. Train 2 carries only your thoughts, including evaluations and commentary, and train 3 carries your urges to act, to pull away, or to make things different.
3. Sitting quietly, begin by thinking of something that you have struggled with lately. Get this difficult situation clear in your mind.
4. Now, closing your eyes, picture the three tracks. Stay on the bridge, noticing if your mind wanders away and what took you away, and gently bring yourself back to the bridge. Avoid judging yourself, but rather congratulate yourself for having noticed the wandering. This is a moment of mindfulness.
5. As you observe the three tracks, notice what is on each train as it relates to your difficult situation. Notice what comes up for you. On a three-column chart, write down what you noticed in each train as you were standing on the bridge.

Source: Adapted from Hayes, S. C., & Smith, S. (2005). *Get out of your mind and into your life: The new acceptance and commitment therapy.* Oakland, CA: New Harbinger.

sharpening judgment and observation skills. These interventions often involve paying attention to environmental elements such as music or aromas as informal meditations.

Mindfulness and Social Work

Social work practitioners are embracing mindfulness on three main levels: as an intervention approach (individual intervention, group work, and community work), as a means for cultivating a positive therapeutic relationship with clients, and for self-care for both workers and family caregivers. As previously discussed, the vast majority of research and publications on mindfulness have occurred in psychology and medicine and on the topic of group intervention approaches.

In many cities across North America and around the world there are many social workers delivering mindfulness-based interventions. In addition, given the uniqueness of social work as a helping profession, social workers may be integrating the concept in new ways. To date, social workers have not discussed or analyzed their work in publications. There are fewer than a dozen publications on the topic by social workers.

I have researched and developed a new approach specifically targeted at severely marginalized people as well as people facing multiple and severe difficulties often resulting in homelessness (Hick & Furlotte, 2009b). Called radical mindfulness training, it builds on existing mindfulness interventions but does so in a way that directly engages participants at the personal, interpersonal, and structural levels. The program was developed with the direct involvement of the target population. In addition, Bien and I have done extensive work examining how mindfulness might have a positive impact on the therapeutic relationship, resulting in a book entitled *Mindfulness and the Therapeutic Relationship* (Hick & Bien, 2008). Finally, Furlotte and I have explored the theory and practice of a combined mindfulness and social justice–oriented social work intervention (Hick & Furlotte, 2009a). This new and unique work aims to link the theory of social justice–oriented approaches to social work with mindfulness and begin to unravel practice approaches within this new terrain. Yuk-Lin Renita Wong (2004) examines mindfulness-based critical social work pedagogy. She examines ideas that are useful for social work practice, but she largely discusses pedagogy and education, as the title of her article, "Knowing through Discomfort: A Mindfulness-Based Critical Social Work Pedagogy," implies. She contrasts "discursive rationality" (which refers to a dominant form of knowledge categories and "knowns" about the world) with "listening rationality." Listening rationality opens us up to the contradictions and richness of being, which are not bound by conceptual ordering. She goes on to present how this has affected her teaching of critical social work ideas to students. She discusses how, when teaching about systemic oppressions, she asked students to stay in touch with and embrace their feelings of discomfort, not to judge them wrong and push them away. Here Wong is really encouraging students to pay attention to internal events and notice how their thinking can be dominated by habitual categories. Wong's exploration of mindfulness and critical social education moves educators toward inquiring into the ways that we construct knowledge, and perhaps providing room for students to discover and honor marginalized knowledge. Other authors outside social work (e.g., Orr, 2002) have similarly discussed the utility of mindfulness in anti-oppressive educational pedagogies.

Coholic discusses how mindfulness meditation can be effective within group work (Coholic, 2006; Coholic & LeBreton, 2007). She has found that learning mindfulness helped the group participants sort through their thoughts more effectively and gain perspective on issues. Specifically, Coholic's participants reported that mindfulness meditation practice assisted them in gaining a deeper level of self-awareness, a less judgmental attitude, a more positive sense of self-esteem, a greater appreciation for life's moments, and increased feelings of gratefulness.

Birnbaum (2005b) discusses mindfulness and the transformation of professional self-concept in social work students. She presents the results of a research study that examines the impact of guided meditation on social work students but does not address issues related to social change or consciousness raising. The study found that meditation has the potential to help social work students become attuned to internal processes, become aware of new information, and explore professional self-image. Her other two articles discuss specific social work interventions involving mindfulness meditation practices. One describes an innovative therapeutic intervention administered in a group-workshop format with suicide survivors (Birnbaum, 2005a), and one discusses the use of mindfulness with adolescents with aggression issues (Birnbaum & Birnbaum, 2004). She found that mindfulness facilitated healing, self-awareness, and growth toward autonomy by helping adolescents connect to their inner voice.

Finally, Thomas Keefe (1975a, 1975b) has explored meditation, Zen, and social work casework. A book by social worker Elana Rosenbaum (2005) presents mindfulness meditation for working with cancer patients.

Several authors explore mindfulness within an explicitly Buddhist context. Loretta Pyles (2005) explores the implications of engaged Buddhism on social work practice and social change work. She found that an engaged Buddhism emphasis on attention to the process of social change is helpful for social work. In Australia, Lai-Kwan Regin (2001) develops the notion of a non-attachment practice stance flowing from the Buddhist idea of emptiness in her doctorial dissertation. She sees social work practice, like all other lived experiences, as constantly changing, with no true boundaries. Canda and Furman (1999) examine the notion of interconnectedness as an extension of social work's idea of person in the environment. An early book by social worker David Brandon (1976) explores the implications of various Zen ideas for social work practice. His discussion is very much about the impacts of being mindful on our work and clients. He emphasizes the cultivation of compassion, a sense of nowness when we truly listen, and an open and egalitarian relationship with clients.

This book builds on this scholarship and experience. Several authors in this book discuss social work's unique contribution to the area of community work and social change and the role that mindfulness might play in this. Many social workers practice in community settings or in social change work. They work on the so-called front lines, directly engaging the institutions of society. I have found that mindfulness has a valuable contribution to make here. Its emphasis on paying attention to process and compassionate listening provides community workers with both an overarching perspective on change and a new range of tools.

Inner, Micro, and Mezzo- and Macro-Practice: Mindfulness at Three Levels

The contribution of mindfulness can be seen as occurring at three levels: within the person, or the inner dimension; in micro-practice (direct intervention with individuals, families, groups, and communities); and in mezzo- and macro-practice (community work and policy). At first glance, these may seem disparate topics, but if one truly holds holistic perspectives, then all levels become simultaneously relevant. Mindfulness has the potential to affect social work at all three levels, and social workers are uniquely using mindfulness at all three levels. Figure 1.1 represents a start at formulating the multilevel role of mindfulness in social work.

Often when people first consider mindfulness, only the introspective or inner work comes to mind. This may be caused by a common misperception of mindfulness as having to do only with formal sitting meditation (this is itself a misconception of formal meditation). Having said this, we must admit that the inner level is important. At the inner level, mindfulness involves a present-moment orientation. This enables us to engage with what is actually happening to us and can preempt our

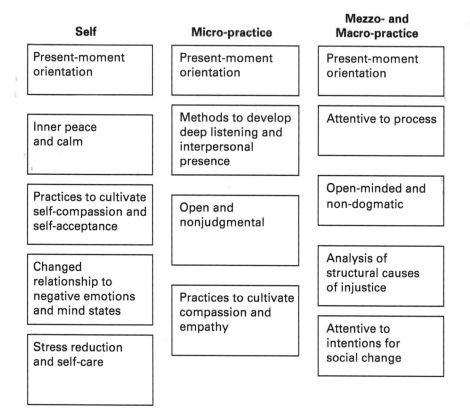

FIGURE 1.1 *The Role of Mindfulness in Social Work*

usual tendency to worry about the past or fantasize about the future. A present-moment orientation can bring inner peace and can facilitate a more attentive approach to working with others. Mindfulness contains practices to cultivate self-compassion and self-acceptance. By allowing and embracing whatever comes up in the present moment, we can change our relationship to negative emotions and mind states. We begin to see thoughts as thoughts, not as facts or as somehow representative of our core personality. All of this enables us as social workers to care for ourselves with kindness. We must learn to care for ourselves before we can effectively care for others.

At the micro-practice level, mindfulness can alter how we interact with others, especially our clients. The present-moment orientation allows us to tune into what is going on within us and around us while we are practicing social work. Over time we begin to realize that much of our inner talk is not accurate or helpful to the client—that we often jump to conclusions and judgments about our clients. By pausing and relaxing into what our clients are saying, we are able to listen deeply—to really be present—not think about what we are going to say next or how we can fix their problems. With mindfulness, we are open to the flow of understanding without judgment and with acceptance. Finally, mindfulness involves practices that actively cultivate compassion and empathy toward others. These are meditations that can be practiced and that grow these seeds within us.

Mezzo- and macro-level practice emphasize community work and making society into a more sustainable and equitable organization. The attention to the here and now allows us to uncover how institutions in society interlink with our everyday actions. During my PhD studies, I studied with Dorothy Smith, who taught me to look at everyday activities to explicate macro relations in society in relation to everyday activities. I have continued with this in my mindfulness work. In addition, when we are mindful, we tend to be more attentive to the details of process, and anyone who has been involved in social change work can attest that process is key. This kind of attentiveness helps us build alliances, enlist additional support, and ensure that all voices are heard. I have found that keeping an open mind and not tenaciously holding onto what I think needs to be done causes a shift in participation and energy. When people truly feel that their voices matter, they tend to engage. Beyond heightened energy and participation, lightly holding opinions allows new and innovative ideas to emerge. More often than not, my initial idea of what might be done is replaced by a hybrid strategy that is a synthesis of ideas. Even then it is important for the group to be mindful of emergent changes in ideas. Community workers need to be nimble and flexible.

Conclusion

Mindfulness is increasingly being employed within social work. This chapter has introduced the definitional terrain for the purposes of research at the more abstract levels. The chapter outlined formal and informal meditation practices. Four brief exercises provided a taste of mindfulness. In many ways, this is the only way to truly know mindfulness. However, as we saw, this has not stopped researchers from developing scales that measure mindfulness. Here we discussed the feasibility of this but at the same time explored how these efforts are leading to intellectual clarity. The measures point us toward the mechanisms at play when one practices mindfulness. Finally, the scholarly work of social workers was reviewed, and we observed the range of perspectives and fields that are being affected. Social work, more than any other profession, is using mindfulness in unique ways in community work and social justice–oriented practice, and as an adjunct to other interventions.

References

Baer, R. A. (2003). Mindfulness training as a clinical intervention: A conceptual and empirical review. *Clinical Psychology: Science and Practice, 10*(2), 125–142.

Baer, R. A. (Ed.). (2006). *Mindfulness-based treatment approaches: Clinician's guide to evidence base and applications.* Burlington, MA: Academic Press.

Baer, R. A., Smith, G. T., & Allen, K. B. (2004). Assessment of mindfulness by self-report: The Kentucky Inventory of Mindfulness Skills. *Assessment, 11,* 191–206.

Baer, R. A., Smith, G. T., Hopkins, J., Krietemeyer, J., & Toney, L. (2006). Using self-report assessment methods to explore facets of mindfulness. *Assessment, 13*(1), 27–45.

Biglan, A., & Hayes, S. C. (1996). Should the behavioral sciences become more pragmatic? The case for functional contextualism in research on human behavior. *Applied and Preventive Psychology: Current Scientific Perspectives, 5,* 243–255.

Birnbaum, L. (2005a). Adolescent aggression and differentiation of self: Guided mindfulness meditation in the service of individuation. *Scientific World Journal, 5,* 478–489.

Birnbaum, L. (2005b). Connecting to inner guidance: Mindfulness meditation and transformation of professional self-concept in social work students. *Critical Social Work, 6*(2). Retrieved December 5, 2006, from http://www.critical socialwork.com/units/socialwork/critical.nsf/EditDoNotShowInTOC/EF84 B5D985393C9285257017001BBEC6

Birnbaum, L., & Birnbaum, A. (2004). In search of inner wisdom: Guided mindfulness meditation in the context of suicide. *Scientific World Journal, 4,* 216–227.

Bishop, S., Lau, M., Shapiro, S., Carlson, L., Anderson, N., & Carmody, J. (2004). Mindfulness: A proposed operational definition. *Clinical Psychology: Science and Practice, 11,* 230–241.

Brandon, D. (1976). *Zen in the art of helping.* London: Penguin.

Brown, K. W., & Ryan, R. M. (2003). The benefits of being present: Mindfulness and its role in psychological well-being. *Journal of Personality and Social Psychology, 84,* 822–848.

Buchheld, N., Grossman, P., & Walach, H. (2001). Measuring mindfulness in insight meditation and meditation-based psychotherapy: The development of the Freiburg Mindfulness Inventory (FMI). *Journal for Meditation and Meditation Research, 1,* 11–34.

Canda, E. R., & Furman, L. D. (1999). *Spiritual diversity in social work practice.* New York: Free Press.

Cardaciotto, L., Herbert, J. D., Forman, E. M., Moitra, E., & Farrow, V. (2008). The assessment of present-moment awareness and acceptance: The Philadelphia Mindfulness Scale. *Assessment, 15*(2), 204–223.

Chadwick, P., Hember, M., Mead, S., Lilley, B., & Dagnan, D. (2005). *Responding mindfully to unpleasant thoughts and images: Reliability and validity of the Mindfulness Questionnaire.* Unpublished manuscript.

Coholic, D. (2006). Mindfulness meditation practice in spiritually influenced group work. *Aretê, 30*(1), 90–100.

Coholic, D., & LeBreton, J. (2007). Working with dreams in a holistic arts–based group: Connections between dream interpretation and spirituality. *Social Work with Groups, 30*(3), 47–64.

Davidson, R. J., Kabat-Zinn, J., Schumacher, J., Rosenkranz, M., Muller, D., Santorelli, S. F., et al. (2003). Alterations in brain and immune function produced by mindfulness meditation. *Psychosomatic Medicine, 65*(4), 564–570.

Feldman, G. C., Hayes, A. M., Kumar, S. M., & Greeson, J. M. (2004). *Development, factor structure, and initial validation of the Cognitive and Affective Mindfulness Scale.* Unpublished manuscript.

Feldman, G., Hayes, A., Kumar, S., Greeson, J., & Laurenceau, J. (2006). Mindfulness and emotion regulation: The development and initial validation of the Cognitive and Affective Mindfulness Scale–Revised (CAMS-R). *Journal of Psychopathology and Behavioral Assessment, 29*(3), 177–190.

Fletcher, L., & Hayes, S. C. (2005). Relational frame theory, acceptance and commitment therapy, and a functional analytic definition of mindfulness. *Journal of Rational-Emotive & Cognitive-Behavior Therapy, 23*(4), 315–336.

Grossman, P., Schmidt, S., Niemann, L., & Walach, H. (2004). Mindfulness-based stress reduction and health: A meta-analysis. *Journal of Psychosomatic Research, 37,* 35–43.

Hayes, S. C. (2004). Acceptance and commitment therapy, relational frame theory, and the third wave of behavioral and cognitive therapies. *Behavior Therapy, 35,* 639–665.

Hayes, S. C. (2005). *Get out of your mind and into your life: The new acceptance and commitment therapy.* Oakland, CA: New Harbinger.

Hayes, S. C., Barnes-Holmes, D., & Roche, B. (Eds.). (2001). *Relational frame theory: A post-Skinnerian account of human language and cognition.* New York: Kluwer Academic/Plenum Press.

Hayes, S. C., Follette, V. M., & Linehan, M. M. (Eds.). (2004). *Mindfulness and acceptance: Expanding the cognitive-behavioral tradition.* New York: Guilford Press.

Hayes, S. C., Strosahl, K. D., & Wilson, K. G. (1999). *Acceptance and commitment therapy.* New York: Guilford Press.

Hick, S. F. (2008a). Cultivating therapeutic relationships: The role of mindfulness. In S. F. Hick & T. Bien (Eds.), *Mindfulness and the therapeutic relationship* (pp. 3–18). New York: Guilford Press.

Hick, S. F. (2008b). My personal journey to mindfulness. *Reflections: Narratives of Professional Helping, 14*(2), 16–23.

Hick, S. F., & Bien, T. (2008). *Mindfulness and the therapeutic relationship.* New York: Guilford Press.

Hick, S. F., & Furlotte, C. R. (2009a). *Bridging the mind and society in social work practice: Mindfulness and social justice.* Manuscript submitted for publication.

Hick, S. F., & Furlotte, C. R. (2009b). *Radical mindfulness training and social wellbeing: Findings from a study with a severely marginalized population.* Manuscript submitted for publication.

Huss, D. B., & Baer, R. A. (2007). Acceptance and change: The integration of mind-fulness-based cognitive therapy into ongoing dialectical behavior therapy in a case of borderline personality disorder with depression. *Clinical Case Studies, 6*(1), 17–33.

Jha, A. P., Krompinger, J., & Baime, M. J. (2007). Mindfulness training modifies subsystems of attention. *Cognitive Affective & Behavioral Neuroscience, 7*(2), 109–119.

Kabat-Zinn, J. (1984). An outpatient program in behavioral medicine for chronic pain patients based in the practice of mindfulness meditation: Theoretical considerations and preliminary results. *General Hospital Psychiatry, 4,* 33–47.

Kabat-Zinn, J. (1990). *Full catastrophe living: Using the wisdom of your body and mind to face stress, pain, and illness.* New York: Dell.

Kabat-Zinn, J. (2003). Mindfulness-based interventions in context: Past, present and future. *Clinical Psychology: Science and Practice, 10,* 44–56.

Kabat-Zinn, J., Lipworth, L., Burney, R., & Sellers, W. (1987). Four-year follow-up of a meditation-based program for the self-regulation of chronic pain: Treatment outcomes and compliance. *Clinical Journal of Pain, 2,* 159–173.

Kabat-Zinn, J., Wheeler, E., Light, T., Skillings, A., Scharf, M. J., Cropley, T. G., et al. (1998). Influence of a mindfulness meditation-based stress reduction intervention on rates of skin clearing in patients with moderate to severe psoriasis undergoing phototherapy (UVB) and photochemotherapy (PUVA). *Psychosomatic Medicine, 60,* 625–632.

Keefe, T. (1975a). Empathy and social-work education. *Journal of Education for Social Work, 11*(3), 69–75.

Keefe, T. (1975b). A Zen perspective on social casework. *Social Casework, 56*(3), 140–144.

Kenny, M. A., & Williams, J. M. G. (2007). Treatment-resistant depressed patients show a good response to mindfulness-based cognitive therapy. *Behaviour Research and Therapy, 45,* 617–625.

Kristeller, J. L., & Hallett, B. (1999). Effects of a meditation-based intervention in the treatment of binge eating. *Journal of Health Psychology, 4,* 357–363.

Langer, E. J. (1989). *Mindfulness.* Cambridge, MA: De Capo Press.

Langer, E. J. (1997). *The power of mindful learning.* Reading, MA: Addison-Wesley.

Langer, E. J., & Moldoveanu, M. (2000). The construct of mindfulness. *Journal of Social Issues, 56,* 1–9.

Lau, M. A., Bishop, S. R., Segal, S. V., Buis, T., Anderson, N. D., Carlson, L., et al. (2006). The Toronto Mindfulness Scale: Development and validation. *Journal of Clinical Psychology, 62*(12), 1445–1467.

Linehan, M. M. (1993). *Cognitive-behavioral treatment of borderline personality disorder.* New York: Guilford Press.

Linehan, M. M., Armstrong, H. E., Suarez, A., Allmon, D., & Heard, H. L. (1991). Cognitive-behavioral treatment of chronically parasuicidal borderline patients. *Archives of General Psychiatry, 48,* 1060–1064.

Ma, S. H., & Teasdale, J. D. (2004). Mindfulness-based cognitive therapy for depression: Replication and exploration of differential relapse prevention effects. *Journal of Consulting and Clinical Psychology, 72,* 31–40.

Marra, T. (2004). *The dialectical behavior therapy workbook for overcoming depression and anxiety.* Oakland, CA: New Harbinger.

Minor, H. G., Carlson, L. E., Mackenzie, M. J., Zernicke, K., & Jones, L. (2006). Evaluation of a mindfulness-based stress reduction (MBSR) program for caregivers of children with chronic conditions. *Social Work in Health Care, 43*(1), 91–109.

Monti, D. A., Peterson, C., Shakin Kunkel, E. J., Hauck, W. W., Pequignot, E., Rhodes, L. et al. (2006). A randomized, controlled trial of mindfulness-based art therapy (MBAT) for women with cancer. *Psycho-oncology, 15*(5), 363–373.

Orr, D. (2002). The uses of mindfulness in anti-oppressive pedagogies: Philosophy and praxis. *Canadian Journal of Education, 27*(4), 477–498.

Praissman, S. (2008). Mindfulness-based stress reduction: A literature review and clinician's guide. *Journal of the American Academy of Nurse Practitioners, 20*, 212–216.

Pyles, L. (2005). Understanding the engaged Buddhist movement: Implications for social development practice. *Critical Social Work, 6*(1), 1–10.

Regin, L.-K. (2001). *Vision of sunyata-wu (void): Towards a processual perspective of social work.* Doctoral dissertation, University of Queensland, Australia.

Robins, C. J., & Chapman, A. L. (2004). Dialectical behavior therapy: Current status, recent developments, and future directions. *Journal of Personality Disorders, 18*, 73–89.

Rosenbaum, E. (2005). *Here for now: Living well with cancer through mindfulness.* Hardwick, MA: Satya House.

Salmon, P. G., Santorelli, S. F., & Kabat-Zinn, J. (1998). Intervention elements in promoting adherence to mindfulness-based stress reduction programs in the clinical behavioral medicine setting. In S. A. Shumaker, E. B. Schron, J. K. Ockene, & W. L. Bee (Eds.), *Handbook of health behavior change* (2nd ed., pp. 126–132). New York: Springer.

Schure, M. B., Christopher, J., & Christopher, S. (2008). Mind-body medicine and the art of self-care: Teaching mindfulness to counseling students through yoga, meditation, and Qigong. *Journal of Counseling & Development, 86*(1), 47–56.

Segal, Z. V., Teasdale, J. D., Williams, J. M., & Gemar, M. (2002). The mindfulness-based cognitive therapy adherence scale: Inter-rater reliability, adherence to protocol and treatment distinctiveness. *Clinical Psychology and Psychotherapy, 9*, 131–138.

Segal, Z. V., Williams, J. M. G., & Teasdale, J. D. (2002). *Mindfulness-based cognitive therapy for depression: A new approach to preventing relapse.* New York: Guilford Press.

Shapiro, S. L., Carlson, L. E., Astin, J. A., & Freedman, B. (2006). Mechanisms of mindfulness. *Journal of Clinical Psychology, 62*(3), 373–386.

Shapiro, S. L., Schwartz, G. E., & Bonner, G. (1998). Effects of mindfulness-based stress reduction on medical or premedical students. *Journal of Behavioral Medicine, 21*, 581–599.

Speca, M., Carlson, L. E., Goodey, E., & Angen, M. (2000). A randomized, wait-list controlled clinical trial: The effect of a mindfulness meditation-based stress reduction program on mood and symptoms of stress in cancer outpatients. *Psychosomatic Medicine, 62*, 613–622.

Teasdale, J. D., Segal, Z. V., Williams, J. M. G., Ridgeway, V. A., Soulsby, J., & Lau, M. A. (2000). Prevention of relapse/recurrence in major depression by mindfulness-based cognitive therapy. *Journal of Consulting and Clinical Psychology, 68,* 615–623.

Tolle, E. (2005). *A new earth: Awakening to your life's purpose.* New York: Dutton.

Williams, J. M., Duggan, D. S., Crane, C., & Fennell, M. J. V. (2006). Mindfulness-based cognitive therapy for prevention of recurrence of suicidal behavior. *Journal of Clinical Psychology, 62*(2), 201–210.

Wong, R. Y. (2004). Knowing through discomfort: A mindfulness-based critical social work pedagogy. *Critical Social Work, 5*(1). Retrieved December 5, 2006, from http://www.criticalsocialwork.com/units/socialwork/critical.nsf/8c20 dad9f1c4be3a85256d6e006d1089/dd7c350ba0866ae785256ec20063c090 ?OpenDocument

CHAPTER TWO

Living Fully: Mindfulness Practices for Everyday Life

Christine Kessen

"No time!" a student exclaims. Discussing an article on risk management in a graduate social work ethics class, I see the frustration on the faces in front of me. I had identified burnout as a major cause of poor social work practice. My suggestion that students take time to address their own needs now sounds feeble. These students are juggling jobs, family responsibilities, and graduate school—how could they *not* be exhausted and depleted at the end of each day? Is there anything I can offer them?

I recall my own practice of mindfulness during spare moments each day. We all have little bits of time, no matter how busy our work and personal schedules, but we often fail to recognize them. Students could begin with their own snatches of time, standing in line at the grocery store, walking to class, or picking up children at school. These moments experienced in mindfulness could benefit anyone. "You have all the time you need," I begin to tell my students. "You have the present moment."

Benefits of Mindfulness

Mindfulness allows us to step outside ourselves and observe our mental processes. With practice, we become less attached to our own thoughts, perceptions, and beliefs. We are able to identify and correct distortions or dysfunctional thoughts (Marlatt & Kristeller, 1999). By learning to see the world as it really is, we develop insight and wisdom. We are able to develop judgments and actions based on the true nature of people and events rather than how we wish them to be.

Seeing our own motivations and ourselves clearly, we may be able to see how we can be helpful in situations involving potential conflict. Through deep listening, wisdom and compassion can develop and lead to benevolent policies, laws, and intergovernmental actions (Kabat-Zinn, 2005). Personal transformation can lead to societal transformation.

Practitioners in the helping professions have reported both personal and professional improvements after mindfulness training. Counseling has improved students' ability to handle stress, as well as their counseling practice (Newsome, Christopher, Dahlen, & Christopher, 2006). Nurses have noted improved work and family relationships (Cohen-Katz et al., 2005). Health care professionals have realized decreased stress and greater self-compassion (Shapiro, Astin, Bishop, & Cordova, 2005). Medical students have reported decreased psychological distress and improved mood states despite increased school pressures as final exams approached (Rosenzweig, Reibel, Greeson, & Brainard, 2003). Medical students and premedical students have experienced decreased stress and increased empathy (Shapiro, Schwartz, & Bonner, 1998). Nursing students have been able to lower their own stress as well as react more empathically with patients without suffering from their patients' negative emotions (Beddoe & Murphy, 2004). Mental health professionals working on an admissions treatment team have improved their work skills by increasing their family friendliness (Singh et al., 2002). Social workers could also realize these benefits.

Mindfulness Practices

So what are the mindfulness practices that bring such benefits? In the words of noted mindfulness scholar Jon Kabat-Zinn, mindfulness "meditation is a way of looking deeply into the chatter of the mind and body and becoming more aware of its patterns. By observing it, you free yourself from much of it" (qtd. in Moyers, 1993, p. 126). Mindfulness practices are both simple in design and easy to understand, yet at times difficult to accomplish. We need to retrain our minds to be in the present moment. After all, we have been conditioning our minds to our unmindful habits for many years. It takes time and effort to change these habits to mindfulness and practice, practice, and more practice. Like all skills, the more we practice, the easier mindfulness becomes to attain. Paradoxically, we already have mindfulness within us—we just have to discover it.

Mindfulness can involve sitting, walking, standing, or the daily tasks of life. We just need to do these activities with moment-to-moment awareness. The following mindfulness exercises can be done in the little bits of time we all have every day. As you begin using these exercises, I believe that your awareness will increase and you will see that you have the choice to expand your mindfulness practices to other parts of your life as well.

BREATH AWARENESS EXERCISE

Wherever I am, whatever I am doing, I simply become my breath. I do not think about breathing but become aware that I am already breathing. I focus on my breath and become aware when I am breathing in, follow my breath throughout my body, and experience the letting go of my breath as it leaves my body. I feel my breath as it enters and leaves my nostrils, as it expands and contracts my chest, as it moves my belly up and down. I do not force my breath or try to slow it down (sometimes I am excited and breathing very quickly). I simply become aware of my breath in my body, and my body slows down on its own. I do not try to control it. I become aware if I am holding my breath (in anger? frustration? fear?) and simply let it go. As my mind wanders, I simply bring it back repeatedly, without judgment or recrimination, to focus on my breath. As my body calms, I find a greater awareness of my own inner life as well as everyone and everything in my immediate environment.

This exercise (detailed in chapter 1) has the remarkable ability to calm me in any situation. The increased awareness frees me from my self-imposed limits, and I feel a wonderful sense of freedom and openness. As I become more aware of others and myself as we really are, compassion arises spontaneously. A reverence for all aspects of life increases with the ability to remain in the present moment. This exercise can be done anywhere at any time and has the potential to bring you back to your true self. It is remarkable in its simplicity. As long as you are alive, this exercise is always available.

MINI BODY AWARENESS EXERCISE

While I prefer to use the forty-five-minute *Body Scan Meditation* CD by Jon Kabat-Zinn (2002) whenever I am home, I have found it helpful to be aware of the sensations in my body at times throughout the day. You can use the mini body awareness exercise (exercise 2.1) in the few minutes of time between clients or at any break in the day. I feel most

EXERCISE 2.1

Mini Body Awareness Exercise

1. Sitting or standing, take a few minutes from your day, consciously shifting your attention away from any daily cares or worries.
2. Turning your attention to your breath, become conscious of your breathing, inhaling and exhaling with increased awareness, becoming centered within yourself.
3. Bring your awareness to one part of your body, perhaps your shoulders, where you may carry your tension, or perhaps your toes, where you may have the least awareness, any part of the body (feet, legs, torso, arms, hands, shoulders, neck, or head) that feels right for you.
4. Breathe in and breathe out, noticing how this part of your body feels, feeling the sensations you find there. Are you tired? Tense? Aching? Tingling?
5. Sink into each sensation, allowing yourself to feel each sensation as fully as you are able.
6. Experience each sensation, and then let go of each sensation, returning to your breath.
7. Release each sensation as you breathe out, experiencing your body anew as you breathe in.
8. Move your awareness to an adjoining area of your body, repeating the process with each area of the body as time allows.
9. Returning to your breath, breathe in and breathe out, remaining aware of your body, accepting your body, accepting who you are.
10. At the end of your designated time, remain in stillness for a few moments, allowing your awareness to return to the room when you are ready.

comfortable doing this exercise sitting or standing at my desk with the door to my office closed. Privacy may not be necessary, but it makes me feel comfortable—do what is comfortable for you.

Concentrating my awareness on the different parts of my body, I mentally feel or experience each area as I breathe in and breathe out several times. Sometimes I experience relief as my muscles release and let go. Other times I become aware of the feelings creating the tension—concern for an ailing pet, worry about not completing a task on time. Now that I am aware of these feelings, I am able to make choices. I can let go of the feelings rather than storing the tension in my muscles.

I must do this activity, like all mindfulness exercises, repeatedly, as I continually remind myself to be mindful, to be aware, and to be present. It is amazing to me that I can forget something so beneficial so easily. That is our human condition, the habits of years of mindless thinking and being.

This exercise helps us to be more aware and accepting of our bodies. As our awareness increases, our ability to make choices increases. While the full benefits of this exercise may take some time to materialize, there are many small benefits each day as you become more mindful. While the goal is not to become less tense, as we become mindful, our bodies naturally release tension. If you find this exercise beneficial, you may want to consider trying the complete body scan found in *Full Catastrophe Living* (Kabat-Zinn, 1990).

SITTING MINDFULNESS MEDITATION

I first learned to meditate using the sitting position, so this position is quite comfortable for me. I suggest trying sitting meditation (see exercise 2.2) for a few minutes a day for several days. You can gradually increase the time as you benefit from it. As you pay attention to your breath, your body will calm and your breathing will naturally become deeper and slower. It is important not to *try* to be calm or relaxed—it will happen spontaneously as you become mindful. During your meditation periods, you may want to try a variety of commonly used words or phrases such as "In" and "Out," "Deep" and "Slow," "Aware of my body," and "Relaxing my body" (Nhat Hanh, 1993).

Many people find it stressful to sit without a planned activity to occupy them. Beginning meditators are often surprised at all the inner activity that arises. "When we actually let ourselves experience the body, we realize that it is not at all solid. Instead, the body can be directly felt as a whirling mass of minute sensations, ebbing and flowing, surging and subsiding, pulsing with the energy of life" (Johnson, 2000, p. 8). These inner movements may consist of thoughts, feelings, plans for the future, regrets from the past, pleasant memories, daydreams, or bodily aches and pains. In meditation, we allow ourselves to be aware of our inner movements, but we do not attach to them. When we find ourselves attached (e.g., planning what to eat for lunch, rehashing an argument, fidgeting in response to an ache or pain), we return to the awareness of our breath. We do not judge or criticize ourselves. We do not try to rid ourselves of what may seem like a distraction even when the thought or feeling is painful. We treat our increased awareness as a valued gift. As we become less attached to our thoughts and feelings, we begin to realize that we are separate from them. They are just thoughts and feelings, not us. The more aware we are of our inner lives, the freer we are in the daily choices we make. Conflicted feelings no longer push us in directions that are harmful to others or ourselves.

EXERCISE 2.2

Sitting Mindfulness Meditation

1. Sit with your back straight to allow for energy flow, perhaps on a straight-backed chair, or sitting a few inches from the back of the chair, or with a cushion between you and the back of your chair. (Note: Sitting meditation on a cushion on the floor is another option.) Designate a set amount of time for the meditation (e.g., thirty minutes).
2. Place your feet firmly on the floor or on a cushion on the floor (if your feet do not reach the floor) with legs uncrossed, putting your hands on your lap or comfortably at your sides, assuming a comfortable position.
3. Sit with eyes closed or cast down to reduce distraction.
4. Silently, gently introduce a word or phrase as you breathe in, such as "Breathing in," and a complementary word or phrase as you breathe out, such as "Breathing out." (Note: For some people, repeating a word or phrase can become a distraction. They prefer to focus their awareness on their breath as they breathe in and then out. Use the practice that is most comfortable for you.)
5. Keeping your awareness with your breath, nourish your body as you breathe in, releasing tension as you breathe out.
6. Stay with the breath, not trying to force the breath, just being in the present moment with the breath.
7. Be aware of your thoughts, not attaching to your thoughts, allowing your thoughts to pass by.
8. Return your awareness to your breath. Be aware of breathing in. Be aware of breathing out.

We are able to recognize hurtful paths and avoid them. Our decisions are more likely to benefit us and all in our environment.

If you find it too stressful to practice sitting meditation even for a few minutes, then this may not be the right activity for you at this time. You may want to try other mindfulness practices such as walking meditation first.

CONSCIOUS WALKING EXERCISE

Since walking has always been one of my favorite activities, walking in mindfulness has become a favorite exercise of mine. Teaching on a university campus, I am frequently walking somewhere: to the library, to my classroom, across campus for a meeting. I used to rush, enjoying the physical activity and mentally planning for the next event at my destination. While I may have benefited from the physical activity, I did not arrive refreshed. I often arrived with preconceived ideas of what I would do, what I would say, and what the next activity would be like. Then I started conscious walking. My favorite walking exercise uses a poem entitled "I Have Arrived" by Thich Nhat Hanh (1996a). I often repeat a line from the poem slowly with each step:

> Breathe in "I have arrived"; breathe out "I am home."
> Breathe in "In the here"; breathe out "In the now."
> Breathe in "I am solid"; breathe out "I am free."
> Breathe in "In the ultimate"; breathe out "I dwell."

Attending to my breath while reflecting on the words of this poem has become my way of returning home to my center. I find that I arrive at my destination feeling more refreshed, more open to my students and colleagues and whatever our current encounter brings.

Conscious walking is a particularly useful exercise during periods of restlessness or agitation. The walking movement itself provides some relief. In this exercise, we simply become aware of each step, slowing our pace if time permits. We feel the sensations of the moment, the air, the ground, our feet, nature, or the objects around us. Some recite a poem like the one I described; others just remain in the present moment. I now look forward to these little spaces of time between my daily obligations. When I can, I plan a few extra moments so that I can extend my walking interlude. When I walk mindfully, I feel grounded. I know who I am.

I suggest trying this exercise whenever you have the opportunity. There is always some time during the day when you need to walk somewhere. Even if you do not have extra time, you can use whatever time you have for a few moments of mindfulness. I have found that even when I am late, I can walk mindfully while rushing. Any pace can be used; just focus on being fully present with each step.

CONSCIOUS STANDING MEDITATION

For some people, standing is a more comfortable posture than sitting or walking. It is also an interesting variation (see exercise 2.3). We all spend some time standing during the day, sometimes just waiting. As in all mindfulness practices, just be aware of what you are doing or not doing. Just be aware of the standing. Stopping your activities can help to unclutter the mind. It is a time to pause, to come back to yourself in your busy day.

You can practice standing meditation in small amounts of time during the day, while you are waiting at the bus stop, standing at a street

---

EXERCISE 2.3

Conscious Standing Meditation

1. Standing with your back straight and your head up, distribute your weight evenly, finding a position that is comfortable for you.
2. Turning your awareness from all previous activities, become aware that you are standing.
3. Looking around you, become aware of your environment—what is the purpose for which you are here at this time today?
4. Consciously standing, become more aware of your space in the world, as you feel more rooted to the earth.
5. Turning your awareness to your breath, become aware of each breath as you breathe in, and each breath as you breathe out.
6. Feeling the calm accompanying your breath, return to your true inner self.
7. At the end of your designated time, when you are ready, return your awareness to your environment.

---

corner waiting for the light to change, or waiting in line at the bank. It can be a powerful way to bring you back to yourself during the day.

HALF SMILE

The half smile consists of simply turning up the corners of one's mouth as if experiencing something pleasant. While it may feel unnatural at first, you will find your mood changing to correspond to the smile. I find that I cannot be angry and practice the half smile at the same time—I have to let the anger go. Practicing the half smile has made me aware of how much anger I hold in my body and how unpleasant it feels.

You can practice the half smile during sitting, standing, and walking meditation or as a separate exercise at any time during the day. I find it helpful to practice the half smile as I change from one activity to another. I place reminders in my appointment book to encourage regular practice. Nhat Hanh (1975) suggests placing reminders on your wall or ceiling so that you remember to practice the half smile when you wake up in the morning. Inhale and exhale three times as you breathe deeply while practicing the half smile. This practice will help you start your day with mindfulness.

Throughout the day, look for opportunities to practice the half smile. You may enjoy practicing while listening to music. Another occasion is when you find yourself becoming irritated or angry. Practicing the half smile at such times can assist you in returning to a mindful state.

When I have difficulty practicing the half smile, I know I am hanging on to anger or past events that I need to let go of. In this way, the half smile makes me aware of any obstacles to remaining in the present moment. I suggest trying the half smile several times a day, as it is a simple exercise. You can practice it at almost any time, and the rewards are great. While I first resisted the half smile, as it felt contrived to me, I have found it to be a powerful exercise.

MINDFULNESS DURING DAILY ACTIVITIES

We can practice mindfulness twenty-four hours a day by bringing awareness to every activity that is part of our daily life. We simply need to focus the mind on the present moment. Following your breath can help to keep the mind from straying. Carry out each task slowly and in a relaxed manner—dusting your study, cutting vegetables for dinner, stacking wood for the fireplace. Be aware of what you are doing when you are doing it. Treat each object you touch with reverence. Notice the touch, shape, and color of each object as you touch it. How does it feel? What a privilege to be here at this moment, touching this object. Think of the materials making up the object. Where do they come from? What people designed, fashioned, developed, and transported this object that I am enjoying at this moment? I thank each person who helped to bring this object to me.

As in other meditation practices, we simply bring the mind back to the present moment whenever it strays. You may want to eliminate unnecessary distractions by turning off the television or radio, and unplugging or turning off the phone when possible. Often we hurry through routine chores, trying to get them finished as quickly as possible. We rush to another activity that we think we will enjoy more or at least dislike less. We need to come to the realization that this moment right now *is* our life (Kabat-Zinn, 1990). Life does not start at some point in the future. If we truly understood this truth, would we not want to be present at every moment?

DAY OF MINDFULNESS

While our intent is to practice mindfulness throughout each day, we find that it is not easy to do. Therefore, setting aside a day to practice mindfulness can be a useful practice. It gives us the time and space to develop mindfulness as a useful habit. We tend to think that our jobs, friends, and family take our time away from us, but in reality, we are just not being mindful. That is why it can be useful to schedule a day or part of a day when we have no obligations to others.

During your day of mindfulness, you engage in the simple activities of daily life with the continued practice of mindfulness. Starting with awareness of your breath as you wake in the morning, you continue to bring yourself back to the present moment. You put aside leisure activities involving others and work activities such as organizing meetings. You get up in the morning, make breakfast, clean the house, walk the dog, and engage in your daily activities with awareness of what you are doing. You do not hurry through your activities to complete them quickly. In fact, it is often helpful to complete your tasks more slowly with your full attention. The change in pace allows us to experience each activity as new. In the present moment, you join with the activity and enjoy it.

Set aside time for the mindfulness meditation practices that you find most useful: conscious walking, sitting mindfulness meditation, conscious standing meditation, the body awareness exercise. You may also want to include activities you particularly enjoy, such as reading poetry or sitting in your garden. Try to observe the day in silence as much as possible. Leave the television, radio, and computer turned off. Let your phone calls go to your answering system. Limit your talking as much as possible. It is important to let go of all expectations, including having a restful day. Your plan for this day is to accept whatever comes. Sometimes the most tumultuous days yield the greatest reward.

Obviously, a day of mindfulness is more than a bit of time, but if you can manage it, I believe that you will treasure it. Try to set aside a day, a week, a month, a vacation day, or whatever day you can, whenever you can. Many people find Saturday to be their best day. In our current fast-paced lifestyle, many of us have relinquished a day of rest once a week in favor of working constantly. A day of mindfulness is a way of strengthening our practice, particularly when we are new to mindfulness. You will find yourself more able to be mindful throughout the rest of your week, particularly when you are confronted with life's challenges.

DEEP LISTENING AND MINDFUL SPEECH

Bombarded with information and noise as part of our daily life, listening in silence allows us to digest what we are hearing (Jeon, 2004). Deep listening is a mindfulness practice that allows us to pass through the surface and see people as they truly are at a deep level. We practice deep listening when we consciously keep an open mind, stop ourselves from making quick judgments, and ask questions in a nonjudgmental manner. In this way, we develop insight and find compassion arising spontaneously. One way of developing the practice of deep listening to others is to practice looking deeply into ourselves. We need to become aware of our own dark side and own it as part of ourselves. "Looking into the mirror, we see, without filter, our capacity for deceit, self-deception, and false grandeur" (Santorelli, 1999, p. 110). This is a humbling, sometimes humiliating process, but one that is necessary for growth. As we practice mindfulness, we begin to accept the self-knowledge that comes to our awareness—our faults, pettiness, and unfair judgments of others. As we see ourselves more clearly, we are able to see others more clearly as well. With this increasing acceptance, our ability to listen deeply to others also increases.

We practice mindful speech when we stop criticizing others, making unkind statements, or repeating hurtful gossip. We do not make or repeat any statements that could cause friction, and we attempt to resolve any conflicts. We think about what we are saying and take responsibility for the consequences of our speech. "The way of meditation only carries that personal disarmament . . . a nonviolent encounter with reality itself. This is the way to understand a simple truth Nhat Hanh has mentioned elsewhere: 'Those who are without compassion cannot see what is seen with the eyes of compassion'" (Forest, 1976, pp. 107–108). With repeated use, these mindfulness practices gradually increase our awareness and compassion, thereby improving both our personal and professional relationships and creating more peace-filled communities.

MINDFUL CONSUMPTION

Mindfulness increases our awareness of what we are consuming on a daily basis. It is a powerful antidote to the automatic responding encouraged by corporate advertising. We learn to appreciate all the aspects of our lives at a deeper level, thereby experiencing a greater sense of fulfillment with life. We become less susceptible to the wish-fulfillment messages (e.g., possessions, sex, or drugs) often contained in modern advertising and entertainment (Rosenberg, 2004).

With mindfulness, we increase our awareness of what we ingest when eating, drinking, listening, and watching (Nhat Hanh, 2001). We stop activities that we do not find health giving, such as eating junk food or watching violent television programs. We are no longer on automatic pilot, consuming, as has been our habit. We are now evaluating our habits. Are we consuming what is healthy for us, for others, for the planet? Caring for ourselves and for others become one. Paradoxically, we are independent of our environment, no longer allowing the noise, clutter, and intrusions of society to do violence to us (Nhat Hanh,

1996b). Yet we recognize that we are not separate from our environment. We become aware that everything we are is interdependent with everything outside us (Rosch, 1997). We recognize that we are our environment and therefore are responsible for the individual and societal effects of our behavior. We engage in mindfulness for our own welfare and the welfare of all of society (Nhat Hanh, 1987).

Mindfulness as Self-Care

Like other helping professions, social work often taxes our inner resources as we care for people confronted with life's most challenging circumstances. Work stress abounds. We can react in unhealthy ways, such as by constricting our muscles, ignoring the unpleasant stimuli, or becoming angry at our plight, or we can react in mindfulness. We have a choice. As Santorelli (1996) reminds us, "stress is a relational *transaction* between a person and her environment" (p. 40). We do not need to be helpless victims of our work stress. Mindfulness practices can be an important form of self-care for the social worker.

Mindfulness practices facilitate continued growth and development. As our awareness of ourselves and our environment increases, we become more perceptive social workers. We are more able to recognize our own afflictive emotions before they interfere with the client-worker relationship. We are less likely to ignore client problems or warning signs when we recognize them in our own daily relationships. We are more able to interact with distressed clients without becoming distressed ourselves.

Despite these benefits, beginning mindfulness practices can be difficult. We may have good intentions and really want to get started but find ourselves not starting or not keeping up the practice. We may tell ourselves that we are waiting for the right time, perhaps when we have less work piled up. Perhaps the sensations, feelings, and self-awareness that occur during meditation make us uncomfortable. We may expect a period of bliss and are disappointed or think that we do not have the skills for this practice. However, in mindfulness, these are only thoughts, part of our awareness. Our thoughts will be a part of us whether we meditate or not (Kabat-Zinn, 2005).

Finding the time, even using the scraps of time in everyday life, can be difficult. I suggest using what time you have, and as you benefit, the time will grow. "You cannot achieve peace and joy by pushing yourself too hard into practices that are not themselves full of peace and joy. The key is to practice in a way that is delightful all along, so that the path and the ultimate destination are the same. If you do this, it will not be difficult to find the time" (Bien & Bien, 2003, p. xix). By striving to live fully in the present moment, you will gain the time of your life!

References

Beddoe, A. E., & Murphy, S. O. (2004). Does mindfulness decrease stress and foster empathy among nursing students? *Journal of Nursing Education, 43*(7), 305–312.

Bien, T., & Bien, B. (2003). *Finding the center within: The healing way of mindfulness meditation.* Hoboken, NJ: John Wiley & Sons.

Cohen-Katz, J., Wiley, S., Capuano, T., Baker, D. M., Deitrick, L., & Shapiro, S. (2005). The effects of mindfulness-based stress reduction on nurse stress and burnout: A qualitative and quantitative study, part III. *Holistic Nursing Practice, 19*(2), 78–86.

Forest, J. (1976). Nhat Hanh: Seeing with the eyes of compassion. In T. Nhat Hanh, *The miracle of mindfulness: An introduction to the practice of meditation* (pp. 101–108). Boston: Beacon Press.

Jeon, A. (2004). *City dharma: Keeping your cool in the chaos.* New York: Three Rivers Press.

Johnson, W. (2000). *Aligned, relaxed, resilient: The physical foundations of mindfulness.* Boston: Shambhala.

Kabat-Zinn, J. (1990). *Full catastrophe living: Using the wisdom of your body and mind to face stress, pain, and illness.* New York: Dell.

Kabat-Zinn, J. (2002). *Body scan meditation* [CD]. Lexington, MA: Stress Reduction CDs and Tapes.

Kabat-Zinn, J. (2005). *Coming to our senses: Healing ourselves and the world through mindfulness.* New York: Hyperion.

Marlatt, G. A., & Kristeller, J. L. (1999). Mindfulness and meditation. In W. R. Miller (Ed.), *Integrating spirituality into treatment: Resources for practitioners* (pp. 67–84). Washington, DC: American Psychological Association.

Moyers, B. D. (1993). Meditation: Jon Kabat-Zinn. In B. S. Flowers (Ed.), *Healing and the mind* (pp. 115–143). New York: Doubleday.

Newsome, S., Christopher, J. C., Dahlen, P., & Christopher, S. (2006). Teaching counselors self-care through mindfulness practices. *Teachers College Record, 108*, 1881–1900.

Nhat Hanh, N. (1975). *The miracle of mindfulness: An introduction to the practice of meditation.* Boston: Beacon Press.

Nhat Hanh, T. (1987). *Being peace.* Berkeley, CA: Parallax Press.

Nhat Hanh, T. (1993). *The blooming of a lotus: Guided meditations for achieving the miracle of mindfulness.* Boston: Beacon Press.

Nhat Hanh, T. (1996a). *The long road turns to joy: A guide to walking meditation.* Berkeley, CA: Parallax Press.

Nhat Hanh, T. (1996b). Please call me by my true names. In A. Kotler (Ed.), *Engaged Buddhist reader: Ten years of engaged Buddhist publishing* (pp. 104–110). Berkeley, CA: Parallax Press.

Nhat Hanh, T. (2001). *Anger: Wisdom for cooling the flames*. New York: Riverhead Books.

Rosch, E. (1997). Mindfulness meditation and the private self. In U. Neisser & D. A. Jopling (Eds.), *The conceptual self in context: Culture, experience, self-understanding* (pp. 185–202). Cambridge: Cambridge University Press.

Rosenberg, E. L. (2004). Mindfulness and consumerism. In T. Kasser & A. D. Kanner (Eds.), *Psychology and consumer culture: The struggle for a good life in a materialistic world* (pp. 107–125). Washington, DC: American Psychological Association.

Rosenzweig, S., Reibel, D. K., Greeson, J. M., & Brainard, G. C. (2003). Mindfulness-based stress reduction lowers psychological distress in medical students. *Teaching and Learning in Medicine, 15*(2), 88–92.

Santorelli, S. F. (1996). Mindfulness and mastery in the workplace: 21 ways to reduce stress during the workday. In A. Kotler (Ed.), *Engaged Buddhist reader: Ten years of engaged Buddhist publishing* (pp. 39–45). Berkeley, CA: Parallax Press.

Santorelli, S. F. (1999). *Heal thy self: Lessons on mindfulness in medicine*. New York: Bell Tower.

Shapiro, S. L., Astin, J. A., Bishop, S. R., & Cordova, M. (2005). Mindfulness-based stress reduction for health care professionals: Results from a randomized trial. *International Journal of Stress Management, 12*(2), 164–176.

Shapiro, S. L., Schwartz, G. E., & Bonner, G. (1998). Effects of mindfulness-based stress reduction on medical and premedical students. *Journal of Behavioral Medicine, 21*(6), 581–599.

Singh, N. N., Wechsler, H. A., Curtis, W. J., Sabaawi, M., Myers, R. E., & Singh, S. D. (2002). Effects of role-play and mindfulness training on enhancing the family friendliness of admissions treatment team process. *Journal of Emotional & Behavioral Disorders, 10*(2), 90–100.

CHAPTER THREE

Mindfulness in Social Work Practice: A Theoretical and Spiritual Exploration

Richard Potter

Spiritual paths are replete with techniques to help adherents let go of the dominating "monkey mind"—the constantly active, evaluating, worrying, anticipating, remembering activity that is going on in our heads—and be open to the present moment and what it has to offer. The "monkey mind" is also the purposeless babbling that is always in the background in our minds. What we know today as mindfulness is one specific and effective method of focusing the mind on the essence of experience, the power of being fully present in one's life. While the term is best known as part of the Buddhist tradition, versions of this practice are common among the spiritual traditions of the world. For example, the Sufi tradition of spiritual development uses the practice of *fikr* to fill the mind with silent repetition of a specific word or phrase, so there is little room left for typical mental processes. The universally desired outcomes of these practices, the development of consciousness and being centered in one's life, are accomplished gradually through a variety of techniques.

This chapter will explore how mindfulness can be an effective technique for social work practice. By enhancing awareness, self-discipline, and sensitivity to their environment, the practice of mindfulness strengthens people's capacity to change personally and also to influence their environment. This exploration will involve looking at a description of the results of mindfulness practice and coupling that with three specific characteristics that are strengthened through the process: awareness, mastery, and sensitivity. We will consider how these outcomes parallel the typical outcomes we seek for our clients.

Chapter 1 made the point that mindfulness does not require the support of any spiritual or religious tradition—that it can be an entirely secular undertaking. This does not mean that mindfulness does not have deep roots in and connections with the spiritual traditions of the world. Most spiritual traditions teach about the need to control, focus, and master the mind and to short-circuit habitual thinking processes, as demonstrated by a few comments from spiritual teachers of the last century. Hazrat Inayat Khan (1978), who brought Sufism to the West in the early twentieth century, stated, "The mind must be one's obedient servant; when it is a master, life becomes difficult" (p. 27). Joe Miller, seen by many as a spiritual "teacher of teachers," taught for the Theosophical Society in the late twentieth century. He translated some of the teachings about the mind into common language; a favorite was "You get more stinkin' from thinkin' than you do from drinkin' but the feel is for real" (communication with the author). When someone asked Ramana Maharshi (2000), the acclaimed mid-twentieth-century Indian yogi, a question, he would often redirect him or her to the query "Who is it that is asking?" (p. x). Ram Das, who as Richard Alpert left his Harvard teaching position and went to India to discover the deeper aspects of human experience, entitled his first book *Be Here Now, Remember* (1971), a phrase that evokes the theme of mindfulness.

As we are beginning to emerge from a time when it was considered essential to separate ourselves from the wisdom of our ancestors, social workers and others who work to alleviate human suffering often are eager to harvest some of this ancient wisdom for modern use. The technique of mindfulness is an important component of this ancient psychology. While the methods of teaching mindfulness may vary, the goal of replacing the seeking, grasping, incessantly active thinking processes of the average person with a more centered, grounded, moment-to-moment awareness is central.

Capacities for increased awareness, mastery, and sensitivity are important aspects of mindfulness. Awareness involves intentionally focusing one's attention on experience in the here and now. It is not thinking, but rather experiencing. Awareness is visceral and sensory and might be described as being "awake" to whatever is happening in the moment. Mastery involves strengthening the capacity to direct one's consciousness to stay awake, and it also imposes a nonjudgmental attitude upon the experience. Sensitivity sinks awareness deeper into our being and environment, opening new vistas of insight and perception that enrich our choices when we are seeking change or the alleviation of pain. Awareness, mastery, and sensitivity become both method and outcome and are at the core of mindfulness, both psychologically and spiritually. We will discuss the psychological significance of these capacities later in this chapter.

Some mid-twentieth-century therapies, especially those that were labeled humanistic in the 1960s and 1970s, had strong mindfulness components. An example of a pioneering therapeutic method that used mindfulness techniques before such techniques were well known is the Gestalt therapy of Frederick Perls, which was popular in the 1970s.

Since the emergence of techniques like Gestalt therapy, social work and psychotherapy have been connecting increasingly with the practice of mindfulness. The last three decades have witnessed the emergence of treatment modalities, as outlined in chapter 1. With the incorporation of mindfulness into clinical practice, considerable empirical support has emerged regarding its effectiveness; this is also discussed in chapter 1. The convergence of evidence-based practice with the reclaiming of ancient psychological strategies may spell the beginning of a new growth spurt in the helping professions.

The Practice of Mindfulness

As we saw in chapter 1, a technique that is almost universal when it comes to developing mindfulness is focusing on the breath as a way to anchor the mind in the moment. Breathing is the most constant, natural, and accessible of our activities. For this reason, it is useful as a focus for awareness. Other reasons for spiritual schools' use of the breath for spiritual practice are related to the belief that breath can be a link between spirit and matter and that the quality of breath has a profound effect on health and consciousness. For our purposes, it is the breathing process as an *anchor for consciousness* that is important.

The basic technique, without the addition of specifics, such as those presented in chapter 1 or those that deal with tradition, purpose, or esoteric issues, is the following brief practice. It can be especially useful for the beginner because it only focuses on one component of the process, the breath.

Exhale deeply. Let the inhalation come naturally. Repeat this a few times. Allow all your attention to focus on the natural rhythm of inhaling and exhaling. Feel the breath in your nostrils as it enters and leaves your body. Let your breath come and go as it pleases. Don't interfere with the natural process—just let it happen. Note the rising and falling of your chest and abdomen. Keep your attention focused, and as thoughts or feelings emerge, simply note them and let them go. Return to the rhythm of your breath. Continue to be aware of the swing of your breath, in and out, back and forth. Do this for ten minutes to begin with, and as you become more comfortable, increase the time to fifteen minutes. Make sure that you don't judge yourself as either bad or good at the practice depending on how well you follow the instructions; simply note your thoughts or experiences and return to the concentration.

This technique is only one of many ways to enter into mindfulness. As noted earlier, a technique of mindfulness can be a guide to help one achieve mindfulness, but it takes time. One learns this very quickly when practicing the technique, because attempting to focus the mind on the moment often leads the mind to rebel. There are often more thoughts to contend with than previously, and new thoughts intrude. One may think, "This is a stupid exercise," or "What am I doing this for? It's beautiful outside and I could be golfing." The body also acts up, and we find ourselves having more itches to scratch and stiffness to stretch out than we would have if we were sitting comfortably, watching television. Usually during the first few attempts we have a moment or two where we feel as if we are getting it. These brief moments lead us to continue to use the technique until we finally reach the point where we are able to maintain mindfulness for a period of time. One should not expect to get to a point where mindfulness is completely solidified as one's typical state. There are few indeed who reach this state of being. The goal is usually to reach the point where mindfulness is a way of being that is present in our personality on an ongoing basis and can be employed when the time is appropriate, just as other ways of being and perceiving are also used when appropriate. At this point a fundamental shift in perspective, labeled "reperceiving" by Shapiro, Carlson, Astin, and Freedman (2006), is taking hold in significant areas of life.

A less technical way of describing a more mindful way of being is *being present in your life*. Mindfulness can then be seen as avoiding the trap of having life be what happens while you are thinking of other things (to alter a well-known quote from John Lennon). If we focus on the outcome sought—being present in your life—rather than the techniques used to create the outcome, we may be better able to see the usefulness of mindfulness in many venues of social work practice.

Three Emergent Qualities

As noted earlier, there are three useful qualities of being—awareness, mastery, and sensitivity—that become strengthened through the practice of mindfulness and being present in your life. The three qualities are also helpful to anyone who is embarking on a process of planned change, and for this reason it becomes increasingly clear why mindfulness techniques are useful in the practice of social work. Let's look briefly at each of these qualities and what they bring to the changing and growing personality.

Awareness is the first mindfulness-related quality that we will explore. Awareness and consciousness are inextricably linked. To be aware of something means that one is conscious of that thing. Psychologically, awareness is often the first step toward dealing with an issue. Spiritually, increased consciousness/awareness is often considered to be the goal of whatever practices are being done, or it may be the goal of life itself (Potter, 2004). Full awareness of each moment is at the heart of the practice of mindfulness, which means that increased consciousness is a goal of mindfulness.

According to spiritual practitioners, those who spend considerable time and effort in the pursuit of spiritual enlightenment, it is self-evident that working with awareness strengthens the capacity for awareness, and that working with consciousness increases consciousness. Awareness, like any other habit of mind, becomes stronger the more it is employed. The habit of awareness stakes out a certain amount of territory and begins to replace the other habits that are there. Awareness becomes a positive, rewarding habit as it gradually limits some less useful habits. Some of the rewards of increased awareness are obvious: increased understanding of one's own actions, issues, and motivations; more access to opportunities for change; feeling more alive; less worry and guilt; and clarity of mind. Less obvious might be some of the more spiritual rewards, such as joy in the ephemeral moment, a peaceful mind and heart, increased perception, and sensitivity.

The second quality that emerges through being mindful is *mastery*. The Indian Sufi Hazrat Inayat Khan (1978) saw the development of mastery as one of the great purposes of life. From a psychosocial perspective, this statement makes a good deal of sense. The spiritual understanding of mastery, which goes beyond the psychological definition related to the ability to perform a certain task, involves a complex of qualities such as self-discipline, self-awareness, ability, and power. According to this perspective, when one attains mastery, one gains power and control over self and the conditions of life. The first condition, control of the self, is considered the precondition for the latter. The wise of many Eastern traditions recognize this quality as being extremely important. Tradition, as relayed by monks at the Copan Monastery in Katmandu, Nepal, tells us that the primary mantra of the Buddha was "Tataya om muni muni, mahamuni so ha" (Potter, 2004). When we recognize that the word *muni* (translated as an invocation of the "master, master, great master") relates to mastery, we become aware that even the Buddha spent much time working to achieve this quality (Potter, 2004). When we begin to realize that the very qualities that are needed to engage fully in the change process involve self-awareness, sufficient self-control to inhibit or initiate behaviors, and some influence over one's environment, the quality of mastery that is developed through mindfulness techniques becomes very important.

Continued practice of mindfulness leads to increased *sensitivity*. Sensitivity is a double-edged sword, for reasons that we will explore. Sensitivity involves growing one's capability of being aware. When one is more sensitive, one experiences more in three different aspects of life: height, depth, and breadth. We can think of the heights as the peak, more refined, sometimes joyful, sometimes exquisite experiences of life. When we become more sensitive to the depths of life, we experience more of the unconscious or partially conscious aspects of the self, as well as a deeper embeddedness in and affinity with the natural and emotional worlds that we occupy. Breadth of experience is the world of empathy with all that is around us, people and things. It is especially in this increased experience of empathy that sensitivity can become painful as well as rewarding.

The rewards of sensitivity may be experienced on spiritual, psychological, and personal levels. Life becomes more full and alive. Individuals become more fully aware of the world and their place in it. Becoming more sensitive to the full experience of life might be described as waking up from a dream of which one was only partially aware. One then begins to feel the full impact of life. As mentioned earlier, one is fully present in life.

This is both the promise of mindfulness and the risk. Many clients of social workers might be seen as too sensitive and lacking in adequate defenses to protect themselves from the harshness of unvarnished reality. Because of the wounds they are carrying, many clients are too unprotected to deal with an increase in their sensitivity. It is therefore important to note that the promise that mindfulness techniques carry is a *gradual* growth that heals wounds and builds capacity based on an emphasis on the strengths of the client in the moment and allowing unhelpful habits to fall away because of lack of use. Rushing the development of mindfulness-related sensitivity could be counterproductive. The oral traditions that surround inner meditative paths often contain stories of those who were adversely affected by too quickly increasing their sensitivity. This author has had the opportunity to watch a highly skilled spiritual teacher work diligently to repair the damage done to one who was too quickly awakened by a previous teacher. His unconditional love and delicate manner helped this young woman repair her defenses and heal her wounds so that she was able to continue to grow spiritually at a more reasonable pace.

Obstacles to Mindfulness

While few would argue with the desirability of achieving a degree of mindfulness in one's life, the obstacles are many. Among the potential barriers, four are particularly challenging. These obstacles—mental habits, cultural conditions, cultural proscriptions, and personal wound-edness—often manifest as components of problematic situations. When an individual begins to overcome such obstacles through the practice of mindfulness, processes of change and growth may open up in unexpected ways. Not only does overcoming these obstacles address clients' problems, but it also helps to create the conditions for improving their lives in general.

When we think of what keeps most people from being happy and able to navigate their lives successfully, mental habits in the forms of patterned ways of thinking, doing, feeling, and experiencing become important avenues of exploration. The tendency to judge is just one of these typical patterns, and it is one that is related to many sorts of psychological and social problems. It might be useful to differentiate between the kind of judgment that we may call discernment and the more common judgmental blame of self and others that can be detrimental on many levels. Discernment is the capacity to make sound choices, guided by experience, knowledge, and insight. It is judgment in the positive sense of the word, while judgmental blame—of either self or others—generally leads to unproductive downward spirals of negativity. Many believe discernment to be at the heart of wisdom.

The types of mental and emotional habits that pull people away from mindfulness are well known and too numerous to mention. They may be seen as identical to habits that prevent people from living healthy, full, meaningful lives. Social workers deal every day with clients who have difficulty getting beyond habitual ways of thinking, perceiving, and doing that have for some reason become their primary methods of responding to their environment. Understanding this can help us understand why mindfulness is so useful in all fields of social work. Inserting mindfulness into a client's repertoire of responses may provide a substitute for the habits that aren't working and may gradually replace them—without focusing on the old mental and emotional habits. The learning of mindfulness may be considered a strengths-based approach, as it is focused on developing positive skills.

Some obstacles to mindfulness are cultural. We who live in the Western world live at a very frantic pace of life that sometimes makes it nearly impossible to focus on the moment. We are usually in too much of a hurry to pay attention to the details of our experience. Instead, we rush from place to place and task to task, never paying much attention to the experience of the process of our lives. We could be judgmental and blame ourselves for not stopping to smell the roses, but that would deny the much larger part of this picture. Our postmodern technological and industrial culture does not easily accommodate individuals who have achieved a high level of self-awareness. Increasing demands of the workplace, along with an emphasis on mindless pastimes and the constant presence of televisions, computer screens, and cell phones, have the ability to keep individuals from ever having to be mindful of anything.

There are cultural proscriptions against mindfulness as well. In the United States, for instance, engaging in reflection, insight, and awareness is often seen as a rather frivolous activity that doesn't measure up to the importance of doing and accomplishing. A consumption-based society requires individuals to focus outwardly on the acquisition of money and consumerism, and insight and self-discipline are often seen as foreign to everyday experience.

Finally, personal woundedness is a strong obstacle to mindfulness. For countless psychological reasons, traumas of all sorts keep people directed either outward or only toward their wounds. Fear of the inner pain, anger toward individuals or groups, anxiety about the future, guilt about the past, and the listlessness of chronic low-grade depression keep many people, and certainly the clients whom social workers encounter every day, from being awake and aware in the moment.

Effective Social Work Practice and Mindfulness

Sogyal Rinpoche (1992) calls mindfulness "bringing the scattered mind home" and says that as we collect the pieces of our mind, three main things occur. First, all the "fragmented aspects of ourselves that have been at war, settle and dissolve and become friends." Second, "negativity, aggression, and turbulent emotions are defused." Third, mindfulness "unveils and reveals" our naturally good heart (p. 61).

By looking at the barriers to mindfulness, one can wonder whether we aren't looking at descriptions of the purposes to which mindfulness can be put to use in social work practice. When we add the elements of awareness, mastery, and sensitivity to Sogyal Rinpoche's three results of mindfulness, we have a good picture of the potential contributions of mindfulness to the strengthening of practice with many client populations. Let's explore some of the ways in which these aspects of mindfulness may be of service to social work clients.

MENTAL HABITS

Dysfunctional mental habits, the realm of many cognitive theorists, are a barrier to mindfulness; mindfulness can help in addressing these habits. One of the primary ways in which mindfulness helps is by helping the client develop the self-discipline required to maintain a focus on awareness. Mindfulness requires focusing awareness on the moment-to-moment experience of life. When one focuses awareness on experience, one can see clearly when certain thoughts and patterns of thinking intrude habitually. It requires self-discipline to return the mind to the moment and away from such intruding thoughts. Through the practice of this process, the client may strengthen self-discipline, the natural antidote to the power of unwanted mental habits.

As described earlier, self-discipline is a part of what spiritual schools refer to as mastery. Continual work with awareness of the moment and mastery over thoughts leads to sensitivity to the experience of life and also to sensitivity to the conditions that lie under the habitual patterns of thought. This combination results in improved self-awareness and can be seen as eventually accomplishing the task of "bringing the scattered mind home." Rinpoche's words provide an apt metaphor for the chaos that inhabits many modern minds: fragmented aspects of the self that have been at war settle and dissolve and become friends. Through the practice of mindfulness, the habitual mental patterns of negativity, aggression, and turbulent emotions are defused. The result of this process is the unveiling and revealing of the "naturally good heart." In a poetic way this describes the outcome that social workers seek for clients who are struggling with psychological issues.

CULTURAL PACE

Our daily lives are often a reflection of our out-of-balance culture. We run about at a frantic pace, lose touch with our basic identities through mindless and sense-dulling work, and fill any free time with activity that takes us away from our inner experience. An important question to ask ourselves is: Would we accept this way of life if we took the time and energy to be aware? What would our world look like right now if a reasonable portion of humanity were truly present in their lives? Jon Kabat-Zinn (2005) comments on the role we each play in the body politic and suggests that our agency is related to our level of inner development. What would each of us be willing to put up with if we really paid attention? Would we continue to create the world we find today? Would our clients stand for the conditions in their lives if they became aware of and sensitive to their "naturally good hearts"? Could being mindful gather the "fragmented self" and "unveil the hearts" of us all? Perhaps concerted social and political actions to create a world that is more sensitive to the needs of aware human beings would become inevitable.

The mastery and self-discipline achieved through the individual practice of mindfulness could begin to serve the purpose of mindful political action and mindful social reconstruction. Perhaps people who are aware, present in their lives, and empowered actually would be less likely to accept oppressive and unfair social conditions. There may be some merit in exploring mindfulness as a strengths-based micro technique that can empower clients to take action in their lives at the mezzo and macro levels as well as at the micro level.

CULTURAL PROSCRIPTIONS

It is clear that the societal proscriptions against awareness and sensitivity serve the status quo. As an increasing number of members of a society fall into the trap of mindless doing without reflection, that society becomes more out of balance. From a spiritual perspective, balance is central to a life well lived. Balance is needed in life between activity and rest, doing and being, striving and surrendering to the process, and balance is needed between the joy of experience and the peace of withdrawal (Potter, 2004). When individuals are constantly pushed to one side of this equation, the society begins to reflect the imbalance, and a vicious circle ensues. As the pressures of consumerism, competition, and orientation to the appearance of things—as opposed to their substance—take over our lives, there is little time left to find a balance of quiet, thoughtful reflection along with reasoned morality. Mindless consuming and mindless doing characterize the so-called ideal citizen of today's hyper-capitalist societies, of which the United States is the prime example.

There are those who try to resist the pull of the consumption-driven society by attempting to return to "the old-time religion," and while the motivations for this choice are laudable, this choice may lead to inherent difficulties with regard to being aware and fully present in one's life. Fundamentalist religions, which are often chosen by those seeking to disengage from consumption-driven society, generally seek to base all activities primarily on religious texts and not upon individual experience. Paying attention to one's moment-to-moment experience may be seen as humanistic, mystical, or otherwise not in keeping with the tenets of the religion and is often discouraged.

Mindfulness techniques and their outcome can be a natural antidote to the above proscriptions. When one becomes aware of and sensitive to oneself and the environment, it becomes more obvious what is life giving and what is life draining. At that point, self-discipline can be engaged to resist cultural proscriptions against being aware and avoid the cultural traps of mindless doing and consuming. Mastery is an effective practice for unveiling one's "naturally good heart" and is inextricably linked to mindfulness practice. Once one's heart is revealed to oneself, one discovers a more essential identity and clearer motivations, and the temptation to believe the cultural myths becomes greatly diminished.

WOUNDEDNESS

Many of the individual clients to whom social workers provide services are suffering from psychological wounds. Whatever framework is used to classify these wounds, whether medical, biopsychosocial, structural, person in environment, or problems in living, the words of Sogyal Rinpoche (1992) seem particularly suited to describe a positive outcome. "Bringing the scattered mind home," defusing "negativity, aggression, and turbulent emotions," and unveiling and revealing "a naturally good heart" are clear descriptions of positive outcomes in counseling and therapy. If we believe the Rinpoche that these are indeed the outcomes of practicing mindfulness, then including this technique as part of an overall treatment plan is not only useful but strengths based.

Earlier in this chapter we discussed the qualities developed by the use of mindfulness, mastery, awareness, and sensitivity. When these qualities are added to the mix, the potential of mindfulness practices becomes clear. These qualities give clients tools to discover their needs and strengths and to live their lives more fully. These qualities are not new, for social workers have been seeking to help clients develop these qualities for the last one hundred years.

Conclusion

Whether the mind is clouded by the unruly habits of the "monkey mind," the frantic pace of modern society, the cultural admonition to not be aware, or personal wounds that prevent one from being able to do what is necessary in life, the practice of mindfulness is emerging as a useful practice, and for some very good reasons. The mindfulness interventions reviewed in chapter 1—such as mindfulness-based stress reduction, dialectical behavior therapy, and mindfulness-based cognitive therapy—may only be the tip of the iceberg.

As an integral part of ancient psychologies, mindfulness has stood the test of time. It facilitates the development of awareness, self-discipline, and a person's sensitivity to self, others, and environment. Whenever mindfulness is part of the method used in the change process, consciousness is developed and strengthened. A sometimes unintended consequence of developing consciousness may be spiritual growth. From a spiritual perspective, when the doctrines of religions fade, the transformation of consciousness becomes a salient goal. As consciousness is transformed, individuals become able to refine perceptions, develop wisdom, and expand their loving hearts.

As social work becomes increasingly strengths based, mindfulness as a part of a strategy for change is a perfect fit. The focus of mindfulness is on awareness, not judging, and not the problem. Clients are empowered to be present in their lives, and as awareness increases, unwanted mental, emotional, and even physical habits diminish.

References

Das, B. R. (1971). *Be here now, remember.* San Cristobal, NM: Lama Foundation.

Inayat Khan, H. (1978). *The complete sayings of Hazrat Inayat Khan.* New Lebanon, NY: Sufi Order Publications.

Kabat-Zinn, J. (2005) *Coming to our senses: Healing ourselves and the world through mindfulness.* New York: Hyperion.

Maharshi, R. (2000). *Talks with Ramana Maharshi.* Carlsbad, CA: Inner Directions.

Potter, R. (2004). *Authentic spirituality: The direct path to consciousness.* St. Paul, MN: Llewellyn.

Rinpoche, S. (1992). *The Tibetan book of living and dying.* San Francisco: Harper.

Shapiro, S. L., Carlson, L. E., Astin, J. A., & Freedman, B. (2006). Mechanisms of mindfulness. *Journal of Clinical Psychology, 62*(3), 373–386.

CHAPTER FOUR

Mindfulness and Reflexivity: The No-Self as Reflexive Practitioner

Laura G. Béres

Mindfulness and taking a reflexive stance allow us to be present to expe-rience another person by observing both what is going on with others and our internal process without judgment, only awareness. As we move to this type of connection with clients in practice, we are more open to listen and allow others the space to open up more. We become more com-passionate with mindfulness and experience more from our heart and bodies than our heads. When we are in tune with our internal process, we can become more self-reflexive as we become more aware and atten-tive to what is happening in the moment. This benefits practice because we begin to de-clutter the judgment and the taken-for-granteds.

—Robin Koop Watson, BSW student[1]

As described in chapter 1, there is a range of different ways of consider-ing mindfulness and incorporating it into social work practice. This chapter defines mindfulness as the practice of intentionally focusing attention on what is occurring in the present moment in a nonjudg-mental manner, with an interest in being rather than doing (Kabat-Zinn, 1990).

I was already keenly interested in reflecting on taken-for-granteds (Chambon, 1999) and critically reflecting on the interaction between power and knowledge (Chambon, Irving, & Epstein, 1999), but I have only recently begun considering the ways in which mindfulness can enrich these reflections. I am somewhat new to the notion of no-self, but practicing mindfulness has naturally brought me to a position of

---

1. On a written test that I recently gave my students, I asked for a description of the link among compassion, mindfulness, and social work practice. One of my students has given me permission to use this answer that she provided. It presents a succinct description of how these practices interrelate.

being curious about no-self. I believe that being open to the possibilities of no-self and particularly fostering a sense of detachment from previously taken-for-granted ideas of the self may assist us in being more present and accepting in our interactions with people in therapy sessions and community settings. This not only would provide a more ethical exchange with the "other," as Levinas, a philosopher of ethics, would suggest (Godzich, 1986), but also can provide us, as social workers and practitioners of mindfulness, with a greater sense of peace and calm.

I have noticed, both within myself and with my social work students, that by being overly attached to our desire to be helpful, we can at times miss the opportunity to be fully present to the other's experiences. We can get so caught up in thinking about what we should say or do next that we miss important information that the other is attempting to convey, or important information that arises within the therapeutic relationship and process. It is true that we need self-awareness in order to catch ourselves wanting to be helpful, but I believe it is also useful to critically reflect upon and deconstruct those desires to be helpful and those ideas about the self. Having reflected upon ourselves and recognized the impacts of social construction, we then may find ourselves wanting to detach from these pressures and find a different way of being with those people who come to consult us. Mindfulness notions, such as non-attachment and compassion, offer us possibilities for incorporating different ways of being into social work practice. Gehart and McCollum (2007), for example, offer a description of engaging with suffering in a more mindful manner. They point out that it is a particularly Western idea that we should be able to live problem-free lives. They suggest that the mental health field has also supported the idea that health is related to a lack of suffering. Drawing upon Buddhist ideas about compassionately engaging with suffering, they then go on to discuss how therapists and clients can feel pressured by Western discourses to end suffering. We can become overly attached to the idea that we must assist in ending suffering and then feel as though we have failed if the suffering and problems do not end quickly through therapy. They provide examples of how, by developing a mindful presence, a therapist is better able to befriend problems rather than battle them, thereby bringing about compassion toward suffering and a willingness to learn from problems. This can lead to the dissolving of problems.

I believe that when we are overly attached to our idea of ourselves as helpful social workers, these attachments may get in the way of our openness to being truly mindful and in the moment with the people who come to consult us. I believe that mindfulness can assist us in being open to the ideas of no-self and, therefore, less attached to a preconceived notion of our professional helpful selves.

Since my background has been in critical reflection, and I am also drawn to mindfulness practices, I will begin by exploring the differences and similarities between mindfulness and various types of reflection. This will highlight how mindfulness can contribute a further dimension to reflexivity. I will then explore different conceptions of the self in order to make clear how different the notion of no-self is from mainstream Western ideas about the self. I am interested in the challenges and possibilities that the notion of no-self provides social workers. If, in fact, there is not a separate self as we have been raised to think of it, then who or what is it that does the reflecting and endeavors to be mindful? The idea that there is possibly no self but rather a stream of thoughts that we put together as a self can be challenging yet liberating at the same time.

I have been incorporating mindfulness exercises into the beginning of a BSW-level course I teach in individual and family therapy. I spend the first three-hour class discussing a range of Buddhist principles and then facilitate a mindfulness exercise, followed by a compassion exercise. We discuss how these approaches may assist in creating an accepting and compassionate classroom experience, and how these ideas may be integrated into the students' developing social work practice. The students are free to choose to continue integrating mindfulness practices into their lives or not but are at the very least encouraged to integrate critical reflection on the taken-for-granteds that are within therapeutic discourses. In the course we review a variety of mindfulness-based interventions (see chapter 1 for an overview). But I am more interested in encouraging students to integrate critical reflection into their practice, and I hope that they may find that mindfulness assists them in developing a reflexive stance. On the other hand, Palmer (2007) has recently shown the relationship between mindfulness and coping with stress, suggesting ways in which incorporating mindfulness into counseling services may assist first-year university students with the transition to university life, but this is not the main reason I incorporate these exercises.

Different Ideas about Reflexivity

I will begin by briefly reviewing three variations of reflexivity as described by D'Cruz, Gillingham, and Melendez (2007), who recently reviewed how social work literature since the 1990s has discussed the concept of reflexivity. They point out that a certain level of confusion has been created because the word *reflexivity* has been used interchangeably with concepts like reflectivity, reflection, and critical reflection. I will focus primarily on their second and third variations, which provide definitions of reflexivity that are useful for this discussion of mindfulness and no-self.

Three Variations of Reflexivity

The first variation of reflexivity that D'Cruz et al. (2007) present is concerned with individuals' ability to process information, assess risks, and make good choices for the future courses of their lives. This approach is described as a skill that can be taught to clients, who can then improve their chances of seizing opportunities and acting on their world. This might be similar to the idea of incorporating mindfulness training for clients in DBT, although in DBT, a balance is sought between accepting and befriending that which cannot be changed and working to change that which can be changed.

D'Cruz et al. (2007) extend this to take into account the social and political causes of individuals' problems. Here it is understood that merely focusing on the development of skills of making reflexive choices makes it possible to blame individuals for making bad choices, rather than acknowledging issues of social power and political domination. Within this second variation, "reflexivity is defined as a critical approach to professional practice that questions how knowledge is generated and, further, how relations of power influence the process of knowledge generation" (D'Cruz et al., p. 77). According to this definition, reflexivity would look to the social construction of knowledge as well as inwardly to find those taken-for-granteds by which we make sense of the world. This shares ideas with Chambon's (1999) descriptions of how to make the familiar visible in our practice. This form of reflexivity fits nicely within social work thinking, where we guard against pathologizing the individual by always remembering that the individual exists within a complex society, with a vast array of pressures and discourses to be negotiated. This would also include deconstructing the discourses that affect our practice.

This second variation of reflexivity examines the concept of relational reflexivity. D'Cruz et al. (2007) suggest that in moving from the personal to the social sphere, reflexivity can also be relational in those situations when "knowledge constructed by practitioners about clients is shared with clients and discussed openly between practitioners and clients" (p. 79). This approach is designed to encourage practitioners to ask questions about the assumptions that their theories generate, and this implicitly challenges the structural power of the practitioner.

For example, I have been providing individual counseling to a single mother for the past year. She had previously received inpatient services

for drug and alcohol addictions and had seen a couple of other therapists regarding self-esteem and family-of-origin concerns. She has been
attending AA meetings regularly each week and has begun to act as a
sponsor to others over the last six months. My practice is most directly
influenced by narrative therapy, and my interactions with this woman
have been structured at times by White's (2007) conversational maps,
which guide conversations from "the known and familiar" to the "possible to know," but also more generally by the underlying assumptions
of narrative therapy. One day as Barb[2] was discussing her frustration
with her father over a recent incident, she was describing being most
frustrated with herself that she had not yet let go of her anger toward
her father, even though she thought she had worked through everything
she needed to and had attempted to move forward. Being mindful of
what was going on in the moment, in terms of her emotions and my
thoughts about how narrative therapy might provide one way of looking
at this situation, I decided to share this framework with her in case it
might be of interest to her. Having asked if she might be interested in
one way of looking at this, I drew a rough sketch on a notepad of how
narrative therapy would visualize the way in which a problem story line
is made up of a series of events, linked over time, according to a plot or
theme. I said that people often come into counseling because of the
problem story line, but in fact there are numerous events in our lives
that we haven't storied. Once we find one event that does not fit within
the problem story line, it may be possible to find other events that also
fit within a new developing alternate story line. She was very excited by
this way of looking at things, realizing that she was not stuck in one
story, or one way of looking at things, but that there were other ways of
being. Many times since then she has mentioned these story lines and
her ability to choose which story line to place herself into. She says that
she wishes more people knew this and so has shared the idea with the
people she sponsors. This was one way of sharing professional knowledge but I think was best done once we had been developing as even a
playing field as possible between Barb and myself for several months.
Within this context, I was able to offer this approach as one of many
ways of looking at it, rather than as the truth that she should accept.

D'Cruz et al. (2007) then move on to discuss the third variation of
reflexivity. They suggest that it is similar to the second but it also
acknowledges the relationship between thoughts and feelings in knowledge creation. Within this variation, emotions are not thought of as having to be repressed but rather are recognized as inherent to professional
knowledge and power. They acknowledge that the relationship between
reflexivity and emotions is complex. Some people may be reflexive and

---

2. Names of clients and identifying information have been changed.

emotional in one situation, when they control their emotional reaction to the environment, or unreflexive and emotional in another situation, when they have numbed themselves to a particular experience. In a third situation they may be reflexive and without feeling, because they have resolved any feeling related to the situation, and then, finally, neither reflexive nor emotional in a fourth situation, because the situation does not provoke an emotional response and is routine enough to be dealt with while they are thinking of something else. They go on to say that reflexive social workers need to be aware of how emotional reactions, particularly anxiety, may at times undermine reflexive abilities. This is similar to my belief that our worry that wanting to be helpful social workers, and our attachment to a notion of the self as a professionally helpful self, can get in the way of our ability to stay mindful and present with the person consulting us. In being anxious about our performance, we may lose our focus on the other and on what is happening in the moment.

This third type of reflexivity is consistent with mindfulness, since mindfulness encourages a noticing of thoughts and emotions, but then also a letting go of them. I would suggest, however, that incorporating these reflexive social work practices with mindfulness would add the option of discerning whether or not it is useful to be transparent about the emotions and thoughts with a client. Rather than noting and then letting go of the emotion or thought without reflection, it may be possible to note the emotion or thought, make a decision as to whether it would be useful to mention, and then let it go if it would not add anything useful to the discussion. This would provide an opportunity for relational reflexivity, as described in the second variation of reflexivity.

Another example from my work with Barb may be useful. The last time I met with her, she told me, with some excitement, that she had signed up for an (expensive) weight-loss program. She said she had previously lost a great deal of weight and although she had put a fair amount of it back on, she believed her best bet for losing weight again would be another weight-loss program. As a feminist therapist, not only do I have concerns about the discourses surrounding appearance and the pressures that women experience regarding the need to be thin in Western society, but I also have concerns about extreme diets. I was aware of these thoughts and, reflecting back, I think in earlier years of my practice I might have jumped into these concerns in an attempt to provide information to my clients. However, this time I was influenced by my desire to be mindful. I stayed in the moment and was present to her excitement and enthusiasm. I remained curious about the program and how she had lost and gained weight previously, rather than influencing the direction of the conversation with what I thought I already

knew. Due to my narrative approach to work, which involves externalizing problems in an attempt to move away from pathologizing conversations, we had already had many conversations about the effects of
alcohol in her life. This involved a type of personification of alcohol as
an external element that we were able to discuss separate from her as a
person, giving her the opportunity to discuss ways of choosing to learn
to control alcohol, rather than letting it control her. As the conversation
about the weight-loss program unfolded, Barb began to talk about the
skills she would be able to learn through her involvement in the program rather than allowing herself to take an easy way out and just be
told what to do. She admitted at this point that she had been worried
about telling people she had joined this particular weight-loss program,
which reinforced my decision not to mention my concerns. We then
discussed how it could be possible to give up control through this system and not learn what was necessary for her to take control of her
weight, but that she could rather choose to learn new skills and a new
approach, which was her preference.

Evidence-based practice, "exhorting practitioners to be objective in
their decision making by the application of 'evidence' derived by
research" (D'Cruz et al., 2007, p. 80), is inconsistent with the second
and third forms of reflexivity. D'Cruz et al. suggest that these forms of
reflexivity invite practitioners to question their claims to knowledge and
introduce uncertainty into practice.

D'Cruz et al. (2007) then go on to discuss critical reflection. In
describing the difference between reflection and critical reflection, they
draw on Fook (1999) and Healy (2000), again pointing out the opportunities for moving away from the dichotomy of theory versus practice,
and valuing the generation of theory from practice experience. Here,
critical reflection is a practice skill that can be taught to practitioners
and students so that they can research their practice. In this approach
a social worker may reflect on a critical incident that occurred in the
past. This would be similar to Schön's (1983) notion of reflection-on-
action. This is an important skill, but not what I mean with regards to
mindfulness and reflexivity, since it does not involve reflexivity in the
moment, but rather after the moment.

Reflexivity, as it is more generally used across the variations, would
be closer to Schön's reflection-in-action, since it occurs in the moment:
"The reflexive practitioner or researcher is constantly engaged in the
process of questioning (self-monitoring) their knowledge claims and
those of others as he/she engages in social interaction and the micro-
practices of knowledge/power" (D'Cruz et al., 2007, p. 82). This type of
reflexivity also has much in common with mindfulness practices, which
occur in the moment, rather than after the fact.

What does Schön say about reflecting-on-action and reflecting-in-action? Are these types of reflection similar to the types of reflexivity that mindfulness may support? Do these ideas offer us any insights about the current state of social work?

Reflecting-in-Action and Reflecting-on-Action

In *The Reflective Practitioner*, published in 1983, Schön begins by describing a crisis of confidence in professional knowledge and a rift between technical rationality and reflection-in-action, which sounds descriptive of some of the tensions within the field of social work today. Students and practitioners continue to request greater links between theory and practice, and schools of social work grapple with the correct balance of critical thinking, theory, and practice skills to cover within a curriculum. Roche (2007), for instance, describes the challenges of attempting to teach postmodern ideas in a modernist university setting. I believe these challenges may be even greater within schools of social work, where we have many pressures to educate for professional practice rather than necessarily encouraging critical thinking or social transformation, and where the history of social work can appear conservative and controlling (Gray & Pozzuto, 2007). Evidence-based practice is promoted by some as the solution to the crisis of confidence in practice, while others suggest this reliance on scientific inquiry is positivist and reductionist in nature.

Schön (1983) describes the usual pattern in professional schools whereby the curriculum generally begins with a common scientifically proven theory base, followed by the application of theory in terms of diagnosing or hypothesizing, and finally by the development of skills through practicum settings. He goes on to problematize these approaches, which have been taken for granted within a model of technical rationality.

Schön (1983) describes and supports a "rebirth of interest in the ancient topics of craft, artistry, and myth—topics whose fate positivism once claimed to have sealed" (p. 48) in place of attempting to become more rigorously scientific in an effort to be more highly regarded. Schön argues for a reconsideration of professional knowledge and a search "for an epistemology of practice implicit in the artistic, intuitive processes which some practitioners do bring to situations of uncertainty, instability, uniqueness, and value conflict" (p. 49). Intuitiveness and a willingness to compassionately embrace uncertainty and suffering are clearly related to mindfulness precisely because they are not about imposing presupposed knowledge but rather are part of a process of being truly present to what is going on in the moment. This also opens up a range of possibilities when it comes to ways of knowing. In one example regarding the use of art, Chambon (2007) describes her explorations regarding ways of communicating and expanding our approaches to knowledge through art forms and art practices. In the same text, Irving (2007) describes his long journey with ambiguity and chaos, saying that "contradictions are not only inevitable but desirable" (p. 243). He also draws upon art, photography, and theater as sites of resistance and creation where we can "establish in an artistic way a social ethic of care in our communities, our universities, our classrooms" (p. 246).

Schön (1983) argues that many professionals "know-in-action" but may have difficulties describing afterward what it is they were doing while acting. He says that both ordinary people and practitioners at times ask themselves, "What features do I notice when I recognize this thing? What are the criteria by which I make this judgment? What procedures am I enacting when I perform this skill? How am I framing the problem that I am trying to solve?" (p. 50). He suggests that if it is common sense to recognize that people know-in-action, then it is also possible to realize that we can think about doing at the same time as we are acting. As an example, he describes good jazz musicians improvising, "feeling" the material, and "making on-the-spot adjustments to the sounds they hear" (p. 55).

Providing descriptions of both reflection-in-action and reflection-on-action, which occurs after the event, Schön argues for the value of these approaches to practice and to the development of theory from practice, much like Healy (2000). His descriptions of reflection-in-action have to do with noting thoughts and asking about what might be taken for granted that has been incorporated from a body of professional knowledge. Reflection-in-action could just as easily involve the noting of emotions and questioning about why we are feeling certain ways. Mindfulness, which assists in the noting of thoughts and emotions, can assist in this reflection-in-action. At times, it may be more beneficial to let go of these thoughts and emotions, but at other times they may inform and improve practice, as I have attempted to point out in the above two examples. In the first, I chose to share the thoughts of which I had become aware. In the second, I chose not to share them.

I will now explore various conceptions of the self, since I have alluded to the possibilities inherent in reflecting upon our assumptions about the self and detaching from conceptions of the professional helpful self. However, I also believe that the more we practice mindfulness or centering prayer (Bourgeault, 2004), the more aware we become of the constant flow of thoughts and emotions, which then leads to questioning and an openness to the idea of no-self.

The No-Self

WHY LET GO OF THE SELF?

I believe that the mainstream approach to the self within therapeutic discourses would suggest that social workers must know themselves well in order to be able to engage meaningfully with another. It is possible to see the traditions of this approach, particularly within psychoanalytic training. I agree that unresolved personal issues might otherwise surface in, and interfere with, a therapeutic relationship. Birnbaum (2005) also provides a description of using mindfulness meditation with social work students in order to teach self-observation and assist students in connecting with their inner voice. This is an important part of social work education, yet at the same time I am also interested in the seemingly contradictory idea that it may also be useful to let go of the self at times.

Godzich (1986) describes Levinas's suggestion that we attempt to let go of our certainties and our "knowledge" in order to engage in an ethical interaction with the other. As a philosopher, Levinas is speaking broadly and not merely about the ethics involved in a therapeutic relationship. However, I believe that his descriptions of this ethical exchange can point toward possibilities within therapeutic relationships. Godzich says,

> Levinas argues that there is a form of truth that is totally alien to me, that I do not discover within myself, but that calls on me from beyond me, and it requires me to leave the realms of the known and the same in order to settle in a land that is under its rule. Here the knower sets out on an adventure of uncertain outcome and the instruments that he or she brings may well be inappropriate to the tasks that will arise. Reason will play a role, but it will be a secondary role; it can only come into play once the primary fact of the irruption of the other has been experienced. And this other is not a threat to be reduced or an object that I give myself to know in my capacity as a knowing subject, but that which constitutes me as an ethical being. (p. xvi)

This gives us, as social workers within a therapeutic relationship, the challenge to be informed by theory and knowledge but not to be so attached to it that we are guided more by it than we are the responsibility to be truly present to the person in front of us. I believe that mindfulness practices that encourage being in the moment make it all the more possible for us to be conscious of theories and knowledge as they flit through our minds as thoughts, but also to be fully present with and experience the other. There will be times when we will need to let go of our commitments to certain theories and allow ourselves to be guided by intuition and the preferences of the person before us. It may also require sitting comfortably with confusion and acknowledging that theories we already know may not be appropriate for this unique situation.

For example, I have been providing individual therapy sessions to Stella for the past seven months. She was referred to me because she wanted to talk about her confusion about her relationship. She has been in her current relationship with another woman for four years but has been drifting apart from her over the past year. She is also attracted to another woman she knows and is having a hard time making a decision about which direction her life should take. Through the use of a narrative therapy approach, much of our interactions have been influenced by White's (2007) conversational maps, which assist people in uncovering their preferences and hopes. Stella has identified that she is feeling stuck between two sets of preferences, both of which are supported by strong discourses. On one hand, she has a preference for being, and being seen as, committed to her intimate relationship and partner. On the other hand, she also has a strong preference for feeling a more intense level of affection and attraction. We touched upon the impacts of her oppression as a lesbian, but she does not believe she is being overly affected by this at this time. Thus we moved into the impact of more general discourses about relationships and commitment and what the primary expectations are in society. Within this context I shared some generalized stories from my experiences with people I have known that I thought offered a range of various options of ways of thinking about the configuration and movement over time of relationships that were less mainstream. At the end of one session I asked, as I usually do, what had struck her the most during our conversation that day and what might stay with her the most. Although narrative therapy does not suggest the use of anecdotes or examples, being mindful of what was going on in the moment and reflexive of the power of discourses, I had decided during this session to follow my intuition and share these stories with her. She said that she found it particularly useful when I shared these types of stories based in my experiences. I had to let go of my worry about not overly influencing her due to my position of power as the therapist and also acknowledge that I did not need to merely adhere to a narrative therapy perspective but could incorporate more. Again in this example we had reached the point in therapy where a comfort level had developed, and I might not share ideas in the same way in the beginning stages.

HOW CAN WE LET GO OF THE SELF IN REFLEXIVE PRACTICE?

Although not coming from a tradition of mindfulness, Levinas's suggestion to let go of what we know in order to engage ethically with the other is of great interest to me. I understand that he does not believe, in fact, that we ever can let go of what we know, but rather that he is suggesting that we not become so attached to our knowledge base that we privilege it over our responsibility to the "other" in front of us. Our knowledge base can become a taken-for-granted, but mindfulness can assist us in being more aware of when our theories and knowledge are influencing us. We can then make decisions about how and when to use these theories. It seems that it would be just as difficult to let go of our self as it would be to let go of what we know.

CHALLENGES TO UNDERSTANDING THE CONCEPT OF NO-SELF

Engler (2003) presents a thorough exploration of the concept of self within psychoanalysis and Buddhism. He begins by reflecting on the criticism of a statement he made twenty years earlier—"You have to be a somebody before you can be a nobody" (p. 35)—by acknowledging how the statement relies upon a developmental model. He would at that time have believed that it was necessary to know yourself before you could let go of yourself in the process of mindfulness. Now he would appear more comfortable with the thought that these two processes may occur together. Drawing upon Western psychoanalytic understandings of the self as well as Buddhist teachings, he goes on to argue for the importance of being both somebody and nobody. In particular, he draws a distinction between the psychological self, in both Western and non-Western cultures, and the ontological self, by which he means the self as existential philosophers understand it. Clearly, psychologists and philosophers with an interest in ontology are interested in the self in different ways and draw upon different discourses. Philosophers are more interested in what it means to exist than in developmental stages, differentiation of the self, or self-esteem. This gives us a way of understanding how it is necessary to know ourselves, psychologically speaking, but at the same time be able to conceive philosophically of how the self or no-self may exist.

Engler (2003) suggests that the notion of a psychologically differentiated self "is a product of the last three or four hundred years of Western civilization: an autonomous individual with a sense of differentiated selfhood having its own nuclear ambitions, goals, design, and destiny" (p. 50). He then points out that even today in Native American cultures and cultures influenced by Buddhism, the sense of self "is much more merged with others in a 'we-sense' that is profoundly different from the separate, autonomous 'I-self' of Western experience. . . . The self is experienced as embedded in a matrix of relations and as defined by those relations" (p. 51). Gehart (2005) has suggested that it is Buddhism's focus on interconnectedness that can assist practitioners of mindfulness in coping with the despair that can be triggered, especially for Westerners, when they contemplate the idea that the self may not exist as a separate, distinct, independent thing. The example she provides is of an apple, which looks fairly solid and separate but would not exist without the apple tree, the air, the rain, the person who picked it, and the transportation that brought it to you. It exists because of a myriad of relationships and connections, just as we do.

What Engler (2003) is more interested in pursuing than the psychologically differentiated self is Buddhism's thoughts on the ontological self: how it is that we exist, philosophically speaking. Although on one hand Buddhism emphasizes and supports individual and personal agency, particularly at the level of encouraging the development of empathy and compassion, at the same time he says that Buddhism aims to show through the observing of moment-to-moment mind states that the self does not exist as an ontological core. In other words, it does not exist as something that can be observed, separate from thoughts, feelings, and interconnectedness.

To this end, Engler (2003) reviews four different types of self-experience. The first two are based on Stephen Mitchell's psychoanalytic thought. I include them here to highlight the multiple ways of thinking about the self. I am not suggesting we abandon these ways of thinking about the self, but rather that we consider the other possible ways of thinking of the self. The first describes the self as multiple and discontinuous, which fits comfortably within a postmodern framework, where we might talk of multiple and fluid identities and where we see that the self can be experienced differently in different contexts and with different people. The second type of self-experience is described as integral and continuous. Within this experience there is a realization that although one may feel differently from day to day, there is an ability to represent an enduring sense of self as "myself" and that this "entity resides deep inside us" (Engler, p. 55).

Engler's (2003) third description of self-experience is "unselfconscious experience," where he describes awareness as non-dual. He suggests this type of experience has been associated with meditative and mystical experiences but also occurs in ordinary situations. These situations are described as those times when "there is full awareness without any reflexive consciousness of self" (p. 59). He quotes Loewald as describing these experiences as "losing oneself": "We get lost in the contemplation of a beautiful scene, or face, or painting, in listening to music or poetry, or the music of a human voice. We are carried away in the vortex of sexual passion. We become absorbed in a deeply stirring play or film, in the beauty of a scientific theory or experiment or an animal, in the intimate closeness of a personal encounter" (p. 59).

Engler (2003) immediately goes on to suggest that this experience is also possible at those moments when a therapist is able to listen empathically in complete attunement without thinking or distraction, which is another good example of how mindfulness can assist us in being more fully present to the other. This would also be an example of experiencing a sensation of interconnectedness, or what Engler describes as dualism.

These first three accounts of self all fit comfortably within Western and therapeutic discourses about the self. It is the fourth experience of self, or no-self, that Engler (2003) suggests is the most unsettling for Westerners to contemplate. Initially drawing upon Freud's observation that the ego can make itself an object, observing itself and criticizing itself, he then goes on to say that what we cannot do is observe our observing self. It sounds a little like a dog chasing its own tail: "If I try, it recedes each time I turn to observe it: I never catch 'it'; I only turn the act of awareness into another object of awareness in an infinite regression. . . . Finally it dawns: detaching our 'self' from awareness in order to observe it is impossible because we *are* that awareness" (p. 66). It is as if the self, thought of as awareness, is a verb rather than a noun and so cannot be pinned down; it is more like a process than an outcome. Fulton (2008), in his descriptions of culturally variable ideas of the self and no-self, describes the sense of continuity of the self as being similar to the way in which our brains string the frames of a movie together into one fluid illusion.

This sense of no-self can be experienced through mindfulness practice, as the *contents* of consciousness are noted as they pass by but are not analyzed in psychoanalytic terms. Rather, the *process* is given attention, and manifestations of the self are seen to arise and pass by. This type of mindfulness, the noting of these moment-to-moment changes, "leads to insight into the nature of all representations of self and reality as construction only and as ungraspable in any real or definitive sense" (Engler, 2003, p. 68). This assists us in beginning to disengage from our attachments to certain thoughts or anxieties as we see that they do not last but rather move on and are replaced by others.

The following description of Engler's has also been helpful for understanding the shift in understanding that can come about with the concept of no-self. He says, "I witness the processes of thinking, feeling, sensing, and perceiving as a series of discrete and discontinuous events, each arising and passing away without remainder. In this experience of complete discontinuous change, a Copernican revolution occurs. 'Things' disappear. What is apparent is only events on the order of milliseconds. Not only is everything changing all the time; there are no 'things' that change. Any notion of an enduring or inherent self, a solid body, a durable perceptual object, even a fixed point of observation like an 'observing self' becomes completely untenable" (Engler, 2003, p. 69).

He then goes on to suggest that the type of awareness brought about by this type of meditation is similar to the reactions a client might experience in the deep work in therapy involving grieving a loss of the sense of self that was previously understood. To Westerners the notion of no-self can bring about a sense of psychological emptiness that can be similar to contemplative Christian experiences of "the dark night of the soul" (Engler, 2003, p. 78), as first described by St. John of the Cross. For Christians, this sense of the dark night of the soul involves a sensation of being let down by all that was previously held dear, as well as feeling completely separate from one's understanding of God. This can be experienced as a profound depression and may also precede new insights and learning. What can alleviate some of this tension and worry about feelings of emptiness brought about by the experience of no-self is a refocusing on the notion of interdependence. Engler (2003) says about no-self, "That doesn't mean that things don't exist or that I don't exist—they do and I do, but dependently: as a form, a patterning, that is nothing more than the totality of our relation with everything else in this moment. They are no-*thing* apart from these relations" (p. 75). So, just as a paradigm shift occurred in relation to an acceptance of the Copernican revolution, and the sun rather than the earth was understood as being in the center of the universe, we are also decentered. The self is not all-knowing and observing of everything that is around it, but rather affected by others' force fields.

How can I interact more compassionately in my social work practice, and how might I see the no-self as assisting with this? If reflexive practice implies tuning into ourselves and reflecting upon the knowledge and skills that we have previously taken for granted, how does the notion of no-self help us in letting go of ourselves in an ethical exchange with the other, as Levinas describes it? The answers may lie in letting go of a variety of attachments: performance anxiety and our attachment to how we think we should be as social workers, what we think we already know about the other, and also what we hope for the therapeutic process regarding the ending of suffering. If we can be open to the possibility of no-self and open to the fact that we are perhaps not much more than a series of fluid thoughts and emotions, we might be better able to be patient and compassionate with ambiguity and suffering. We may witness and experience these things with less of a struggle to control. Ironically, when we become less attached to the idea of fixing the problems that are presented to us, the problems are more likely to dissolve. In my therapy work and spiritual life, I grapple with this notion of no-self as much as I am attracted to it. However, I have currently decided to live with the ambiguity and confusion this causes, since I am drawn to the possibilities it offers me. I have already begun to experience a greater ease with attempting to let go of expectations for certain outcomes in my personal and social work lives. This has ironically meant that at times more than I could have hoped for has occurred.

Engler (2003) concludes by saying that the extent to which we cling to and operate out of the illusion of continuity and sameness (i.e., cling to the idea that there is some sort of independent static self) "will inhibit and constrict our ways of being, as compromise formations always do" (p. 79). If we can stop clinging to our sense of self as independent and stop clinging to the goals we have set for the self, then this detachment may free us to be more present in moment-to-moment exchanges. Fulton (2008) describes this as a shift away from taking things personally.

Kwee (2003) and DelMonte (2003) also discuss the relationship between no-self and the possibilities for nurturing a state of detachment in order to be more present to the other in the therapy setting.

NO-SELF AND DETACHMENT

Like Schön, Kwee (2003) problematizes positivist approaches, describing postmodernism as a worldview that "questions logical positivism and scientific generalizations that go beyond space-time/culture and challenges the objectivist-rationalist viewpoint" (p. 182). Kwee's descriptions of his approach of "NeoZEN, a clinical psychological approach to Buddha's pristine words" (p. 181), sound consistent with narrative therapy approaches and also with Engler's description of the no-self. He says, "We are self-reflexive time binders capable of projecting events from the past to the present or to the future. To be means to be constructed in a coherent story. Thus self is viewed as a narrative construction, an I-me-mine that is relative, contextual, interdependent, and foremost: impermanent" (p. 182).

Kwee (2003) goes on to discuss the mind/body. He suggests that being aware of the perishable body allows us to think of how our nails and hair grow and to accept radioactive isotope studies that suggest that "98% of all bodily atoms are renewed within one year. . . . The solid body is not only impermanent and changes by drugs/medication, it is also the physical locus from which we experience out interrelations" (p. 186). According to his reasoning, if the solid body is changeable, then the mind, which cannot be found and the existence of which cannot be proved, surely must also be changeable and impermanent. "Thus we are full of experience but empty of self. . . . Fortunately we can create provisional permanence. In fact, this is an amazing human quality. The problem arises when we believe or become attached to that permanence" (p. 186). He later moves on to make the link between meditation and emptiness, whereby meditation leads to an enlightened self-interest, which "is a loving kindness/friendliness that keeps the middle way between egotism and altruism. It is a loving self-interest first to be better able to give more to others" (p. 188).

DelMonte (2003) also discuses mindfulness as a process of moving toward freedom from attachment. He says,

> Meditational mindfulness is also used to observe the psychic nature of felt attachments, with their complex interwoven webs of emotional, cognitive, attitudinal and behavioral subcomponents. In observing the very construction of consciousness in this non-attached (i.e. non-grasping or non-identificatory manner) practitioners [of meditation] hope, at least temporarily, to move beyond the pull of our unbridled yearnings. . . . Freedom is where craving is converted into mindful choice. If cravings are invariably suppressed then we are no freer than if we always yield to them! . . . Mindfulness meditation encourages an opening to higher consciousness. In this way it is similar to some forms of prayer. (p. 160)

In fact, Bourgeault (2004), discussing "centering prayer," says, "The practice of meditation is indeed an authentic experience of dying to self—not at the level of the will, however, but at the level of something even more fundamental: our core sense of identity and egoic processing methods that keep it in place. . . . When we enter meditation . . . we let go of our self-talk, our interior dialogue, our fears, wants, needs, preferences, daydreams, and fantasies. These all become just 'thoughts,' and we learn to let them go" (p. 81).

In one of my favorite passages by Merton (2003), he says, "I wind experiences around myself and cover myself with pleasures and glory like bandages in order to make myself perceptible to myself and to the world, as if I were an invisible body that could only become visible when something visible covered its surface" (p. 37). He later goes on to describe a need for detachment from these experiences we wind about ourselves, but also from other pleasures and ambitions that might appear to be more noble and less worldly. In fact, he says, "You will never be able to have perfect interior peace and recollection unless you are detached even from the desire of peace and recollection. You will never be able to pray [or meditate] perfectly until you are detached from the pleasures of prayer" (p. 211).

Conclusion

If I were to draw a diagram of my view of the connection among mindfulness, reflexivity, and no-self, I would place mindfulness at the top and in the center of the diagram. I would then draw two arrows coming away from it, one pointing toward reflexivity and the other toward no-self. Then at the bottom, I would have reflexivity and no-self both contributing to a form of social work practice that is more situated in the moment-to-moment process. I believe that mindfulness can enhance our reflexivity as social workers. I also believe that the more we experience mindfulness and the impermanence of our thoughts and feelings, the more apt we are to experience a sense of no-self. I am suggesting that these experiences can assist us in being less attached to our previously taken-for-granted ways of thinking and being and so more open to other possibilities for ourselves and for those people who come and consult us.

References

Birnbaum, L. (2005). Connecting to inner guidance: Mindfulness meditation and transformation of professional self-concept in social work students. *Critical Social Work, 6*(2). Retrieved July 29, 2007, from http://www.criticalsocial work.com/units/socialwork/critical.nsf/EditDoNotShowInTOC/EF84B5D 985393C9285257017001BBEC6

Bourgeault, C. (2004). *Centering prayer and inner awakening.* Cambridge, MA: Cowley.

Chambon, A. S. (1999). Foucault's approach: Making the familiar visible. In A. S. Chambon, A. Irving, & L. Epstein (Eds.), *Reading Foucault for social work* (pp. 51–81). New York: Columbia University Press.

Chambon, A. S. (2007). Between social critique and active reenchantment. In S. L. Witkin & D. Saleebey (Eds.), *Social work dialogues: Transforming the canon in inquiry, practice, and education* (pp. 203–226). Alexandria, VA: Council on Social Work Education.

Chambon, A. S., Irving A., &. Epstein, L. (Eds.). (1999). *Reading Foucault for social work.* New York: Columbia University Press.

D'Cruz, H., Gillingham, P., & Melendez, S. (2007). Reflexivity, its meanings and relevance for social work: A critical review of the literature. *British Journal of Social Work, 37*(1), 73–90.

DelMonte, M. M. (2003). Mindfulness and the deconstruction of attachments. *Constructivism in the Human Sciences, 8*(2), 151–171.

Engler, J. (2003). Being somebody and being nobody: A reexamination of the understanding of self in psychoanalysis and Buddhism. In J. D. Safran (Ed.), *Psychoanalysis and Buddhism: An unfolding dialogue* (pp. 35–79). Boston: Wisdom.

Fook, J. (1999). Critical reflectivity in education and practice. In B. Pease & J. Fook (Eds.), *Transforming social work practice: Postmodern critical perspectives* (pp. 195–208). St. Leonards, Australia: Allen and Unwin.

Fulton, P. R. (2008). Anatta: Self, non-self, and the therapist. In S. F. Hick & T. Bien (Eds.), *Mindfulness and the therapeutic relationship* (pp. 55–71). New York: Guilford Press.

Gehart, D. R. (2005). *Mindfulness in therapy: Integrating Buddhist concepts in therapy.* Paper presented at the Catching the Winds of Change Conference, Halifax, Nova Scotia.

Gehart, D. R., & McCollum, E. E. (2007). Engaging suffering: Towards a mindful revisioning of family therapy practice. *Journal of Marital and Family Therapy, 33*(2), 214–226.

Godzich, W. (1986). Foreword. In M. de Certeau, *Heterologies: Discourse on the other* (pp. vii–xxi). Minneapolis: University of Minnesota Press.

Gray, M., & Pozzuto, R. (2007). Can a conservative profession like social work have an emancipatory practice? In S. L. Witkin & D. Saleebey (Eds.), *Social work dialogues: Transforming the canon in inquiry, practice, and education* (pp. 113–143). Alexandria, VA: Council on Social Work Education.

Healy, K. (2000). *Social work practice: Contemporary perspectives on change.* London: Sage.

Irving, A. (2007). Inhabiting the off-frame: Social workers as connoisseurs of ambiguity. In S. L. Witkin & D. Saleebey (Eds.), *Social work dialogues: Transforming the canon in inquiry, practice, and education* (pp. 227–248). Alexandria, VA: Council on Social Work Education.

Kabat-Zinn, J. (1990). *Full catastrophe living: Using the wisdom of your body and mind to face stress, pain and illness.* New York: Dell.

Kwee, M. G. T. (2003). NeoZen: A "structing" psychology into non-self and beyond. *Constructivisim in the Human Sciences, 8*(2), 181–203.

Merton, T. (2003, 1961). *New seeds of contemplation.* Boston: Shambhala.

Palmer, A. (2007). *Mindfulness, stress and coping styles among university students.* M.Ed. thesis, University of Western Ontario.

Roche, S. E. (2007). Postmodern call and response: Social work education in the modernist university. In S. L. Witkin & D. Saleebey (Eds.), *Social work dialogues: Transforming the canon in inquiry, practice, and education* (pp. 299–325). Alexandria, VA: Council on Social Work Education.

Schön, D. A. (1983). *The reflective practitioner: How professionals think in action.* New York: Basic Books.

White, M. (2007). *Maps of narrative practice.* New York: Norton.

CHAPTER FIVE

Watching the Train: Mindfulness and Inner Dialogue in Therapist Skills Training

David A. Paré, Brian Richardson, and Margarita Tarragona

Knowing that we can slow things down to determine where our questions are stemming from is both exhilarating and frustrating.

My inner dialogue is such an integral part of my counseling process that I have difficulty articulating it . . . yet when you sit and look at your hand, and really look at it, you see all of these weird lines, and it becomes something completely foreign.

I strongly believe my role as a counselor is to stimulate thought and help clients reach their own conclusions. I think I chose to respond differently when I found my inner dialogue was becoming too judgmental or when I was taking on a stance of fixing the client.

The quotes above are samples of reflections from student therapists on their experiences of attending to their inner dialogues in the midst of a therapeutic conversation. The task of directing their attention inwardly during a session reaps a rich range of reflections, from exasperation with conflicting impulses to delight at the discovery of what becomes visible when one slows down and attends to the moment at hand. Their comments capture some of the paradoxes and possibilities unveiled by mindful attention to therapeutic conversation.

In this chapter, we share some of our experiences in applying mindfulness to therapist training. The aspect of mindfulness practice we are most concerned with here is the way it promotes an exquisitely fine-grained awareness of experience as it unfolds, moment by moment. More specifically, we will reflect on how mindfulness practice renders more visible to practitioners what one of our students described as the ongoing train of thought that accompanies the outer dialogue of therapeutic conversations. In this chapter we will take a look at that "train" and how to relate to it in specific ways in order to enhance the therapeutic relationship. Furthermore, we will explore some ideas and exercises related to mindfulness and inner dialogue in therapeutic conversations.

Attention, Intention, and an Ethic of Care

Our interest in mindfulness as it relates to therapeutic conversations is at the service of a more fundamental priority—the promotion of ethical relationship practices as a core feature of practitioner training. The imperative to do no harm is central to ethical codes in the helping professions; however, it is not the adherence to codes we refer to in invoking the word *ethics* (Strong, 2005), but a more general and ubiquitous ethic of care (Crocket, Kotzé, & Flintoff, 2007). The development of one's therapeutic practice is a lifetime's work, and fully ethical practice is an aspiration rather than a destination. It is a fundamental aspiration, however, because it relates to our accountability to the person across from us in a therapeutic conversation. Mindfulness as refined and compassionate attention serves this aspiration for many reasons and is an important tool in therapist training.

We believe the possibility of minimizing unanticipated harm to clients increases as therapists attend more closely to what they are experiencing, both externally and internally, in the course of their work. The intention to do no harm is a necessary starting point but in itself is insufficient to ensure care-filled practice. In the course of our careers as therapists, we have heard numerous stories from clients about hurtful experiences they have had in therapy. It is unlikely their therapists generally *intended* harm, and so how can this have occurred? A therapist's intentions can be sabotaged when he or she overlooks a pained look or a pregnant pause, which leads the therapist to lose step with a client's mood or meaning. Alternately, therapists may fail to notice their own emotional response to a situation, a response that leads them to avoid or hone in on a particular detail without consideration for the impact on the client. Or they may not be fully aware of a deeply entrenched belief that persuades them to champion some goal contrary to clients' preferences. These blind spots can otherwise be understood as failures of attention, of practice that is insufficiently mindful. When we notice more, we are able to make more informed decisions: *attention supports intention* in this respect.

Donald Schön's (1983, 1987) seminal work on reflective practice has influenced our work here: our aim is to promote increased reflexivity on the part of practitioners by inviting them to be more mindful in their practice. This involves awareness of the subtle nonverbal cues within the room, as well as the broader cultural discourses originating outside the room (Hare-Mustin, 1994), which influence how we go forward at every utterance. This is not to suggest that practitioners must settle for nothing less than full awareness—a sort of "enlightenment or nothing" position. Nor do we presume that therapists can achieve certainty that their actions, however well intended, are without harm. But this ongoing striving for an ethic of care in the sense we are describing it here is central to our therapist training, and mindfulness practice supports that aspiration. In this chapter we will say more about how we introduce mindfulness into our teaching—especially pertaining to the therapist's inner dialogue—elaborating further on our purposes as they relate to ethical relationship practices.

Counseling as Conversation: Exoticizing the Domestic

At the outset of our skills training we suggest to graduate students that, previous career experience aside, they all have long histories of practice directly relevant to their professional training. Drawing on social constructionist premises (Gergen, 1994, 1999), we make sense of therapy as conversation (Anderson, 1997; Eaton, 1998; Labov & Fanshel, 1977; Strong, 2006), in which meaning is jointly constructed between therapist and client, utterance by utterance, as the conversation unfolds (Anderson, 1997; Anderson & Gehart, 2006; Shotter, 1993). We remind students that it is their long-developed, well-honed abilities to be helpful to others through conversation that brings them to the program.

This is the good news. However, we also acknowledge that, as Langer (1989) has discovered through dozens of ingenious experiments, it can be more difficult to notice and make distinctions about what we are doing when the task is familiar than when it is novel. Engaging repeatedly with the familiar can lead to what Langer calls a "mindlessness" (p. 11) characterized by automatic, unreflected action. In this mindless state, there is little discernment regarding experience. We act on impulse and are more likely to fall back on rigid categorizations and to prematurely foreclose the weighing of options. Langer's observations about how a mindless orientation leads to rigid categorization resonate with Schön's (1983) description of practitioners who act from theories and models unreflectively: They "carry a danger of misreading situations, or manipulating them, to serve the practitioner's interest in maintaining his confidence in his standard models and techniques. When people are involved in the situation, the practitioners may preserve his sense of expertise at his clients' expense" (p. 45).

Mindfulness applied to therapeutic dialogue offers much to counter-act these tendencies. It starts with encouraging in our students a fine-grained attention to what they experience through their eyes and ears, moment by moment in dialogue. This is the "bare attention" referred to by Epstein (1995) in his integration of Buddhism and psychotherapy: the invocation to "pay precise attention, moment by moment, to exactly what you are experiencing, right now" (p. 110).

Early in our classes, we introduce students to the raisin exercise mentioned by Hick in chapter 1. The discovery of a raisin's complexity of color, shade, shape, texture, odor, and taste opens students up to the nuances presented in each therapeutic moment. It is not as though those nuances are available only to the trained practitioner. On the con-trary, they constitute a wide range of information readily available to the observer but most often overlooked. Bennett-Goleman (2001) speaks of studies that show that most people stop hearing the sound of a metronome after ten clicks—the phenomenon literally drops out of their experience in its repetitive familiarity. On the other hand, experi-enced meditators continue to be aware of the sound for four times as long (Bennett-Goleman, 2001). It is that attention to their experience that we encourage in our students with a number of variations on the raisin exercise, such as directing them to listen to a client without speaking and to direct their attention exclusively to nonverbals.

Predictably, students report the discovery of cues previously unno-ticed—variations in voice tone and body posture, facial expression, cadences and rhythms of speech. They also frequently report that the act of attending to these knocked them off balance, as it were, disrupt-ing conventional conversational practices and rendering the familiar strange. This is what the anthropologist Bourdieu (1988) referred to with the phrase "exoticizing the domestic"—an orientation of wonder and curiosity that unveils the complexity and variation of phenomena that might otherwise be taken for granted. Becoming mindful opens us to an array of previously unnoticed phenomena. In the short term, this can be overwhelming; in the longer term, as we shall see as this discus-sion unfolds, much of the newly discovered information recedes into the background, where it is available but does not hamper practice. Witnessing this process unfold with our students has provided insight into the challenges of expanding our awareness while we are engaged in complex tasks such as therapeutic dialogue.

Noticing Discourse from a Position within Discourse

The openness to that which makes each person unique is an orientation we encourage in our teaching. It stands in contrast to an expert stance characterized by predetermined categories, labels, and explanations that frame our experiences and our views of the client. For us, this orientation relates to an ethic of care because it guards against us inadvertently supplanting clients' meanings with our own, an act that might arguably be described as a form of violence. Elsewhere, this therapeutic posture is described as "not-knowing" (Anderson, 1997), "beginner's mind" (Epston, 1993), and "curiousity" (White, 1997). Despite this diversity in terminology, we find here a shared theme—an openness to being surprised, a holding lightly to presuppositions, a relinquishing of certainty. All of these are congruent with a mindful orientation, with "bringing a gentle curiosity to something" (Segal, Williams, & Teasdale, 2002, p. 227) as a means to greeting the moment and meeting the person before us in his or her exquisite uniqueness.

In this chapter we want to share some reflections about how this posture of wonder can be brought to a very specific aspect of the wide range of phenomena open to awareness: our inner dialogue in the midst of therapeutic conversation. Mindfulness literature often speaks of letting go of discursive mind chatter, which may include unsolicited mental mail in the form of preoccupation with the past or future, self-judgment, and self-criticism. This letting go creates space to attend more fully to what Epstein (1995) calls a "raw sensory event" (p. 110). It also promotes a quiescence in which practitioners may bring their attention back to their thoughts, this time with intention and discernment, to note the various options presented to them in their inner dialogue—the potentially productive features of discursive mind. And so we encourage students to apply the same bare attention to inner dialogue that they do to, for instance, the nonverbals in a therapeutic exchange.

Overtly, one-on-one therapy conversations are single dialogues between two persons. When one makes space for the covert, however—taking into consideration the inner experience of the two conversants—there are at least three dialogues going on (Anderson, 1997). Taking this notion further, we believe there are multiple and often contradictory dialogues available to a therapist's attention. In a sense, "the I fluctuates among different and even opposed positions" (Hermans, 2004, p. 19). Some of these positions have the potential to be harmful to clients. Awareness of inner dialogue, like awareness of other sensory impressions, supports practitioners in acting in ways that are congruent with the intention to be helpful.

To make meaning of what we notice when we attend to it—even something as apparently straightforward as a facial expression or tone of voice—we nevertheless have to rely on a historically and culturally situated interpretive repertoire. This repertoire provides us with a myriad of frames or filters, otherwise referred to as "lenses" (Hoffman,

1990), "voices" (Bakhtin, 1984; Penn & Frankfurt, 1994), or "discourses" (Fairclough, 1992; Paré, 2002). Attending to inner dialogue sheds light on this extensive repertoire—these ideas, beliefs, values, concepts, and so forth—which influences the meanings we make of the moment at hand.

Some of that repertoire is the outgrowth of institutional knowledge making—the innumerable theories, constructs, categories, and labels generated by twentieth-century psychology. A client becomes tearful, and one therapist seeks to intensify the emotion through an empty chair exercise. A client expresses an unhelpful belief, and another therapist hears irrational self-talk and steers the conversation toward disputing the cognition. There are many other varieties of frequently unnoticed discourses that have an impact on how we respond in therapeutic conversations. Some relate to professional codes and legal statutes—for example, in relation to reporting abuse to authorities. Gender discourses often come into play, as well, and may lead us in conversations with families to turn to mothers for nurturance, and fathers for discipline. Some of our own long-standing values and beliefs traceable to particular experiences may also influence what we attend to, as when we automatically hear accounts of work stress as equivalent to our father's workaholism, or we turn a conversation about quitting smoking into a critique of advertising and the perils of capitalism under the influence of Marxist ideas informing our politics.

These are of course just a few of the infinite possible sources of influence, frequently unnoticed, that impinge on the unfolding therapeutic conversation. Rober, Elliott, Buysse, Loots, and De Corte (2008) identified 282 varieties of inner dialogue in a study of eight therapy sessions. While they found that "the therapist gathers information, constructs hypotheses, and tries to formulate therapeutic goals" (p. 48), the authors' qualitative study demonstrated that "the therapist also doubts, hesitates, senses what the client experiences, notices the client's resources, is surprised, and so on" (p. 48). None of this happens in a vacuum. Hare-Mustin (1994) refers to the "mirrored room" to describe the culturally embedded repertoires of sense-making that reflect back at us from all sides as we attend to and speak with the people who consult us. Mindfulness practice allows therapists in training to notice these discourses while acknowledging that they always do so from a place within discourse.

Choosing that place is central to ethical practice. Morson and Emerson (1990) cite the work of Mikhail Bakhtin, who depicts inner experience as a struggle between discrepant voices which speak from different positions and are also invested with different degrees and kinds of authority. Noticing and attending to inner dialogue thus helps a practitioner to "find [his or her] own voice and to orient it among other voices, to combine it with some and to oppose it to others, to separate [his or her] voice from another voice with which it has inseparably merged" (Bakhtin, 1984, p. 239). We see this as an important component of developing a reflexive practice (Schön, 1987).

Consider the example of a therapist who hears a client speak of frequent arguments with his or her partner. This week they yelled at each other every day but Thursday, when they avoided an argument by walking away from a heated exchange and reconvening later to more calmly talk through their issue. Turning their attention inward, the therapist might notice various strands of dialogue. One might be speculation about how the relational conflict may be the outgrowth of trauma originating in childhood, a focus on what is "broken." Taking up this strand might lead the conversation toward an exploration of childhood trauma and a curiosity about what dysfunctional patterns are being duplicated in the current relationship, and so on. A second strand might feature identification of Thursday's events as a personal victory, a celebratory moment rife with promise. Taking up that strand might lead to an exploration of how the couple managed to avoid yelling, what skills they may have drawn on in doing things differently, what this development might say about their commitment to peaceful relations, and so forth. These are distinct "trains," and they lead to very different places. A therapist who is not mindful will "board" one or the other without the experience of having chosen to do so, in much the same way that the mind undeliberately latches onto discursive strands during meditation practice and draws us away from attention to the breath. Doubtless, different readers may favor one or the other of the two conversational directions cited here; the point is that intentional selection from inner dialogue supports practice congruent with an ethic of care.

In the parlance of emerging approaches integrating mindfulness practice with cognitive therapy, we therefore invite students to experience "decentering" (Segal et al., 2002, p. 38) themselves in relation to their trains of thought—to watch those trains from the platform, as it were. From here, the thoughts can "be seen as passing events in the mind that [are] neither necessarily valid reflections of reality nor central aspects of the self" (Segal et al., 2002, p. 38). However, we do not advocate that practitioners merely dismiss these thoughts en masse. Like all other data in their field of awareness, this is useful information. Selecting what to respond to and what to ignore is all at the service of being helpful through conversation.

Slowing the Train Down through a Pedagogical Exercise

Anderson stresses the importance of pauses in conversation in order to open space for inner and outer dialogues (Anderson & Gehart, 2006).

The first author has devised a pedagogical exercise designed to open this space (cf. Paré & Lysack, 2006). It is focused on inner dialogue with master's-level students in their core therapy skills course. The exercise is one of several practice-based assignments in the full-semester course and calls upon students to conduct a therapy session with one of their classmates and record their inner dialogue during that conversational exchange.

The exercise is fashioned to slow conversations down and to provide a window for observing inner dialogue. In one variation, we introduced a text-based medium in order to create the possibility for a dialogic exchange in slow motion. Students were paired up (as "therapist" and "client") and began a conversation outside class. The conversation provided the beginning of a conversational exchange in which the client broadly outlined the presenting concern being brought forward. The face-to-face contact also made it possible for client and therapist to develop some degree of rapport through direct verbal contact.

The students were then instructed to continue the conversation online—talking by typing, as it were. As registrants in the course, they had access to a WebCT site to do this, though most opted for more familiar public chat rooms on the Internet. The assignment instructed students to record their inner dialogue at the time it came up. Following each utterance from their clients, the therapists were asked to type notes in their word processors offline (thoughts, feelings, images, ideas, etc.)[1] prior to typing a response to the other student in order to remind themselves of their inner dialogue later. The students were then instructed to combine the online exchange and the offline notes on each utterance in a written assignment. In a more recent course, students did a variation of this assignment. Instead of conversing online, they conducted the exercise face to face, with both therapist and client pausing to jot down inner dialogue after key utterances. Our aim here is not to summarize the considerable qualitative data that emerged from these studies of student responses, but rather to reflect more broadly on the pedagogical challenges associated with encouraging mindful attention to activities previously performed automatically.

Slowing an activity down makes it possible to turn one's attention to features of the activity that are typically overlooked. Reporting on the inner-dialogue exercise, some students described the luxury of having time to reflect; others recounted how they came to be more comfortable with and to value the pauses and silence the exercise demanded.

---

1. Inner dialogue is frequently characterized solely in cognitive terms, that is, as self-talk (cf. Morran, 1986; Morran, Kurpius, & Brack, 1989). We believe the notion of dialogue extends beyond cognitions—it is the meaning making we do in response to anything in the field of perception—and so we were deliberate in not limiting students' attention to cognitions alone.

The inner dialogue itself took many forms, from speculating about details of the client's story or the possibility of implementing a particular intervention to fretting about a perceived lack of direction in the session or noticing hunger or boredom.

In many cases, attention to inner dialogue provided the students with useful information for making adjustments in accordance with their preferred therapeutic positioning. This included reflecting on the direction of the session, as in "Before I can delve further, I need to get a better idea of how she feels 'restricted.' This would give me a clearer picture of what she is going through at the moment." Other opportunities for making adjustments arose when students caught themselves doing more of the work than they considered helpful: "[He] needs to come to his own conclusions and I am to facilitate or guide him." In attending to inner dialogue about the prospects of encouraging a client to take steps, a student concluded: "I will be curious and ask if he might be ready to join a club or a team."

These are examples of intentional practice informed by inner dialogue. By turning their attention inward, students were presented with further options, making selections based on their preferred directions. Many students, like Nancy,[2] found their discoveries surprising: "I never noticed that such thoughts and feelings were occurring while I listened to someone else. Being aware of this was a powerful experience." Nancy described the experience as exhilarating. This noticing by the students of particular patterns in their practice and in their reflections on their practice will usefully inform their ongoing work.

But the students did not uniformly cite the benefits of the exercise. Like dancers who fumble when encouraged to count the beat so as to refine their steps, many spoke of being overwhelmed by the new information entering their awareness. Some found themselves "losing connection" with their clients as a result. Irene spoke of feeling overwhelmed by the potential complexity of the work itself: "I would like to feel good about my role as a therapist and not second-guess myself at all times. What did I learn from this session? Honestly, I learned that counseling is a lot harder than it seems. It is more than 'how does that make you feel' questions, like people think."

For Irene, the familiar task of having a talk was rendered exotic, and in the process, she lost touch with her own long-standing ability to be present and connected to the other through conversation. Reflections like Irene's have led us to ponder deeply the connection between mindfulness and what appears at first glance to be a contradiction between intentionality and responsivity in therapeutic conversations. It would be useful for us to briefly explore this distinction before sharing some

---

2. Student names were altered to preserve confidentiality.

closing reflections on mindfulness and inner dialogue as it pertains to pedagogy.

Intentionality and Responsivity in Dialogue

One distinction that surfaced in this research is between practice characterized by *intentionality*, primarily informed by active choice making involving selecting from options presented through reflection (as described here) and practice mostly oriented to *responsivity*, primarily informed by the client's contributions, utterance by utterance (T. Strong, personal communication, May 23, 2007). It is certainly possible to engage with either aspect of practice mindfully. With the former, we attend to a repertoire of conversational options that may open a crack to new possibilities; with the latter, we attempt to stay as close as possible to client meanings. Lowe (2005) highlights this distinction in writing of practice more oriented to "structured methods" and preconceived question sequences versus practice characterized primarily by spontaneous responsivity to unanticipated "striking moments."

Useful as the distinction between responsivity and intentionality is, it suggests an unnecessary polarization. We do not believe the two are at odds; indeed, neither aspect of practice is sufficient in itself. With regard to responsivity, Lynn Hoffman (2006) describes a range of contemporary "conversational" or "dialogical" approaches[3] embodying "the art of witness." These approaches emphasize the importance of being with the client, of following the conversation closely and responding to the client's narrative moment by moment and joining together in a mutual inquiry. Anderson (2006) says: "Listening is . . . a participatory activity that requires responding to try to understand. . . . It requires checking with the other to learn if what you think you heard is what the other person hoped you would hear" (p. 36). Being intentional (i.e., reflecting on choices and making decisions as to how to position oneself with regard to sometimes conflicting options) without being responsive could lead to practice dominated by therapist meaning making and could be unhelpful or inadvertently harmful.

On the other hand, being responsive without being intentional is also insufficient. Responsivity calls upon therapists to examine what meaning they are making of what they are hearing in order to attend to what is informing their choices to go forward in the conversation. Merely responding unreflexively on the assumption that what we say will always be right if it feels right is perilous. "Withness" does not happen

---

3. Hoffman mentions the work of Harlene Anderson and Harry Goolishian, Tom Andersen, Peggy Penn, Jaakko Seikkula, Mary Olson, and Chris Kinman, among others.

in a vacuum. As White (2007) says, our very approach to therapeutic conversations is informed by some sort of guiding idea that informs how we listen and what we notice, "although very often these guiding ideas have become so taken for granted and accepted that they are rendered invisible and unavailable for critical reflection" (p. 6).

A guiding idea may not always be an explicit thought expressible in discursive terms. Some forms of knowing are more elusive and difficult to capture in words—and certainly not all of our teaching focuses on inner dialogue. But we are interested in encouraging students to be mindful of the variety of knowledges available to them, and these include not just the subtle form of knowledge, sometimes thinly described as intuition, but other knowledges as well. These may be ideas about gender or family patterns and their influence on actions, to name but a couple of potentially endless forms of knowledge that might inform the conversation at hand. As therapists acquire experience, these knowledges may increasingly be associated with repertoires of potentially useful questions and intervention options honed by the therapist him- or herself or others, consistent with the practitioner's values and appropriate to the circumstances at hand. White (2007) likes to employ the term *map* to characterize this repertoire. For beginning therapists, it is difficult to summon up these maps in the therapeutic moment (Stoltenberg & Delworth, 1987), and more so to choose from them deliberately in a manner congruent with their overall ethical intentions. The journey toward more complex[4] practice involves the development of the ability to do this while maintaining a conversational flow, being responsive, and staying connected to clients. It is a demanding journey, however: learning to be responsive while also staying in touch with multiple possibilities presented through attending to inner dialogue takes time. As one student reflected, the word *practice*, as in *therapeutic practice*, has more than one meaning.

Mindfulness, Tacit Knowledge, and Flow

Therapeutic practice is rife with paradoxes, and certainly the issues associated with therapist pedagogy discussed here are not exempt. As we have seen, we are advocating for an expansion of awareness that, in the short term, may detract from rather than enhance therapist flexibility. As therapists attempt to be more mindful in their practice, they initially stumble and find it more difficult to be responsively present.

---

4. Despite its occasional usage in the field (cf. Jennings & Skovholt, 1999; Murphy, Cheng, & Werner-Wilson, 2006), the word *mastery* suggests that what we feel is an unattainable endpoint and is an individualistic term that fails to capture the collaborative, relational process of therapy.

But it is through doing this that they learn to increase their options while staying true to their ethical intentions. And here what appears to be a second paradox surfaces. The development of intentional practice involves rendering conscious material previously unnoticed, but it also leads over time to the expression of what Polanyi (1975) has called "tacit knowledge." While engaging with therapeutic maps is initially very challenging to novice therapists, more experienced practitioners are able to incorporate them into their repertoires to the degree that they become second nature and retreat into the background of attention.

Take, for example, the therapist who through attention to inner dialogue has come to distinguish between conflicting ideas about clients who have survived abuse. One strand of inner dialogue may be centered on the notion of dysfunction and may initiate conversation that leads clients to view themselves as deficit ridden by childhood trauma. A second strand of inner dialogue may highlight the various skills of living acquired through the adversity faced by persons who have been abused, which might promote talk that leads clients to experience themselves as resourceful. In our own experience, the latter view plays out more usefully in practice, and we typically prefer to be informed by it as we go forward in therapeutic conversations. It might lead to questions such as "How did you manage to realize that you weren't responsible, despite being told otherwise?" or "Who would have predicted that you would survive this, and what might they tell me about what qualities have supported you in that?" As our own practices have unfolded over time, questions such as these come more easily, with less need for conscious deliberation over disputing strands of inner dialogue. However, we see this tacit knowledge (ready availability of particular question sequences) as an accomplishment, the product of sustained mindful attention to conversational options, rather than a gift.

Earlier in our practice, identifying the crossroad where we might join with the client in two very different conversations was somewhat of a revelation, and selecting the direction that meshed with our preferred ethical posture was the fruit of sustained training, reading, and practice. More recently, we are inclined to gravitate toward curiosity about client knowledges, skills, and resources without so often making that conscious choice. This is not necessarily a good thing to the extent that we could become complacent in our practice and overlook openings ripe with meaning. But it is the expression of tacit knowing, similar to what Schön (1987) calls "knowing-in-action" and akin to the knowledge of, for example, how to ride a bicycle. At first it is necessary to pay attention to the placement of one's feet on the pedals, maintenance of an upright posture, and so on. Over time, this knowledge is embodied and takes care of itself.

There is a movement toward complexity here along two continua: (1) awareness of the options available in the task at hand and (2) ability to access them. The evolutionary progression is as follows: unaware/ unable → W aware/unable →W aware/able →W unaware/able. We do not mean to suggest that one's practice always unfolds with such precise linearity, but these pairings loosely capture the trend we are discussing, where the "unaware" in the final pair refers not so much to what is unavailable, but to what is available without conscious and deliberate effort.

To achieve the highest levels of performance of any task requires much practice: consider again the accomplished dancer who, along with a partner, expresses a wide range of human emotion while responding to the partner's subtle movements. The technical skills here take years to master. The expression "Prepare, prepare, prepare, and then be spontaneous" captures the lead-up to this exquisite moment. In that moment of expression, the knowledge is merely *performed*, without discursive thought.

Csikszentmihalyi (1991, 1997) has studied this optimal moment for thirty years and uses the term *flow* to describe the state that resonates with descriptions of practitioners (e.g., cyclists, dancers, therapists) in a moment of mastery. Among the features of flow, Csikszentmihalyi cites deep concentration and being in the present, a sense of letting go of control and losing one's ego, and an altered perception of time,

Rønnestad and Orlinsky (2005) found that therapists who have practiced for many years and whose work is rewarding and characterized by what they call "healing involvement" frequently experience in-session moments of flow. This is not the case for therapists in training when they are engaged in attempting to enlarge their repertoires. How, then, can therapists be trained to be mindful of options presented by various therapeutic maps without sacrificing the apparently non-discursive expression of tacit knowledges, the experience of flow? Our own conclusion is that the former makes the latter possible. When we attend deliberately to tasks long performed mindlessly, we are temporarily impaired in our performance of those tasks. But it is for a worthy longterm cause. To experience flow in the performance of highly complex tasks such as therapy requires considerable rigor, despite the feeling of effortlessness that might eventually be experienced in the moment.

Closing Thoughts: Mindfulness, Flow, and Pedagogy

Given the staggering complexity and the dialogic nature of therapeutic conversations, we are not waiting for the emergence of empirically validated treatments. However, we are interested in training new therapists to practice with the welfare of the person across from them informing their actions as much as possible. This is about an ethic of care, and this chapter has examined the role of mindful attention to inner dialogue in that quest.

It is common to advocate qualities such as compassion, nonjudgment, and hopefulness in therapeutic relationships. Achieving this, however, requires more than the mere aspiration, and this is where mindfulness comes in. When we respond automatically in therapeutic conversations, our responses are sometimes guided by unnoticed ideas that are incongruent with our preferred relational style. When we selectively attend with curiosity to the stream of ideas, thoughts, impressions, and the like—the internal dialogue—while engaging in an outer dialogue, we are more able to let go of that which does not serve our intentions to be helpful, and to benefit from that which does.

We do not mean to assert that therapy is all about attending to inner dialogue, and we hope we have made it clear that in merely doing that, we risk losing touch with the client altogether. But we do believe that what goes on internally deserves our attention as practitioners, and we continue to develop pedagogical exercises that refine this attention.

Our research on mindful attention to inner dialogue has led to a variety of interesting situations, some somewhat paradoxical in nature. For instance, we have encountered the dilemma of how attending to inner experience may disconnect us from outer experience. But we have also identified how it becomes possible, over time, to pay attention and to select from inner dialogue during therapeutic conversations in a less effortful manner. When this happens, our ethic of care becomes more tacit, blended into the wholeness of our practice. We come to more fully embody our values and are freer to act spontaneously without fear of inadvertently harming the other. Mindfulness practice supports this evolutionary movement from awkward self-consciousness to a fuller practice featuring expanded attention to both inner and outer experience.

References

Anderson, H. (1997). *Conversation, language and possibility.* New York: Basic Books.

Anderson, H. (2006). Dialogue: People creating meaning with each other and finding ways to go on. In H. Anderson & D. Gehart (Eds.), *Collaborative therapy: Relationships and conversations that make a difference* (pp. 33–41). New York: Routledge.

Anderson, H., & Gehart, D. (Eds.). 2006. *Collaborative therapy: Relationships and conversations that make a difference.* New York: Routledge.

Bakhtin, M. (1984). *Problems of Dostoevsky's poetics*. Minneapolis: University of Minnesota Press.

Bennett-Goleman, T. (2001). *Emotional alchemy: How the mind can heal the heart*. New York: Three Rivers Press.

Bourdieu, P. (1988). *Homo academicus* (P. Collier, Trans.). Stanford, CA: Stanford University Press.

Crocket, C., Kotzé, E., & Flintoff, V. (2007). Reflections on shaping the ethics of our teaching practices. *Journal of Systemic Therapies, 26*(3), 29–42.

Csikszentmihalyi, M. (1991). *Flow: The psychology of optimal experience*. New York: Harper Perennial.

Csikszentmihalyi, M. (1997). *Finding flow: The psychology of engagement with everyday life*. New York: Basic Books.

Eaton, J. (1998). Gadamer: Psychotherapy as conversation. *European Journal of Psychotherapy, Counselling and Health, 1*(3), 421–433.

Epstein, M. (1995). *Thoughts without a thinker: Psychotherapy from a Buddhist perspective*. New York: Basic Books.

Epston, D. (1993). Internalized other questioning with couples: The New Zealand version. In S. Gilligan & R. Price (Eds.), *Therapeutic conversations* (pp. 183–189). New York: Norton.

Fairclough, N. (1992). *Discourse and social change*. Cambridge, MA: Polity Press.

Gergen, K. (1994). *Realities and relationships*. Cambridge, MA: Harvard University Press.

Gergen, K. (1999). *Invitations to social construction*. Thousand Oaks, CA: Sage.

Hare-Mustin, R. (1994). Discourses in the mirrored room: A postmodern analysis of therapy. *Family Process, 33*, 19–35.

Hermans, H. J. M. (2004). The dialogical self: Between exchange and power. In H. J. M. Hermans & G. Dimaggio (Eds.), *The dialogical self in psychotherapy* (pp. 13–28). New York: Brunner/Routledge.

Hoffman, L. (1990). Constructing realities: An art of lenses. *Family Process, 29*(1), 1–12.

Hoffman, L. (2006). The art of "withness": A new bright edge. In H. Anderson & D. R. Gehart (Eds.), *Collaborative therapy: Relationships and conversations that make a difference* (pp. 63–79). New York: Routledge.

Jennings, L., & Skovholt, T. (1999). The cognitive, emotional, and relational characteristics of master therapists. *Journal of Counselling Psychology, 46*(1), 3–11.

Labov, W., & Fanshel, D. (1977). *Therapeutic discourse: Psychotherapy as conversation*. New York: Academic Press.

Langer, E. J. (1989). *Mindfulness*. New York: Addison-Wesley.

Lowe, R. (2005). Structured methods and striking moments: Using question sequence in "living" ways. *Family Process, 44*(1), 65–75.

Morran, D. K. (1986). Relationship of counselor self-talk and hypothesis formulation to performance level. *Journal of Counseling Psychology, 33*, 395–400.

Morran, D. K., Kurpius, D. J., & Brack, G. (1989). Empirical investigation of counselor self-talk categories. *Journal of Counseling Psychology, 36*, 505–510.

Morson, G. S., & Emerson, C. (1990). *Mikhail Bakhtin: Creation of a prosaics*. Stanford, CA: Stanford University Press.

Murphy, J. M., Cheng, W., & Werner-Wilson, R. J. (2006). Exploring master therapists' use of power in conversation. *Contemporary Family Therapy, 28*, 475–484.

Paré, D. A. (2002). Discursive wisdom: Reflections on ethics and therapeutic knowledge. *International Journal of Critical Psychology, 7*, 30–52.

Paré, D. A., & Lysack, M. (2006). Exploring inner dialogue in counsellor education. *Canadian Journal of Counselling, 40*(3), 131–144.

Penn, P., & Frankfurt, M. (1994). Creating a participant text: Writing, multiple voices, narrative multiplicity. *Family Process, 33*, 217–231.

Polanyi, M. (1975). Personal knowledge. In M. Polanyi & H. Prosch (Eds.), *Meaning* (pp. 22–45). Chicago: University of Chicago Press.

Rober, P., Elliott, R., Buysse, A., Loots, G., & De Corte, K. (2008). What's on the therapist's mind? A grounded theory analysis of family therapist reflections during individual therapy sessions. *Psychotherapy Research, 18*(1), 48–57.

Rønnestad, M. H., & Orlinsky, D. E. (2005). Therapeutic work and professional development: Main findings and practical implications of a long-term international study. *Psychotherapy Bulletin, 40*, 27–32.

Schön, D. (1983). *The reflective practitioner: How professionals think in action.* New York: Basic Books.

Schön, D. (1987). *Educating the reflective practitioner: Toward a new design for teaching and learning in the professions.* San Francisco: Jossey-Bass.

Segal, Z. V., Williams, J. M. G., & Teasdale, J. D. (2002). *Mindfulness-based cognitive therapy for depression: A new approach to preventing relapse.* New York: Guilford Press.

Shotter, J. (1993). *Conversational realities: Constructing life through language.* London: Sage.

Stoltenberg, C., & Delworth, U. (1987). *Supervising counselors and therapists: A developmental approach.* New York: Jossey-Bass.

Strong, T. (2005). Constructivist ethics? Let's talk about them: An introduction to the special issue on ethics and constructivist psychology. *Journal of Constructivist Psychology, 18*(2), 89–102.

Strong, T. (2006). Counselling as conversation: A discursive perspective. *Alberta Counsellor, 28*(2), 21–27.

White, M. (1997). *Narratives of therapists' lives.* Adelaide, Australia: Dulwich Centre Publications.

White, M. (2007). *Maps of narrative practice.* New York: Norton.

CHAPTER SIX

The Contribution of Mindfulness Practice to the Development of Professional Self-Concept in Students of Social Work

Liora Birnbaum

The use of mindfulness meditation in teaching social work represents a shift in social work education toward a broader holistic approach that utilizes bodily, cognitive, and emotional personal experiences in the learning process (Canda & Smith, 2001). The social work literature tends to be limited to describing the emotional and educational benefits associated with mindfulness meditation, among them emotional regulation, enhanced community and self-awareness, and an enriched teaching curriculum. Although these benefits have been studied and documented, it is not clear how mindfulness produces them.

Meditation is a complex of disciplines that encompass a wide range of emotional and attentional regulatory training practices that may enhance physical and psychological well-being. Among these various practices, mindfulness is described as an open (or insight) meditation, which involves an ongoing observation of the content of experience from moment to moment (Lutz, Slagter, Dunne, & Davidson, 2008).

Because meditation involves altered states of consciousness, it entails a wholesome, direct, and often intuitive way of knowing in addition to the familiar cognitive-intellectual methods of learning (Jung, 1969; Tart, 1990; Wilber, 1977). This higher state of consciousness is accompanied by changes in brain-wave activity (Anand, China, & Singh, 1961; Kasamatsu & Hariri, 1966; Lutz, Greischar, Rawlings,

Ricard, & Davidson, 2004), and meditation practiced daily may open one up to a transcendent reality (e.g., Kabat-Zinn, 2005) or, as William James and Carl Jung called it, to the universal or collective unconscious (Jung, 1969; Perry, 1996).

Recent research sheds light on changes in biological processes that are associated with reported changes in mental health in response to mindfulness meditation. These biological mechanisms that involve brain functioning have not been systematically explored (Davidson et al., 2003; Davidson & Lutz, 2008), and no attempt has been made to connect them to the professional development of social workers.

This chapter explores the way in which mindfulness may mediate the development of professional self-concept in students of social work, with the aim of providing a scientific explanation to this process. The significance of such an explanation is that it addresses the practice of mindfulness in a manner that is neither spiritual nor phenomenological. The chapter includes evidence that positive emotions can be learned in the same way that one becomes proficient at a sport (Lutz, Brefczynski-Lewis, Johnstone, & Davidson, 2008).

The implications for students of social work is that they can learn to initiate independent use of their brains (and consciousness) in order to expand the repertoire of ways in which they experience and perceive themselves in the course of their studies.

Integrating Mindfulness into Training Programs

The inclusion of mindfulness practice in our social work training program allowed novice social workers to be introduced to new ways of utilizing their consciousness in the service of self-knowing. However, topics such as consciousness studies and the use of intuition are largely ignored in the academic world and are usually considered fully legitimate only in programs with a distinct spiritual or transpersonal orientation. Consequently, most graduates continue to enter the field ignorant of the function and utility of the possible activation of different parts of the brain in different states of consciousness for their own benefit as well as for the benefit of others. These brain functions could be used in the service of emotional regulation, self-awareness, and other traits that can promote the development of students' professional selves.

We find ourselves facing questions worth exploring regarding the possible connection among consciousness, the physiological mechanism activated in a meditative state, and the potential for transforming students' professional self-concept. The illustrations here are based primarily on three qualitative pilot studies in which students were exposed to formal (meditative) and informal (nonmeditative) mindfulness in the course of their social work curriculum. These teaching experiences have been studied and documented (Birnbaum, 2005, 2006, 2007).

Upon consent, fifty first-, second-, and third-year students (thirty-seven women, thirteen men; mean age = twenty-five years) participated in the first project (Birnbaum, 2005). Of the fifty participants, thirty-five met only once for an in-class workshop, while fourteen first-year students and one second-year student met for three additional sessions (on free mornings) at three-week intervals. The main goal of this project was to allow for acquaintance with one's "inner environment," to practice meditative breathing, and to foster an initial relationship with inner (higher) wisdom.

In the second project (Birnbaum, 2006) participants were fifty third-year students (forty-three women, seven men; mean age = thirty-five years) who were asked to integrate informal (everyday state) mindfulness into the first term's paper after learning about it in an intervention class. The goal here was to see whether mindfulness is associated with new ways of self-inquiry and conceptualizing therapeutic and supervisory relationships.

The third project (Birnbaum, 2007) was initiated by twelve third-year students (seven women, five men; mean age = twenty-seven years) and followed the previous project's methodology. The goal here was to allow for a long-term experience of formal mindfulness while exploring the subjective sense of being. In this project students were exposed (in class or in group) more intensively to authentic reading about related topics, such as what consciousness is, attention to breathing, and leaving the meditation (Kabat-Zinn, 1994).

As the scope of the new findings is wide, this chapter will limit discussion to information that corresponds with our own findings. We will provide an integrative explanation for processes associated with the use of mindfulness as a training tool that may expand students' self-perceptions.

Enhancing Positive Emotions

One effect of regular meditative practice is the enhancement of sensitivity to self and others. The basic technique of inner observation uses techniques that are aimed at enhancing positive emotions such as kindness, generosity, compassion, and empathy. Consistent practice may result in enhanced self-love and an improved ability to visualize the suffering of others. The goal is to weaken egocentric (therefore fixated) traits so that more aware behaviors might arise more frequently and spontaneously. Such traits among social workers can be beneficial to practice.

Our goal with our students was to practice self-observation. At that initial stage we did not know what to expect and therefore were surprised to discover that the vast majority of the participants specified experiencing positive emotions directed at the self, sometimes accompanied by bodily representations, which intuitively rose in the course of meditation (Birnbaum, 2005). Of the fifty participants, forty-five reported experiencing physical, imaginary, or emotional occurrences that they interpreted as positive. Some described radiating warmth around them, clear enhanced energy or a sensation of love, or compassion for self, and some felt hugged; fifteen participants reported feeling closeness to their own self, and eight experienced feelings of happiness, joy, and excitement (Birnbaum, 2005).

Davidson and Lutz were the first to use functional magnetic resonance imaging (fMRI) to indicate that positive emotions such as loving-kindness and compassion can be learned in the same way that one gains proficiency at a sport (Davidson et al., 2003; Lutz, Brefczynski-Lewis, et al. 2008; Lutz, Slagter, et al., 2008). Their ongoing studies investigated a group of Tibetan monks and lay practitioners who had been practicing meditation for a minimum of 10,000 hours. In one case, the researchers worked with sixteen monks who had cultivated compassion meditation practices (Lutz, Brefczynski-Lewis, et al.). Controls were sixteen age-matched lay practitioners with no previous training in meditation.

In this study and other studies they conducted (e.g., Davidson & Lutz, 2008), the fMRI scans revealed significant activity in the insula and cingulate cortices (a region near the frontal portion of the brain that plays a key role in bodily representations of emotions), and this activity appeared when the long-term meditators were generating compassion. Studies have shown that this area of the brain is important in processing empathy, especially in perceiving the mental and emotional states of others.

Compassion and empathy are no doubt essential skills for social workers in general, and especially for recent graduates at the beginning of their work. According to the traditional supervision model, these emotions are usually expected to be present in the supervisory relationship (Friedlander, Costello, & Kabos, 1984; Holloway, 1988). These models generally see the supervisee as developing through phases, shifting gradually from a passive to an active mode of operation, and finally reaching calm and collegiality with the supervisor.

While this description may be valid, it tends to rely heavily on the supervisory relationship as the context in which progress is embedded and depends specifically on the image of the good enough supervisor as an "emotional provider" (Watkins, 1992). In other words, these models suggest an other-related framework that builds on the supervisor's ability to show empathic feelings like compassion. In our perception, we are looking at an innovative way of teaching students to generate positive emotions toward themselves and become more autonomous in building their professionalism. We do not suggest that mindfulness should replace the warm relationship with the supervisor, although, undoubtedly, it has the capacity to promote self-care behavior.

As one student put it with reference to supervision, "I can turn my emotions into a creation. . . . Usually discovering things about myself is painful and causes me to shut down. In meditation the transition was easy, full of light, joy, and wholeness." Moreover, the trained Tibetan meditators in this research had baseline increases in gamma synchrony and amplitude (Lutz, Slagter, et al., 2008), which suggest long-term changes in their brains brought about by years of meditation. The great significance of this fact is that emotional (and later behavioral) changes are apt to last longer among people who practice mindfulness consistently. The practical implication is that students can be taught to regulate their brain activity through their own will to enhance desirable qualities through a purely deliberate mental activity.

Exploring Altered States of Consciousness

One of the immediate outcomes of our mindfulness projects was students' exploration of the nature of altered states of consciousness and the potential for knowing embedded in them. We taught our students basic mindfulness techniques and encouraged them to add a creative component of seeking the voice of their higher self for guidance. Most of the students reported receiving intuitive messages in the course of meditation that expanded on their self-awareness (Birnbaum, 2005, 2007). Some described intuitive insights as a feeling of "just knowing," as if "someone" were delivering the information to them. Some were connected to bodily sensations and some carried a more sophisticated nature of innovative insight. Two types of intuitive insights were evident among our students. One type emerged while students were in a meditative state: "I felt a lot of love surrounding me . . . and peace. . . . It was like meeting myself without masks. . . . Information arrived." "Your inner center is your heart. . . . It needs more love and less [reliance] on your rationality." The other type emerged from the reflective writing carried out after meditation: "It has occurred to me that I have a tendency to get emotionally enmeshed with others and enmeshment brings fear. . . . That's something to consider with clients and supervisor" (Birnbaum, 2007).

On a philosophical-spiritual level, we agree with Tolle's (2002) belief that insights should be treated as a manifestation of creativity that is embedded in a consciousness state of thinking/not-thinking or thinking and silence. A physical explanation is offered by Conte (2008), who, in "Testing Quantum Consciousness," refers to Bore's atomic theory. Conte says that mental states of human beings follow quantum mechanics, and he refers both to physical processes and to the basic foundation of our mind's entities. Like C. G. Jung, Bore also culminated in the formulation of a theory of mind-matter synchronization, stating that some laws and principles of quantum systems can be applied to our complex cognitive systems. The phenomenon of experiencing intuitive knowledge in the course of meditation is well known, and I suggest that it can be explained by quantum theory, should we accept a nontraditional theory of causality. Quantum mechanics involves, among other things, the relationship among reality, the act of observation, and the observer. Physical experiments show that an observed particle employs several unusual scientific qualities. First, it is capable of knowing which direction to take in the course of the experiment and thus might have consciousness. Second, it is un-localized, meaning that its behavior might influence a certain space from a distance. Third, it possesses an unexplained capacity to move from one point to another without any apparent explicable pattern. Whether accepted or not, quantum theory and its implications have placed one fact beyond dispute: there is no way to distinguish between ontology and epistemology; when human consciousness observes any phenomenon, it becomes a participating part in that phenomenon itself.

Lutz et al. (2004) assume that in terms of brain function, the meditative state marked by enhanced gamma synchrony represents an immersion of the subjects in this (meditative) fundamental luminosity. In such a state, large brain networks are changed, and new connections made (Davidson et al., 2003; Lutz, Brefczynski-Lewis, et al., 2008), and it seems like consciousness enables itself to "shift to a different mode." This kind of "just knowing" is a conscious occurrence that cannot be anticipated. It is similar to a quantum leap. Our students were instructed to shift gradually from the meditative state to what we have identified as a transitional state using nonjudgmental intuitive writing.

In general we found that while some students preferred to keep the experience to themselves and remain silent, others felt a need to share their meaning-making process. They seemed to be busy developing insights by going over their growing awareness and asking questions like: What do certain thoughts mean when they appear closely with certain body sensations and visual images? What do these thoughts and intuitions say about the *real* me, my abilities, motivations, relationships, and so forth (Birnbaum, 2005, 2007)?

Some of the written reports exhibited insightful self-apprehension, and this raised the possibility of interplay between intuitive and cognitive processes. The ability to develop insights in the form of knowledge about the self seems to emerge from the messages themselves, which are then taken a step further by students. Shifts in perception become apparent as awareness of new ideas regarding the personal self are interpreted in a broader way. Some of the insights expressed by the students were "I realize I chose to become a social worker in order to please my father," "I know I have to work on my control needs and search for my inner freedom before I can get involved in a psychological relationship," and "My anxiety of becoming a new mother represents my anxiety of not being a good enough therapist" (Birnbaum, 2005). To sum up, we believe that human consciousness serves as a channel through which new knowledge may be obtained, since in different states, it uses mechanisms capable of mediating between the physical and the metaphysical reality. We use the term *metaphysical reality* to refer to any inquiry that examines the ultimate nature of reality and existence, including the relationships between mind and matter and substance and attributes, and the mind-body problem (Loux, 2006).

Mindfulness and Emotional Regulation

The research found that, in addition to helping participants gain insight, mindfulness can have a significant calming effect, helping students regulate their anxieties. This could be the result of a self-nurturing part that they discovered in themselves—a part capable of intimacy and love (Birnbaum, 2005). This newly acquired skill helped ease the challenge of having to pay attention and comply with external systemic demands while staying attuned to one's self and maintaining an emotional inner balance.

Our advanced students who voluntarily participated in an eight-week mindfulness group were exposed to meditation techniques in a more detailed way, including the labeling aspect of the observation. *Labeling* refers to the cognitive activity of giving thoughts and emotions a label, such as "critical mind' or "anger," as they arise during meditation. Labeling aspects of experience is a central feature of historical and contemporary accounts of mindfulness (Creswell, Baldwin, Eisenberger, & Lieberman, 2007) and may represent one mechanism for the salutary effects of mindfulness practice. Creswell et al. provide the first neural evidence for associations among mindfulness, affect labeling, and improved neural affect regulation. These findings are consistent with historical accounts of mindfulness that suggest that affect-labeling practices encourage individuals to treat affective states as "objects" of attention, thus promoting a certain amount of detachment from these negative states.

In the third session of our meditation groups, students observed themselves going through an emotionally charged situation of looking at certain fears, or elements that feed these fears. Some were able to connect the anxiety and the fear that surfaced in the meditation to current aspects of their private lives—"I tend to focus on negative feelings in relation to my fetus," "I'm not good enough for it"—or to their professional lives: "I'm afraid of my field supervisor, I feel small and unskilled next to her, when we have an argument I'm afraid I'll just disappear." With some, observing and labeling the unpleasant cognitions at close range activated a reduction of its emotional intensity. "Fear is here, helplessness too. Feeling small, first I tried focusing on the fear itself[,] trying to figure out its source. . . . I continued looking at it. . . . Then I felt an immediate relief . . . felt free" (Birnbaum, 2007).

We recognized students' ability to look at the eye of the storm, right before the magic happens and the negative feeling fades away (Kabat-Zinn, 1994). Epstein (1995) describes how the ability to shift attention to a succession of objects of awareness allows the meditator to enter into states described as either terror or delight. Creswell's findings made an important contribution to the existing mindfulness literature by suggesting one neurocognitive pathway that may link mindfulness meditation practices with reduction in negative affect and mood disturbance. These findings support the existence of one of the most basic powers of mindfulness—the "power of the now" (Tolle, 2002)—as a healing force. According to Tolle, the power of the moment lies in the ability to remain present even through difficult feelings and thoughts, while consciousness is free of any pattern of thinking. True coping with harsh moments in either the past or present really occurs when we can "observe our behavior, reactions, moods, thoughts, feelings, fears and desires as they arise without judging, analyzing or criticizing" (Tolle, p. 77). These are states that do not often unfold in psychotherapy. Tolle feels that ideally, the work of meditation is in one sense the work of developing an ego that can experience terror without fear and delight without attachment. With this distinction in mind, we noticed a decrease in emotionally reactive behaviors among students who described the creation of a safe space that enabled them to observe all occurrences from a distance. "Suddenly I can see a new angle to things even in daily events. There is a sense of wholeness in me which I would like to preserve." "Concentrating on my breathing creates a huge comforting safe place inside me; an amazing, pleasant feeling" (Birnbaum, 2007).

In general, the students' reports revealed shifts in the way they experienced the self. Overall, they exhibited a new and relaxed sense of being during the independent free meditations, which was quite differ-ent from their usual state of feeling tense and overwhelmed. As one student commented, "I felt a very warm feeling in the area of my heart, a sense of liberation, like there is lots of air in me which raises me up." "I feel I'm not going anywhere . . . not intending to do anything. All I want is open space, quiet, and freedom."

These findings are very significant regarding people's emotional bal-ance. In meditation, the observer seems to be able to create an inner space that allows both a safe distance and a detachment from reactive patterns such as anxiety. In addition, this ability provides social workers with a unique emotional instrument to hand over to their clients. Aside from the physiological changes, these findings allow a new way of client empowerment as they suggest that regulating one's emotional state can be taught in a relatively simple way that can greatly support and enhance any emotional procedure.

Conclusion

The idea that the brain is constantly changing as a result of our life experience has been studied by a group of leading researchers from the University of Wisconsin (Creswell et al., 2007) and from UCLA (Lutz, Slagter, et al., 2008). In a series of innovative studies, these researchers have determined the underlying changes in biological processes that are associated with reported changes in mental health during medita-tion, for example, enhanced positive emotions and decreased negative emotions. Their findings support the view that attention is a trainable skill that can be enhanced through the mental practice of mindfulness (Davidson & Lutz, 2008). Additional research revealed the relationship between the act of labeling in meditation and emotional regulation, especially reducing anxiety. These studies pave the way to our under-standing the answers to such questions as: How much can we trans-form our minds? What are the ramifications of this new knowledge in reference to self-development?

Those physiological mechanisms that activate mental and emotional processes happen to be highly relevant to the profession of social work, possibly acting as self-directive mechanisms by which practitioners and students may improve not only their self-awareness, but also their pro-fessional skills. Our own studies with students of social work revolved around the way in which mindfulness may mediate professional devel-opment through the gradual transformation of self-concept. Gaining self-control and autonomy over the above neurophysiological proc-esses may assist in that.

Our teaching experience and student feedback indicate that integrating mindfulness into professional training programs generally means bringing the self forward and encouraging students to observe it and rely on it as a trustworthy way of learning and knowing. Most exciting to students was the appearance of intuitive messages in the workshops, insights of a personal nature that highlight professional dimensions of the self. Exposure to mindfulness demonstrated a process of self-knowing that relies on cognitive, emotional, and intuitive skills used by students in various states of consciousness. It introduces a new and unusual line of experiential self-inquiry and self-guidance to intervention courses. It challenges students to think about learning techniques that, in the past, were considered non-academic.

We found that experiencing the transformative nature of consciousness and being exposed to the underlying premises of mindfulness helped broaden students' role perspective, allowing them to view themselves as mediating new ways of approaching life and its meaning. Our students were able not only to meet new aspects of themselves, but to actively entertain the possibility that their role in this world may be different from what they previously thought.

Our impression is that programs that are progressive enough to integrate consciousness studies and mindfulness practice in their training will launch more open-minded and broadly skilled social workers who not only have read about holism but will also know how to translate this concept into useful tools in their everyday work.

References

Anand, B. K., China, G. S., & Singh, B. (1961). Some aspects of electroencephalographic studies in yogis. *Electroencephalography and Clinical Neurophysiology, 13*, 452–456.

Birnbaum, L. (2005). Connecting to inner guidance: Mindfulness meditation and transformation of professional self-concept in social work students. *Critical Social Work, 6*(2). Retrieved January 10, 2006, from http://www.critical socialwork.com/units/socialwork/critical.nsf/EditDoNotShowInTOC/EF84 B5D985393C9285257017001BBEC6www

Birnbaum, L. (2006, April). *The use of different states of consciousness in social work training.* Paper presented at Toward a Science of Consciousness international conference, Tucson, AZ.

Birnbaum, L. (2007). The use of mindfulness training to create an "accompanying place." *Social Work Education, 27*(8), 837–852.

Canda, E., & Smith, E. D. (2001). *Transpersonal perspectives on spirituality in social work.* New York: Haworth Press.

Conte, E. (2008). Testing quantum consciousness. *Neuro Quantology, 6*(2), 126–139.

Creswell, J. D., Baldwin, M. W., Eisenberger, N. I., & Lieberman, M. D. (2007). Neural correlates of dispositional mindfulness during affect labeling. *Psychosomatic Medicine, 69,* 560–565.

Davidson, R. J., Kabat-Zinn, J., Schumacher, J., Rosenkratz, M., Muller, D., Santorelli, S., et al. (2003). Alterations in brain and immune function produced by mindfulness meditation. *Psychosomatic Medicine, 65,* 564–570.

Davidson, R. J., & Lutz, A. (2008). Buddha's brain: Neuroplasticity and meditation. *IEEE Signal Processing Magazine, 25*(1), 172–176.

Epstein, M. (1995). *Thoughts without a thinker.* New York: Basic Books.

Friedlander, L. R., Costello, R. M., & Kabos, J. C. (1984). A developmental model for teaching and learning in psychotherapy supervision. *Psychotherapy, 21,* 189–196.

Holloway, E. L. (1988). Models of counselor development or training models for supervision: Rejoinder to Stoltenberg and Delworth. *Professional Psychology, 19,* 138–140.

Jung, C. G. (1969). *The structure and dynamics of the psyche* (R. H. Hull, Trans.). Princeton, NJ: Princeton University Press.

Kabat-Zinn, J. (1994). *Wherever you go, there you are: Mindfulness meditation in everyday life.* New York: Hyperion.

Kabat-Zinn, J. (2005). *Coming to our senses: Healing ourselves and the world through mindfulness.* New York: Hyperion.

Kasamatsu, A., & Hariri, T. (1966). An electroencephalographic study on the Zen meditation. *Folia Psychiatria et Neurologica 20,* 315–336.

Loux, M. J. (2006). *Metaphysics: A contemporary introduction* (3rd ed.). London: Routledge.

Lutz, A., Brefczynski-Lewis, J., Johnstone, T., & Davidson, R. J. (2008). Regulation of the neural circuitry of emotion by compassion meditation: Effects of meditative expertise. *Plos One, 3*(3), e1897.doi:10.1371.

Lutz, A., Greischar, L. L., Rawlings, N. B., Ricard, M., & Davidson, R. J. (2004). Long-term meditators self-induce high amplitude gamma synchrony during mental practice. *Proceedings of the National Academy of Sciences, USA, 101*(46), 16369–16373. Retrieved December 5, 2005, from http://www.quantom consciousnessorg/EEGmeditation.htm

Lutz, A., Slagter, H. A., Dunne, J. D., & Davidson, R. J. (2008). Attention regulations and monitoring in meditation. *Trends in Cognitive Sciences, 12*(4), 163–169.

Perry, R. B. (1996). *The thought and character of William James.* Nashville, TN: Vanderbilt University Press.

Tart, C. T. (1990). *Altered states of consciousness.* New York: Harper.

Tolle, E. (2002). *The power of the now.* Prague: Carcur.

Watkins, C. E. (1992). Psychotherapy supervision—the separation-individuation process: Autonomy versus dependency issues. *Clinical Supervisor, 10,* 111–121.

Wilber, K. (1977). *The spectrum of consciousness.* Wheaton, IL: Quest Books.

CHAPTER SEVEN

Subjective Well-Being, Mindfulness, and the Social Work Workplace: Insight into Reciprocal Relationships

Susan M. Graham and John R. Graham

The profession of social work operates within the context of multiple social levels—the individual, community, and institutional levels. Along with the complexity attached to practicing amid these multiple social levels, practitioners are presented with individual challenges and situations that have been shown to weigh negatively on the workplace and the individual practitioner. As a result, emphasis is placed on the negative repercussions and limitations of the work. Moving away from focusing on these limitations, we find it useful to unravel the interconnected and reciprocal relationship between mindfulness and subjective well-being (SWB), as these two concepts relate to the social work workplace and the profession in general. Social work practitioners could take on unique roles in their respective workplaces as leaders by adopting some of the promising characteristics associated with mindfulness and potentially improving overall individual and workplace SWB. Furthermore, drawing on the role of social work practice in the present social environment, we seek to begin expanding the discourse related to SWB and mindfulness beyond the individual to encompass the community and institutional levels of society.

A great deal of research on the experiences of social work practitioners focuses on detrimental things, such as burnout, blunted employee morale, and workplace turnover. The resolution of these problems is frequently conceived at the societal level—for instance, ensuring sufficient funding for social services; at the community level—perhaps introducing preventative measures that respond to social needs; and at the agency level—when, for example, an executive director and board adopt workplace policies that seek greater work-and-life balance. But individual practitioners, too, are important instigators of change at these mezzo and macro levels of intervention. Our profession, likewise, encourages all individuals to seek positive changes in their environments, and this imperative applies to practitioners as much as it should to their clients. And yet insufficient attention is often given to social worker well-being—in and outside the workplace.

As a modest corrective, this chapter seeks to understand better the reciprocal relationship between mindfulness and the social scientific concept of SWB. Both, together, are intricately connected with how social workers might understand with greater depth what ancient philosophers called "the good life." The chapter is divided into four sections. The first briefly identifies the reciprocal relationship between the key concepts of mindfulness and SWB. Most scholarship concurs that SWB represents how people evaluate their lives and includes measures of life satisfaction, a lack of depression and anxiety, and positive moods and emotions. The second section elaborates on this theoretical literature on SWB, as it connects or does not connect with mindfulness. The third section analyzes SWB in relation to social work practice—particularly the workplace, as this is one immediate locus where social workers may begin to be better to themselves (and, more particularly, the workplace could be better to them). The final section briefly discusses future imperatives for incorporating SWB and mindfulness in social work practice and research. Positive social worker SWB has everything to do with effective mindfulness practice. In the end, a closer relationship between SWB and mindfulness, we believe, lays groundwork for positive interactions with clients, potential human betterment for worker and client, and commensurate possibilities for positive social and individual change.

Reciprocal Relationship between Mindfulness and SWB

This first section identifies the interconnectedness between mindfulness and SWB. After a review of relevant literatures, we find that the cultivation of mindfulness in social work has the potential to increase levels of SWB, but through analysis of the fundamental characteristics of being mindful, the act of being mindful, and the outcomes attained as a result of being mindful, it becomes apparent that SWB and mindfulness are related. Each is distinct, yet there is overlap between the two; one way of understanding the two is to consider overlapping Venn diagrams. Not all SWB is reciprocal with mindfulness, but some is. A reciprocal relationship becomes evident through discussions relating to decision making, personal disposition, and the overall enhancement of positive states of mind. The presence of SWB is directly linked to the ability to practice techniques that enable individuals to be mindful.

Our chapter is one of the very first to consider the relationship between SWB and mindfulness. And much of what we argue is inherent in mindfulness and relevant to SWB is based on our own appreciation of both domains. Indeed (and, we believe, in the spirit of mindfulness itself), the following pages are consciously tentative, if not speculative, for the field is relatively wide open for fulsome empirical research into the relationship between these two robust analytical categories. But we begin with two writers who wisely point out the following: "Cultivation of mindful awareness of each moment is believed to lead to increased self-awareness and the ability to make adaptive decisions about handling difficult and problematic situations as they arise, as well as increased enjoyment of pleasant moments" (Baer & Krietemeyer, 2006, p. 10). SWB, the positive emotions and moods that are associated with it, higher satisfaction with life, and the reduction of stress and anxiety are all examples of the "increased enjoyment of pleasant moments" with which these authors correlate mindfulness. But SWB, to stress a point, is not the absence of suffering any more than mindfulness is the absence of difficulties. "Adaptive decisions" is likely the key point in this particular quotation. And positive SWB is a useful artifact and tool of these decisions.

As other contributors to this book point out, mindfulness involves important attitudes—and many, we believe, are positively associated with SWB. "Mindful attention includes a stance of compassion, interest, friendliness, and open-heartedness toward experience" (Baer & Krietemeyer, 2006, p. 3). One of the leading psychological theorists of SWB describes the imperative of high-SWB people to render the meaning of both "happy and unhappy moments, the tapestry they weave, and the strengths and virtues they display that make up the quality of [one's] life" (Seligman, 2002, p. 7). The great thinkers—from the Noble Buddha to Seneca to Schopenhauer—agree that life involves suffering. Mindfulness allows a person to experience deep SWB, as well as the awareness that there are ups and downs in life and that not all moments can be up ones; this is a realistic stance toward the reality of suffering. Part of the approach is reaching out to others, and sharing our common humanity and the suffering that is anchored to this. Mindful people can be "available to anyone for reducing suffering and encouraging the development of positive qualities, such as awareness, insight, wisdom, compassion, and equanimity" (Kabat-Zinn, 2003, p. 14). Part of that mindful compassion is inherent in accepting ourselves—cultivating an attitude of friendly curiosity, interest. A big part is discernment: accepting those things in oneself and those things external to the self that one should accept, and changing those things one should change (Baer & Krietemeyer, 2006).

Another mindful stance is keen sensitivity to the unexpected. "The workplace is full of unexpected stumbling blocks that can get in the way" of what we think we should be doing. "To a mindful manager or employee, these become building blocks" (Langer, 1989, p. 134). It is the serendipity—the unexpected—that can often be the most profitable, and perhaps, too, the most robust for SWB. Mindful people are open to new information, appreciative of more than one perspective, and continuously seeking new categories for understanding their world, rather than rigidly relying on those that are static and old (Langer, 1989). The mindful imperatives to view all problems as challenges, to deeply investigate oneself (Gunaratana, 2002)—these are things that in turn may allow for positive construction and acting upon the unexpected. Disposition has everything to do with SWB; scholarship is clear that positive people who are able to optimistically construct their worlds are likely to have higher SWB.

But there is more. Precisely because mindfulness skills are required in emotion regulation and distress tolerance and SWB is associated with positive moods and emotions, we believe that mindfulness provides insight into some of the concrete skills that get us to greater possibilities of high SWB. Two categories of skills may be particularly salient, the first of which is: What does one do when being mindful? Here, we have the acts of observing, mindfully noticing the rise and fall of internal phenomena, and participating in our interior and exterior worlds. The other skill set focuses on how one is when being mindful: being non-judgmental, attentive, and discerning are effective means of cultivating mindfully positive SWB (Baer & Krietemeyer, 2006).

Ultimately, as Langer (1989) points out, exchanging unhealthy mind-sets for healthy ones and increasing generally mindful states—these are the lasting and transformative potentials of which all of us are capable, and yet few seek in depth. But mindfulness can enhance positive states of mind—states of mind that we suspect are anchored to higher poten-tial for SWB. The ability to control one's attention—to stop obsessing about the past, the future, or current difficulties (to the detriment of full and productive responses to these difficulties): these are anxiety-reducing stances that surely influence SWB—a concept deeply reflec-tive of low anxiety (Baer & Krietemeyer, 2006). Without paying attention to these things, writes an often-cited mindfulness writer, we may be "driven by deep-seated fears and insecurities" (Kabat-Zinn, 2005, p. 5). These, in turn, may build over time, eventually "leaving us feeling stuck and out of touch. . . . We may lose confidence in our ability to redirect our energies in ways that would lead to greater satisfaction and happiness" (p. 5).

Two concluding comments emphasize those things that are not related to both SWB and mindfulness. The first is the role of judgment in better promotion of both SWB and mindfulness. For instance, in mindfulness a significant component consists of the act of being non-judgmental, based primarily on the premise that a person cannot only have positive judgments with an absence of negative judgments (Kabat-Zinn, 1990). Segal, Williams, and Teasdale (2002) demonstrated this point in research that sought to determine the effectiveness of cognitive therapy practices for patients with multiple depressive episodes; they found that being nonjudgmental was more effective for the research participants than treatment that aided individuals to have more positive judgments of themselves. In contrast, a core foundation of SWB is the act of developing positive judgments about one's experiences.

Related to judgment and the second point of difference between SWB and mindfulness is their relationship with the constructs of pleasure and happiness. Pleasure, as it is related to SWB, is understood as a mere momentary experience, and happiness comes about due to ongoing momentary experiences—both pleasant and unpleasant. Literature describing mindfulness, however, suggests that trying to avoid all unpleasant experiences is impossible, and it would seem that attempts to avoid them would lead to judgments—both positive and negative. Mindfulness would emphasize the cultivation of acceptance by taking each moment, embracing it, and being with the moment—essentially trying to avoid imposing our ideas about how the moment should be different (Kabat-Zinn, 1990). In the case of mindfulness, it presents a fundamental shift in the way that we relate to our moment-to-moment experiences.

Exploring the Meaning of SWB

We begin now to develop a greater awareness of what is meant by SWB. It becomes apparent that SWB is simply more than just personal happiness and is directly affected by both internal and external conditions. Furthermore, a voluntary condition is present when we identify the reasons for variations in levels of SWB, which is directly linked to mindfulness. Following this general discussion, we ask how it is possible to relate SWB to our ongoing lives. Seeking an answer to this question reaffirmed some of the underlying points identifying the interconnections between SWB and mindfulness.

SWB is properly understood to mean happiness. Little social work research, to date, has examined SWB (Graham, Trew, Schmidt, & Kline, 2007), and so other disciplines provide very helpful background. Like many social scientific concepts, SWB means different things to different authors. It is, first, subjective, as it depends on people's self-reporting. It may vary over a person's life and is also a continuum concept, ranging from positive levels to negative levels (Kim-Prieto, Diener, Tamir, Scollon, & Diener, 2005). As suggested by Sheldon and Lyubomirsky (2006), the hallmark of well-being is positive affect: for purposes of this chapter, SWB is understood as a positive concept, as opposed to its negative: subjective *ill-being*. Here we need to emphasize where SWB and mindfulness part company: mindfulness teachings point out that grasping for and clinging to the pleasant leads to suffering. And so the key is to discern what is mindful SWB and what is not. SWB is understood to be multidimensional—a continuum of positive/negative affect, satisfaction with specific life concerns, satisfaction with life as a whole, and satisfaction with other matters of human experience beyond these (John, 2004). With over 800 citations, Diener, Emmons, Larsen, and Griffin's (1985) definition of SWB is perhaps the most widely accepted: SWB involves how satisfied people are with their experiences of positive and negative emotions and with their lives overall. SWB is popularly understood to mean happiness, but the two terms are far from synonymous. SWB refers to people's evaluation of overall life satisfaction as well as momentary affective states such as mood and feelings. This evaluation concerns both positive and negative affect (Eid & Diener, 2004). Happiness, on the other hand, refers to a transitory state of well-being characterized by emotions ranging from contentment to intense joy—a worthy and constructive concept in one's pursuit of subjective well-being.

Abraham Lincoln has been attributed to the following maxim, which in our view expresses an understanding of the link between subjective well-being and mindfulness—"Most folks are about as happy as they make up their minds to be" (Lincoln, 2005, p. 17). Yet, according to Seligman (2002), achieving an enduring level of happiness is dependent on three factors. The first involves one's genetic predisposition to a "specific level of happiness or sadness" (p. 47; see also Sheldon & Lyubomirsky, 2006). This factor is generally considered beyond our influence; however, Easton (2006) briefly touches on new brain research and reports of neurological findings suggesting that we can possibly *rewire* our brains for happiness. In any case, we can strive to live at the top of our happiness range through the coordination of the two other aspects.

The second factor addresses our external circumstances; some of these are altered more easily than others. Seligman (2002) and others (Diener, 2000; Nettle, 2005) have found that circumstantial variables such as being married, being religious, having a rich social network, and living in a wealthy democracy (where GNP exceeds $8,000 per person) positively influence our level of happiness and satisfaction with life. The avid pursuit of more money, staying healthy, becoming highly educated, or moving to a sunnier climate have relatively no effect on our sustainable level of happiness. Length of life, however, has been found to reflect positive life perspective. One remarkable study was able to follow up on a cohort of nuns over sixty years after they completed autobiographical sketches as they entered the nunnery. It found that 90 percent of the nuns who had expressed high levels of positive emotion in their early reflections lived to be eighty-five, whereas only 34 percent of the less happy nuns were still alive at this age (Danner, Snowdon, & Friesen, 2001). Although working to alter our external circumstances accounts for "no more than between 8 and 15 percent" of our happiness (Seligman, 2002, p. 61), it may be worth consideration. This point merits great emphasis in relation to a mindful recognition of limits of external circumstances.

The final factor influencing our pursuit of happiness is a "voluntary variable" (Seligman, 2002, p. 62): our disposition regarding the past, the present, and the future—this is where mindfulness comes in. Attending to the SWB continuum mentioned earlier, emotions about our past can range from contentment or pride to bitterness or anger. The classical Freudian perspective suggests that our reactions to events are based on a subconscious energy that is distinct from our conscious responses. According to psychoanalytic thought, people may respond positively or negatively to a particular life event because of intrapsychic baggage extending to the first several years of their lives. Many more recent social scientific theories, however, support a more evidence-based here-and-now context for human motivation and behavior. The Stress Reduction Clinic at the University of Massachusetts Medical Center, for example, has been providing training in the practice of mindfulness for decades. Here, the process of paying attention and the implications of how the mind and body interact are seen as intimately interconnected, ultimately influencing our health and wellness (Kabat-Zinn, 1990). As far as SWB is concerned, in accepting that cognition may influence feelings, theorists produce powerful means for people to make sense of their lived experiences and to construct these in ways that are positive to their well-being.

But how might we understand SWB in our ongoing lives? Nettle (2005) provides useful insight. His construct of a hierarchy of happiness allows each level to include and build upon previous levels. Level 1 happiness refers to momentary feelings or moods that are often described by words such as *joy, ecstasy, pleasure,* and *flow.* The second level considers the judgments one makes about both positive and negative moments through their "comparison with alternative possible outcomes" (Nettle, p. 19): these are revealed through words such as *optimistic, confident, proud, trusting,* and *hopeful.* The highest level of Nettle's happiness hierarchy entails approaching Maslow's pinnacle of self-actualization. Within this third level, one would derive satisfaction from experiencing "personal growth, purpose, mastery of one's environment and self-directedness" (Nettle, p. 23). Self-actualization is often paired with a more objective characteristic: that of being open to new experiences. It is evident, then, that the level of happiness we choose to focus on influences our outlook on life.

A 2006 BBC television series on happiness suggested that people have difficulty stabilizing their level of happiness for two reasons: comparison and habituation. The first can be seen in our tendency to evaluate what we have, what we do, where we live, how much money we make, and so forth, in relation to our situation. We may currently experience great satisfaction; however, as our status/possessions/circumstances shift, we alter our assessment criteria, which results in a new set of comparisons. The passage of time is also relevant to our ability to adapt to our environment, often making the intense feelings (both positive and negative) fade with time. Lottery winners, as well as persons who sustained debilitating injuries, have been tracked. In both instances, the previous levels of happiness were recovered within less than a year. Here we need to emphasize a subtle nuance. Nettle (2005) writes favorably about comparisons in one's mind, which help one discern positive outcomes. At the same time, comparisons of one person's circumstances to another's can be highly detrimental both to mindfulness and to SWB. And so the whole process of comparing can be helpful and unhelpful, circumstances depending.

SWB and Social Work Workplace and Social Work Practice

This section expands on the characteristics and conditions of mindfulness and SWB outlined above, as they relate to the work environment. We argue that leaders within the work environment who harness practices and thoughts related to mindfulness can have an extended impact on the work environment, essentially encouraging the development of positive SWB. We clarify that the presence of burnout and job satisfaction are only components of the entire discussion relating to SWB in the workplace and suggest the need to go beyond these discussions to identify more specific factors affecting levels of SWB in people. Building on literature that presents the unique characteristics of the social work profession, we move beyond this discussion of burnout and job satisfaction to highlight the role of social workers in the present social environment, and the necessary leadership role practitioners could undertake within this environment to facilitate workplace SWB.

Work is as essential to success as water is to a boat; one can subsist without the other, but together their potentials are more fully realized. For most citizens of the Global North, work is an essential component of a fulfilling life. In fact, Lyubomirsky, King, and Diener (2005) posit three domains intrinsic to success: social relationships, health, and work life. If satisfaction with work is a component of SWB and the hallmark of well-being is positive affect, then it is imperative that organizational leaders work to create cultures where happiness can be advanced. Overell identified several features of the workplace that have a high correlation with happiness: "autonomy over how, where, and at what pace work is done; trust between employer and employee; procedural fairness; and participation in decision making" (qtd. in Delamothe, 2005, p. 1490). Creating a work environment that encompasses these qualities takes a reflective, caring leader, and one who can model and encourage an institution to carry out these SWB-enhancing values.

To these ends, SWB is a useful concept. Indeed, Csikszentmihalyi (2004) suggests that leaders begin by providing a unified vision that builds a better future and gives life meaning—a foundation to SWB. His strategies encourage leaders to provide "an environment where *flow* and *complexity* can thrive" (p. 18; emphasis added). By collaboratively identifying clear goals that are responsive to the changing conditions, by providing immediate feedback that frames the experience positively, and by matching the challenge of the job with people's recognized strengths, social work administrators may begin to create a setting where more positive SWB is sought (see also chapter 4).

Social work has long been seen as a stressful occupation, and burnout has received the attention of many researchers (Halbesleben & Buckley, 2004; Maslach, 1982). Caregiver role identity has been related to burnout, depression, professional impairment, and failure to seek help for personal problems (Siebert & Siebert, 2005). However, individual factors alone are not sufficient to explain all cases of burnout, as is illustrated by the fact that individual coping strategies were not found to be related to the level of burnout experienced (Stevens & Higgins, 2002). Organizational factors such as workload burden (Coyle, Allebach, & Krueger, 2005; Levert, Lucas, & Ortlepp, 2000), the influence of funding sources (Arches, 1991), inadequate administration, and a lack of social support, particularly within the organization (Graham et al., 2007), have also been shown to have an impact on burnout across the helping professions. Across fields of work, individual differences in disposition (Judge & Hulin, 1993), locus of control (Koeske & Kirk, 1995), job values (Habich, 1986), and personality (Lounsbury, Loveland, Sund-strom, Gibson, Drost, & Hamrick, 2003) have been linked to levels of job satisfaction.

Job satisfaction (or dissatisfaction) can have an impact on employee health and turnover, and like burnout, it is influenced by many different factors, both positive and negative. Job satisfaction is influenced by individual differences such as disposition, locus of control, job values, and personality (Lounsbury et al., 2003). The social work environment, with its combination of scarce resources, advocacy, and accountability, introduces a number of factors that should influence job satisfaction. Perceived autonomy has an impact on job satisfaction (Jayaratne, Vinokur-Kaplan, & Chess, 1995), as does role conflict and role clarity (Carpenter, Schneider, Brandon, & Wooff, 2003), decision authority, flexibility, and impact on others (Carpenter, 1999). Organizational con-ditions are also strong predictors of job satisfaction and the intention to leave. Issues such as the perceived quality of supervision and perceived workload, perceived autonomy, role conflict and role clarity (Carpenter et al., 2003), decision authority, flexibility, and impact on others (Car-penter, 1999) have all been found to have a serious impact on the job satisfaction of social workers (Acker, 2004). In addition to influencing service delivery, job satisfaction has been shown to have connections to overall life satisfaction, perhaps due to the mediating influence of core self-evaluations (Rode, 2004), thus influencing the overall SWB of individuals.

Research has successfully identified a number of factors that have been shown to have a positive impact on SWB in the workplace. Simple holiday taking has been shown to have a positive impact on SWB (Gil-bert & Abdullah, 2004), while the perception of support (Jayaratne, Himle, & Chess, 1988), exposure to employee involvement practices (Mackie, Holahan, & Gottlieb, 2001), and effective supervision (Cearley, 2004) have been linked to positive outcomes and feelings of well-being. In the helping professions, practitioners have been shown to benefit psychologically from the helping role (Lazar & Guttman, 2003) and from opportunities for continuing education and professional development (Laufer & Sharon, 1993; Marriott, Sexton, & Staley, 1994; Roat, 1988). Indeed, there are many factors that can have a positive influence on both job satisfaction and overall SWB. The level of job satisfaction expe-rienced by social workers has been correlated with the quality of service to clients (Packard, 1989). However, job satisfaction is only one aspect of overall well-being, albeit with established connections to overall life satisfaction (Hart, 1999). Understanding how organizations can enhance the overall well-being of social workers may enhance job satisfaction and may have a greater impact on employee productivity and commit-ment than focusing on job satisfaction alone. Thus it is important to go beyond job satisfaction to consider the factors that influence the SWB of social workers (Graham et al., 2007).

Social work education and its professional development, perhaps more so than any other line of work, should reflect the values that professionals seek to pass on to their clients. In this framework, emphasizing how overwhelming life can be is not what we desire to inculcate in others: instead, we seek to encourage a passion for living, a comprehensive sense of wellness. As social workers, *we* need to know how to emphasize our strengths and capacities and experience wholeness and interconnectedness as we strive for fundamental balance in our lives. Many variables, both internal and external to the individual, can come to influence SWB. Dysfunctional thought processes have been shown to influence SWB (Judge & Locke, 1993), along with personality and cultural factors (Diener, Oishi, & Lucas, 2003; Gutierrez, Jimenez, Hernandez, & Puente, 2005; Hayes & Joseph, 2003), religious observance (Poloma & Pendleton, 1990), explicit self-esteem (Schimmack & Diener, 2003), relationship harmony (particularly for women; Reid, 2004), and goal attainment (Kehr, 2003). As well, occupational congruence and work setting congruence have been related to SWB (Lachterman & Meir, 2004). SWB supports productivity, socially desirable behaviors, and positive physical and mental health (Keyes & Waterman, 2003). A number of factors have been shown to have a positive impact on SWB in the workplace. Not only are social workers a part of today's manic society (Holden, 2005) of turbo-capitalism (Graham, Swift, & Delaney, 2008), but we are called to seek social justice and to facilitate the well-being of all society—social workers included.

A great deal of scholarship, particularly in the United Kingdom, emphasizes the de-skilling of social work and the routinized nature of practice—much of which is seen as an artifact of neoconservative managerialism (Harris, 1998; Jones & Novak, 1993). As professionals, we need to be more than just managers or performance-driven professionals. Hargreaves and Fink (2006) advise that leaders respect their roles as citizens in the community who "lead to serve and promote the good of all" (p. 20). Emotional understanding, as posited by Stoll, Fink, and Earl (2004), encourages leaders to "read the emotional responses of those around them and create emotional engagements and bonds with and among those with whom they interact" (p. 108); these behaviors are reflective of SWB. But we must be cognizant of the considerable institutional and broader community constraints that impinge upon social workers, and that make the realization of professional discretion, let alone SWB, difficult.

But there are modest possibilities for hope. The impact of *one* worker, within *one* workplace environment, can create a ripple effect, leaving a lasting imprint, positive or negative, on the surrounding communities (cf. Sparks, 2005). Malcolm Gladwell's book *The Tipping Point* popularizes a lot of social scientific research on how organizations and other human systems change. Change, scholars argue, may be contagious: "Simply by finding and reaching those few special people who hold so much social power, we can shape the course of social epidemics" (Gladwell, 2002, p. 259). It is critical, then, that social workers' effect be both practical and positive. By understanding how SWB is promoted through the positive energy of our environment, perspective, and daily activities, such as mindfulness, social workers can engage in more positive living and working.

As social workers, ours is a labor of love, an emotional labor—where our work involves embracing and accepting our own emotions while attending to other people's feelings (Hick, 2005). Our success in ensuring high-quality, sustainable SWB among social workers is perhaps dependent on what Sparks (2005) refers to as "the final two percent . . . that cluster of experiences that literally change the brains" of social workers—the experiences that "produce new habits of mind and behavior" (p. 19). Leadership can work to engage in activities that address the overall SWB of the setting, thereby having a significant positive effect on the entire workplace culture.

Gladwell (2005) supports a method of unconscious influence in his book *Blink*. Referred to as "priming," the method affects the recipient and influences the behavior of others. By commenting on the creativity of counseling practices, for example, leaders can foster an atmosphere of risk taking. In using priming and SWB, however, leaders must maintain a sense of optimism, a characteristic that Peterson (2000) states is "linked to good mood, perseverance, achievement, and physical health" (p. 45). The founder of the Happiness Project, Robert Holden (2005), states that happiness "brings out the best in us. When we are happy we relate better with others. We feel more connected, we are less afraid and we are more confident. Our inner happiness . . . attracts happy relationships. When we are happy we work better. . . . [We] are likely to be more productive, more creative, more successful and, also, experience less stress, less depression and less mental illness. True happiness enables us to be more successful" (p. 112). Is it not worth our energy, then, to strive to live at the top of our happiness range and purpose to lead others on this same journey toward self-actualization?

Self-knowledge is critical to the social worker as he or she seeks to build SWB within the workplace. Holden (2005) likens self-knowledge to "the jewel in the crown of success" (p. 55). As counselors, we can model, mentor, and coach others in the values of mindfulness; we can even use some of our professional development time to encourage guided reflections and sharing. The key to promoting SWB through professional development is to attend to the SWB needs of participants. Seligman (2002) suggests that "by learning about each of the three different kinds of happiness [past, present, and future], you can move your emotions in a positive direction" (p. 62). As professionals, and as leaders, we need to assist our colleagues in ensuring that they reflect on the past in a positive way, think about the future with optimism, and fully experience the joys of the present.

Future Imperatives for SWB and Mindfulness in Social Work

This chapter's conclusion merely represents an end to this particular discussion as much more research and fruitful inquiry are necessary to understand the necessity of the application of mindfulness in the realm of social work practice and social work workplaces. We conclude with some final thoughts relating to individual applicability in light of the community and institutional environments in which so much of social work practice takes place, to hopefully inspire a continuation of this discussion.

One wise observer states the following: "Burnout, a problem in a wide variety of workplaces from emergency rooms to corporations, is compounded by mindlessness" (Langer, 1989, p. 148). But burnout, like so many problems social workers face, is multifaceted. There is a lot of mindlessness associated with burnout: from the underfunding of social services to the inordinate expectations agencies and communities have of practitioners to the continued inability of society to respond properly to many of the structural issues that contribute to the social problems that are part of social workers' professional lives. The present chapter has addressed the connection between mindfulness and subjective well-being. As an exploratory piece, it has provided social workers with a direction rather than a destination. We suspect that mindfulness practices of moment to moment—nonjudgmental awareness and acceptance—may well increase the probability of improved levels of happiness and ultimately overall SWB. Likewise, through meditation, we can begin weaving the strands necessary to create the tapestry within which we live and work. These and other strategies certainly merit further research, and empirical scholarship regarding the relationship between mindfulness and SWB practices remains to be done.

But there remains a profound danger: that some may assume the way forward is through individuals—and only individuals—attempting to leverage these pockets of light and hope. Individuals are important. But the institutional and community structures in which they operate

are equally, if not at times more profoundly, significant in helping to
create those contexts that best enhance mindfulness and ultimately
SWB. The social work academy, too, has vital roles to play, and its growing commitment to spirituality and social work as a viable topic of analysis is entirely hopeful, too (Coates, Graham, & Schwartzentruber, 2007;
Graham, 2006, 2008; Graham, Coholic, & Coates, 2006). A great deal of
work remains to be done. An essential beginning point, as with any
topic related to mindfulness (and we argue, to life in general), is to have
a community of open-minded seekers interested in knowing and
understanding more. This, in turn, stands to make our experiences
more vivid and our lives more real. Indeed, mindfulness encourages us
to become sensitive to how our bodies are being affected by physical
and social environments, by our actions, and even by our own thoughts
and emotions. Learning to listen to our own bodies is vital to improving
health and quality of life. The happy social worker—the happy person
in general—has insight into body and mind, well enough to work at
optimizing his or her health. Surely this catalyst toward healing is a
viable strategy for social workers, particularly in this time of tremendous workplace stress and social need.

References

Acker, G. M. (2004). The effect of organizational conditions (role conflict, role
    ambiguity, opportunities for professional development, and social support)
    on job satisfaction and intention to leave among social workers in mental
    health care. *Community Mental Health Journal, 40*(1), 65–73.
Arches, J. (1991). Social structure, burnout, and job satisfaction. *Social Work, 36*(3),
    202–206.
Baer, R., & Krietemeyer, J. (2006). Overview of mindfulness- and acceptance-based
    treatment approaches. In R. Baer (Ed.), *Mindfulness-based treatment
    approaches: Clinician's guide to evidence base and applications* (pp. 3–27).
    New York: Elsevier.
Carpenter, J., Schneider, J., Brandon, T., & Wooff, D. (2003). Working in multidisci-
    plinary community mental health teams: The impact on social workers and
    health professionals of integrated mental health care. *British Journal of
    Social Work, 33*(8), 1081–1103.
Carpenter, M. C. (1999). Job rewards and concerns for social workers: The impact
    of changes in funding and delivery of mental health services. *Smith College
    Studies in Social Work, 70*(1), 69–84.
Cearley, S. (2004). The power of supervision in child welfare services. *Child &
    Youth Care Forum, 33*(5), 313–327.
Coates, J., Graham, J. R., & Schwartzentruber, B. (Eds.). (2007). *Canadian social
    work and spirituality: Current readings and approaches.* Toronto: Canadian
    Scholars' Press.

Coyle, E., Allebach, J., & Krueger, J. (2005). A systematic review of stress among mental health social workers. *International Social Work, 48*(2), 210–211.

Csikszentmihalyi, M. (2004). *Good business: Leadership, flow, and the making of meaning.* Toronto: Penguin.

Danner, D., Snowdon, D., & Friesen, W. (2001). Positive emotions in early life and longevity: Findings from the nun study. *Journal of Personality and Social Psychology, 80,* 804–813.

Delamothe, T. (2005). Happiness: Get happy—it's good for you [Editorial]. *British Medical Journal, 331,* 1489–1490.

Diener, E. (2000). Subjective well-being: The science of happiness and a proposal for a national index. *American Psychologist, 55*(1), 34–43.

Diener, E., Emmons, A., Larsen, R., & Griffin S. (1985). The satisfaction with life scale. *Journal of Personality Assessment, 49*(1), 71–75.

Diener, E., Oishi, S., & Lucas, R. E. (2003). Personality, culture, and subjective well-being: Emotional and cognitive evaluations of life. *Annual Review of Psychology, 54,* 403–425.

Easton, M. (2006, June 26). *The happiness formula.* Retrieved September 14, 2006, from http://news.bbc.co.uk/1/hi/programmes.happiness_formula/

Eid, M., & Diener, E. (2004). Global judgements of subjective well-being: Situational variability and long-term stability. *Social Indicators Research, 65,* 245–277.

Gilbert, D., & Abdullah, J. (2004). Holiday taking and the sense of well-being. *Annals of Tourism Research, 31*(1), 103–121.

Gladwell, M. (2002). *The tipping point: How little things can make a big difference.* New York: Little, Brown.

Gladwell, M. (2005). *Blink: The power of thinking without thinking.* New York: Little, Brown.

Graham, J. R. (2006). Spirituality and social work: A call for an international focus of research. *Aretê, 30*(1), 63–77.

Graham, J. R. (2008). Who am I? An essay on inclusion and spiritual growth through community and mutual appreciation. *Journal of Religion, Spirituality, and Social Work, 27*(1–2), 5–24.

Graham, J. R., Coholic, D., & Coates, J. (2006). Spirituality as a guiding construct in the development of Canadian social work: Past and present considerations. *Critical Social Work, 7*(1), 1–17.

Graham, J. R., Swift, K., & Delaney, R. (2008). *Canadian social policy: An introduction* (3rd ed.). Toronto: Prentice Hall.

Graham, J. R., Trew, J., Schmidt, J., & Kline, T. (2007). Influences on the subjective well-being of practising social workers. *Canadian Social Work, 9*(1), 92–105.

Gunaratana, B. (2002). *Mindfulness: In plain English* (Updated and expanded ed.). Somerville, MA: Wisdom.

Gutierrez, J., Jimenez, B., Hernandez, E., & Puente, C. (2005). Personal and subjective well-being: Big five correlates and demographic variables. *Personality & Individual Differences, 38*(7), 1564–1569.

Habich, R. (1986). Job values, realities of the workplace, and job satisfaction: The problem of weighting of demands in explaining job satisfaction. *Zeitschrift für Soziologie, 15*(4), 278–294.

Halbesleben, J., & Buckley, M. (2004). Burnout in organizational life. *Journal of Management, 30*(6), 859–879.

Hargreaves, A., & Fink, D. (2006). *Sustainable leadership.* San Francisco: Jossey-Bass.

Harris, J. (1998). *The nurture assumption: Why children turn out the way they do.* New York: Free Press.

Hart, P. M. (1999). Predicting employee life satisfaction: A coherent model of personality, work and non-work experiences, and domain satisfactions. *Journal of Applied Psychology, 84*(4), 564–584.

Hayes, N., & Joseph, S. (2003). Big 5 correlates of three measures of subjective well-being. *Personality and Individual Difference, 34*(4), 723–727.

Hick, S. (2005). *Social work in Canada: An introduction.* Toronto: Thompson.

Holden, R. (2005). *Success intelligence.* London: Hodder & Stoughton.

Jayaratne, S., Himle, D., & Chess, W. (1988). Dealing with work stress and strain: Is the perception of support more important than its use? *Journal of Applied Behavioural Science, 24*(2), 191.

Jayaratne, S., Vinokur-Kaplan, D., & Chess, W. (1995). The importance of personal control: A comparison of social workers in private practice and public agency settings. *Journal of Applied Social Sciences, 19*(1), 47–59.

John, L. (2004). Subjective well-being in a multicultural urban population: Structural, and multivariate analyses of the Ontario health survey well-being scale. *Social Indicators Research, 68,* 107–126.

Jones, C., & Novak, T. (1993). Social work today. *British Journal of Social Work, 23*(3), 195–212.

Judge, T., & Hulin, C. (1993). Job satisfaction as a reflection of disposition: A multiple source causal analysis. *Organizational Behavior and Human Decision Processes, 56*(3), 388–421.

Judge, T., & Locke, E. (1993). Effects of dysfunctional thought processes on subjective well-being and job satisfaction. *Journal of Applied Psychology, 78*(3), 475–490.

Kabat-Zinn, J. (1990). *Full catastrophe living: Using the wisdom of your body and mind to face stress, pain, and illness.* New York: Delacorte Press.

Kabat-Zinn, J. (2003). Mindfulness-based interventions in context: Past, present, and future. *Clinical Psychology: Science and Practice, 10*(2), 144–156.

Kabat-Zinn, J. (2005). *Wherever you go, there you are: Mindfulness meditation in everyday life.* New York: Hyperion.

Kehr, H. M. (2003). Goal conflicts, attainment of new goals, and well-being among managers. *Journal of Occupational Health Psychology, 8*(3), 195–208.

Keyes, C., & Waterman, M. (2003). Dimensions of well-being and mental health in adulthood. In M. H. Bornstein (Ed.), *Crosscurrents in contemporary psychology* (pp. 477–497). Mahwah, NJ: Lawrence Erlbaum Associates.

Kim-Prieto, C., Diener, E., Tamir, M., Scollon, C., & Diener, M. (2005). Integrating the diverse definitions of happiness: A time-sequential framework of subjective well-being. *Journal of Happiness Studies, 6,* 261–300.

Koeske, G., & Kirk, S. (1995). The effect of characteristics of human service workers on subsequent morale and turnover. *Administration in Social Work, 19*(1), 15–31.

Lachterman, B., & Meir, E. (2004). The impact of work setting congruence on well-being. *Journal of Career Assessment, 12*(2), 150–168.

Langer, E. (1989). *Mindfulness.* Cambridge, MA: Da Capo Press.

Laufer, Z., & Sharon, N. (1993). Continuing education programs (CEP), an image of the professions: The case of social work. *Higher Education, 26*(3), 267–274.

Lazar, A., & Guttman, J. (2003). Therapists' benefits from conducting psychotherapy: The case of social workers. *Research on Social Work Practice, 13*(6), 705–723.

Levert, T., Lucas, M., & Ortlepp, K. (2000). Burnout in psychiatric nurses: Contributions of the work environment and a sense of coherence. *South African Journal of Psychology, 30,* 36–43.

Lincoln, A. (2005). *The wit and wisdom of Abraham Lincoln: A book of quotations.* Mineola, NY: Dover Publications.

Lounsbury, J. W., Loveland, J. M., Sundstrom, E., Gibson, L., Drost, A., & Hamrick, F. (2003). An investigation of personality traits in relation to career satisfaction. *Journal of Career Assessment, 11*(3), 287–307.

Lyubomirsky, S., King, L., & Diener, E. (2005). The benefits of frequent positive affect: Does happiness lead to success? *Psychological Bulletin, 131*(6), 803–855.

Mackie, K., Holahan, C., & Gottlieb, N. (2001). Employee involvement management practices, work stress, and depression in employees of a human services residential care facility. *Human Relations, 54*(8), 1065–1092.

Marriott, A., Sexton, L., & Staley, D. (1994). Components of job satisfaction in psychiatric social workers. *Health and Social Work, 19*(3), 199–205.

Maslach, C. (1982). *Burnout: The cost of caring.* Englewood Cliffs, NJ: Prentice Hall.

Nettle, D. (2005). *Happiness: The science behind your smile.* New York: Oxford University Press.

Packard, T. (1989). Participation in decision-making, performance, and job satisfaction in a social work bureaucracy. *Administration in Social Work, 13*(1), 59–73.

Peterson, C. (2000). The future of optimism. *American Psychologist, 55*(1), 44–55.

Poloma, M., & Pendleton, B. (1990). Religious domains and general well-being. *Social Indicators Research, 22*(3), 255–276.

Reid, A. (2004). Gender and sources of subjective well-being. *Sex Roles, 51*(11–12), 617–629.

Roat, J. (1988). The effects of continuing education on staff performance. *Journal of Continuing Social Work Education, 4*(4), 26–30.

Rode, J. (2004). Job satisfaction and life satisfaction: A longitudinal test of an integrated model. *Human Relations, 57*(9), 1205–1230.

Schimmack, U., & Diener, E. (2003). Predictive validity of explicit and implicit self-esteem for subjective well being. *Journal of Research in Personality, 37*(2), 100–106.

Segal, Z. V., Williams, J. M. G., & Teasdale, J. D. (2002). *Mindfulness and cognitive therapy for depression.* New York: Guilford Press.

Seligman, M. (2002). *Authentic happiness: Using the new positive psychology to realize your potential for lasting fulfillment.* New York: Free Press.

Sheldon, K., & Lyubomirsky, S. (2006). Achieving sustainable gains in happiness: Change your actions, not your circumstances. *Journal of Happiness Studies, 7,* 55–86.

Siebert, D., & Siebert, C. (2005). The caregiver role identity scale: A validation study. *Research on Social Work Practice, 15*(3), 204–221.

Sparks, D. (2005). The final 2%: What is takes to create profound change in leaders. *National Staff Development Council–JSD, 26*(2), 8–15.

Stevens, M., & Higgins, D. (2002). The influence of risk and protective factors on burnout experienced by those who work with maltreated children. *Child Abuse Review, 11*(5), 313–331.

Stoll, L., Fink, D., & Earl, L. (2004). *It's about learning (and it's about time): What's in it for schools?* New York: Routledge Falmer.

CHAPTER EIGHT

Mindfulness-Based Practices in Group Work with Children and Youths in Care

Diana Coholic and Julie LeBreton

This chapter explores mindfulness-based training with children living in foster care (ages eight to fifteen). Presently there is no research on using mindfulness in this area. We present an outline of our program, detailing specific activities that are appropriate for and have been proved effective with this population, and examine some of our preliminary conclusions based on our experience delivering the program.

Research that examines mindfulness practice with children is just beginning to emerge, and evidence in the literature regarding the helpfulness of mindfulness practice for children is sparse. As Semple, Reid, and Miller (2005) state, despite the promise of mindfulness training in adult psychotherapies, there are no studies that extend these findings to children. In a pilot study, these researchers studied a six-week group with five children identified as anxious. They found that mindfulness can be taught to children and holds promise as an intervention for anxiety. Birnbaum (2005a) concurs that very little has been written about the use of mindfulness meditation with adolescents. She found mindfulness meditation helpful for adolescents in their search for self-awareness, meaning, and life purpose and contends that teaching mindfulness to young people provides them with

This research is funded by the Sick Kids Foundation and the Social Sciences and Humanities Research Council of Canada.

an effective life skill that can turn into a major resource. There are two research teams (both based in the United States) that are exploring the effectiveness of mindfulness-based practices for children and youths. One team is developing a mindful awareness program for teenagers with ADHD (Zylowska & Smalley, 2008), and the other is exploring the possibility that children can reap benefits from practicing mindfulness by way of a mindfulness-based stress reduction course for children in the fourth through sixth grades and their parents (Goldin & Saltzman, 2007). Certainly, there has been some other exploration that has focused on mindfulness-based parent training, and calls have been issued for empirical research in this area (Dumas, 2005; Singh et al., 2006). As well as exploring how mindfulness practice can shape parenting practices, which has attracted popular interest, Goodman (2005) discusses how mindfulness can help a practitioner develop "psychotherapeutic presence" with children (p. 199). Finally, there is also some evidence of mindfulness training in school-based programs in order to reduce stress (Napoli, 2005; Wall, 2005), and in nursing practice to help children deal with pain management (Ott, 2002). Currently, there is no literature that explores mindfulness-based training with children in care with child protection, who typically have significant difficulties and life challenges (Boyd Webb, 2006a). However, while the research in this area is emergent, there is substantial information regarding the facilitation of meditation with children and we have utilized this material as a base from which to develop our group work (Fontana & Slack, 2002; Jenkins, 1996; MacLean, 2004; Viegas, 2004).

Since 2005, we have been studying the helpfulness of holistic arts–based and experiential group work for the development of self-awareness and self-esteem. Our primary focus has been with children in care with the Children's Aid Society of the districts of Sudbury and Manitoulin, although we have also facilitated five groups with adult women. The group program that we have developed makes use of a myriad of creative and expressive arts methods, but mindfulness-based practices underpin all the group processes (Coholic, 2005, 2006; Coholic, Lougheed, & LeBreton, in press). The group context and methods create novel experiences and an environment in which group participants can be encouraged to explore their viewpoints, feelings, and behaviors in order to develop their self-awareness and improve their self-esteem. Mindfulness practice is an integral component of the group program, although its practice, particularly with children with significant difficulties, is different from the practice that occurs in work with adults. Some of these differences and our experiences working with children in care are the focus of this chapter. First we describe the group program and its goals, linking this with the practice of mindfulness, and then we provide some examples of the mindfulness-based practices that are facilitated in the group work with the children in care.

Description of the Group Program

Our group program emerged from a desire to study the processes and helpfulness of spiritually sensitive/holistic social work practice. Studying group practice was and remains more feasible than studying individual practice at this point in our knowledge development in this new area. For instance, there are few social workers who identify themselves as working with a spiritually sensitive practice, especially in northeastern Ontario, where services and practitioners are sparse to begin with. Many of the techniques that we use are often taught in a group format (France, 2002; Kabat-Zinn, 1990). Indeed, the use of creative activities has long been part of group practice (Tilly & Caye, 2004). The group also provides an opportunity for children to learn from each other's experiences, and to gently challenge one another to develop alternative narratives of their experiences. Certainly, the benefits of group work have long been established and include learning interpersonal skills, cooperating in pursuit of a shared goal, learning about values through comparison with others, and alleviating isolation (Whitaker, 1975).

The group required an overall purpose, and we chose to focus on the development of the participants' self-awareness and self-esteem, which is a basic aspect of most helping approaches and a building block for good mental health and wellness. Importantly, the goal is useful for most client groups. Thus, we knew that the group could be adapted and studied with different population groups such as children in care, Aboriginal women, and women dealing with addictions. It is important to study how holistic practice works with various groups because social work practice is so varied. The uniqueness of the group program comes from its incorporation of spiritually sensitive practices. It is arts based and experiential because these sorts of practices can be an outlet and expression for, and connection to, unconscious thoughts, beliefs, feelings, and behaviors. Also, spirituality is often described as an experience and/or feeling that is difficult to express or capture in words. Self-awareness and insight arise from an ability to pay attention to one's anxieties, fears, and other feelings, which often reside in the unconscious mind. As Frattaroli (2001) contends, we can think of this process as simply getting in touch with a feeling or, more profoundly, as listening to the soul.

We depend on a multitude of experiential exercises that are integral to many spiritually sensitive approaches for the purposes of building self-awareness and self-esteem (France, 2002; Wilner, 2001). These include guided imagery; dream work; drawing, painting, working with clay, and making collages; and mindfulness practices, which all help participants develop insight and self-understanding. Expressive and creative methods are particularly useful or even essential to use in work with children in care, who have experienced severe life challenges and/or trauma, as these children usually work to avoid talking about their stressful experiences (Boyd Webb, 2006b). Also, children do not communicate the way adults do, as many of their thoughts and feelings are expressed nonverbally through creative activity such as play (Goodman, 2005). All the group processes and exercises are in harmony with Kabat-Zinn's (2003) definition of mindfulness meditation practice: activity that encourages awareness to emerge through paying attention on purpose, in the present moment, and nonjudgmentally to the unfolding of experience moment by moment. Certainly, the awareness that develops from mindfulness meditation does not have to be limited to meditation (Bishop et al., 2004). Thus, the idea of mindfulness shapes the group's exercises. This is particularly true for the groups we deliver to children in care, as will be discussed later in this chapter.

We began with a group program that consisted of six weekly sessions of two hours each. However, we have now moved to a twelve-week model. This shift occurred for several reasons, including the desire of the children to keep attending the group. Also, we have learned that six sessions is not adequate time for these children to explore and develop their self-awareness and to learn to incorporate some of the group techniques into their lives. Based on feedback from the children and their foster parents, schools, and child-care workers, and our own experiences, the children who have attended twelve sessions benefit more in terms of feeling better about themselves and understanding themselves better, and reports are that their behaviors at home and at school are more positive and less disruptive. Importantly, as the weekly sessions progress, we can engage them with more depth and complexity in the work of the group. It usually takes six sessions before the children can actively listen to and focus on one another and the group facilitators. The observation of one youth who attended twelve weeks of the group illustrates this well: "The first time I think I was distracted. . . . I sort of knew [other participants] so we fooled around a lot. . . . I was able to focus more on it the second time."

Mindfulness, Self-Esteem, and Self-Awareness

Self-awareness can develop from a connection with one's feelings and/or unconscious processes and learning to pay attention to this material (Birnbaum, 2005b). In fact, mindfulness in contemporary psychology has been adopted as an approach for increasing awareness (Bishop et al., 2004). As Goodman (2005) argues, most of our experience is "deep" in a field of preconceptual and preverbal awareness, and people can learn to "abide calmly in that domain during mindfulness practice" (p. 205). While self-awareness in and of itself may not directly lead to greater self-esteem, we believe that developing self-awareness and understanding is an important element in this process. In fact, self-awareness and self-esteem are often linked in the helping literature. As Sadao and Walker (2002) state, self-esteem is closely tied to knowing oneself and one's capabilities. Berger (2005) argues that in order to develop self-esteem, which she equates with self-acceptance, we have to connect with ourselves, with all of what makes us who we are. This connection occurs when we learn about and express our feelings, which are often held in the unconscious. Silvia and O'Brien (2004) acknowledge that self-awareness has a bad reputation in social-clinical psychology because of its ties to negative affect (for example, people can become locked in a cycle of self-criticism and rumination) but argue that without self-awareness, one cannot experience high self-esteem, and that its contributions to constructive human functioning are significant.

While self-esteem can fluctuate, some argue that it is essentially a realistic and appreciative opinion of oneself (Schiraldi, 2001). The development of a healthy sense of self-esteem can be a complex process influenced by many factors. While we think that uncovering insights (developing self-awareness) and connecting with one's "inner voice" (a deep level of consciousness where one's authentic values and needs are held [Birnbaum & Birnbaum, 2004]) can engender a better sense of self-esteem, learning not to judge oneself too critically and learning appreciation are also an important component of this process. As Olendzki (2005) contends, people calibrate their self-esteem by constant comparison with others, and as a consequence, people can feel impoverished in the face of abundance. The improvement of self-esteem is not often presented as an outcome of learning mindfulness. Instead, the focus is usually on developing acceptance, self-compassion, and positive well-being (Brown & Ryan, 2003; Stewart, 2004). However, some authors do discuss the connections between self-esteem and these other concepts. For instance, Morgan and Morgan (2005) state that due to the tendency toward low self-esteem among Western meditation students, instructors should teach loving-kindness practice to beginning students. Also, Smith (2004) explains that learning self-acceptance and self-compassion may be particularly important for older people whose self-esteem is negatively affected by ageism. However, some contend that self-esteem in the West is based on how much we stand out or are special. Their argument is that a need for high self-esteem may encourage narcissistic, self-absorbed behavior. Therefore, developing self-compassion is stressed because "you don't have to feel better than others to feel good about yourself" (Neff, n.d.).

While self-esteem and self-compassion are different concepts, we hope that both are being improved for the children by way of their involvement in the group. Our understanding of self-esteem is in harmony with Schiraldi's (2001) definition. He explains that people with self-esteem believe they are neither more nor less than human. Aware of their faults, they are quietly glad to be who they are and view others as equals. The choice to frame the group's goal as improved self-esteem can be explained by a few factors. When we first developed the group program, mindfulness was deemed an important component in helping people develop their self-awareness, but it was not the group program's sole focus. Also, the client groups we work with, such as children in care, typically begin the group with low self-esteem caused by the multiple oppressions, traumas, and challenges they have suffered in their lives (Sadao & Walker, 2002; Simmons & Weinman, 1991). Moreover, the outcome of improved self-esteem is easily measured because several well-established self-reporting tools exist for both adults and children/youths, such as the Multidimensional Self-Esteem Inventory (O'Brien & Epstein, 1988), which we use with adults, and the Piers-Harris Children's Self-Concept Scale (Piers, Harris, & Herzberg, 2005), which we use with children and youths, pre- and post-group. Certainly, the recent development of self-compassion scales (Neff, 2003) may influence the future development of the group program and its goals.

Mindfulness-Based Practices with Children in Care

In our work with adults, mindfulness practices were facilitated by meditations, writing exercises, other arts-based activities, mindful walking and eating, group exercises, and homework (daily practice and reading outside of the group). Learning mindfulness helped these participants become more self-aware; increase their self-esteem; stop judging their thoughts, feelings, and experiences; deepen their feelings of experience and appreciation; and feel more connected to their spirituality (Coholic, 2006). To date, our experience with children in care is that due to their challenging life situations, it is difficult for them to focus on their breathing for any length of time, or even to close their eyes, especially when sitting together in a group. It takes them longer to develop trust, their feelings are often chaotic and intense, they have difficulty listening to one another and the group facilitators, and they generally feel or experience a lack of control (which is sometimes based in present reality—that is, a few of the children were involuntarily moved from their foster homes during the groups to new foster homes). As Boyd Webb (2006a) explains, children taken into care have typically suffered multiple losses; they expect a continuation of their abusive, neglectful experiences, they blame themselves for the abuse or neglect, and they have poor self-esteem. Indeed, there are serious concerns regarding the health, and particularly the mental health, of children in care and their future ability to participate fully in society. Children in care carry a high burden of difficulties caused in part by the consequences of abuse, family breakdown, and being taken into care. Unfortunately, they remain at high risk for poor long-term functional outcomes well into adulthood (Racusin, Maerlender, Sengupta, Isquith, & Straus, 2005). For example, they are particularly at risk of suicide, and they have higher rates of mental health problems than children who are not in care (Charles & Matheson, 1991). Clearly, they constitute a population of children in dire need of psychosocial services, especially preventative types of intervention.

As a result, the mindfulness exercises with children in care are more basic and shorter than is usually the case. Similarly, Semple et al. (2005) kept breathing exercises in their children's group brief and in line with the children's capabilities. While they were able to incorporate three-minute seated breath mediations at the beginning and end of a group session, we find that even shorter meditations are more possible for the children in care. However, other clinical observations made by Semple et al. were consistent with our experiences, for example, the importance of group rules, and the difficulty children have closing their eyes while sitting together in a group. They concluded that mindfulness exercises with children need to be more active and sensory focused, and that abstract concepts have to be concretized. Their hypothesis that the primary mechanism of mindfulness is self-management of attention is certainly reflected in some of the mindfulness activities we have developed. As they argue, a foundation of attention is essential for the observation of thoughts, emotions, and body sensations. Goodman (2005) explains how she taught a nine-year-old girl to notice her feelings, thereby learning that she did not always have to believe her thoughts: "She could choose to let them be, to let them go" (p. 207). Thus, helping children in care to pay attention and listen to their thoughts, sensations, and feelings is a good beginning point in work with children and youths. It should be mentioned that many of the children (particularly the boys) who attend our group are also diagnosed with attention deficit disorders, which may make it even harder for them to focus. Given the difficulty that children in care have in paying attention not only to themselves but to each other, it is essential to develop group exercises that aim to improve their ability to listen and pay attention.

One simple process that we have built into the group is a progressive relaxation exercise in which children are taught to tense up and then relax different parts of their bodies and their breathing. Goodman (2005) explains that relaxation can be used to release excess tension, and then the cultivation of mindful awareness can be facilitated by a focus on one of the five senses. Accordingly, in one exercise, the facilitators brought to the group assorted materials that could be ripped, for example, paper, tinfoil, plastic bags, newspaper, cardboard, and sandpaper. The children were encouraged to closely examine the materials for a few minutes and then to close their eyes. While their eyes were closed, a facilitator would tear one of the materials and the children had to guess which one had been torn. The children also took turns ripping an item for the rest of the group, and some even became creative by tearing more than one material at the same time. This exercise encouraged the children to focus on and be mindful of what they were hearing, and to become aware of how much information they can retain in a short amount of time. The children found delight in challenging their own awareness of sound. Another exercise also attuned to helping the children develop mindful listening skills encouraged them to write down everything they were conscious of hearing over a period of three minutes. The children noted that they could hear breathing (their own and others'), doors opening and closing, the beep of a watch, the click of a pen, and the sound of their own writing, among other things. In our experience, the lists are never identical. For example, one child heard someone burp and another child thought the same sound was a laugh, while yet another child noticed the heater and another focused on the fan. In comparing the lists, the facilitators could highlight the choices that we make in what we choose to focus on and how we might perceive the same stimuli differently. The children appeared satisfied when they noted something that the others did not or if they perceived it differently, perhaps indicating some awareness of their individuality or uniqueness.

We also try to fully utilize spontaneous teaching moments. For example, one time when the children and the facilitators went outside for a break, they noticed a raccoon behind a chain-link fence. The children really enjoyed noticing everything about the raccoon and they were encouraged to be mindful of their observations. Later, in group discussion, the children expressed their worries about the raccoon. They wondered if he felt lost, unloved or scared, and they worried that he felt alone, perhaps projecting some of their unconscious feelings onto the raccoon. Also, the image of the raccoon was used to encourage the children to contemplate the masks they wear in their lives. Another activity that takes place outside is the game Camouflage (a version of hide-and-seek). The children are challenged to be mindful in their hiding places—that is, they are encouraged to notice any bugs running on the ground, the colors of the leaves, or the sound of the wind. During one game, a facilitator and a child were hiding close to each other, and the child became quite excited as she showed the facilitator a perfectly preserved dried flower that she deemed to be "the most beautiful flower in the world." We later expanded on this experience by asking the children to draw pictures of different items from the view of an ant to help them develop a different perspective of something ordinary. Due to their challenges, helping the children become mindful of their feelings is especially difficult. Consequently, we use exercises that encourage them to learn about and pay attention to their emotions. In one exercise they were encouraged to draw a circle full of their feelings and to indicate within the circle how much time they spent during the day feeling each emotion. One participant developed a pie chart, while another child used different sizes of the feeling words to depict her experience with each emotion. In group discussion, we validated their feelings and also encouraged them to think about what they could do to experience more of the emotions they enjoyed the most—how could these take up more space inside the circle (and in their lives)? For many of the children, paying attention to, noticing, and reflecting on their feeling experiences is a new skill and practice. But overall, they really enjoy these sorts of activities. This activity has also been assigned as homework in order to encourage the group participants to utilize what they are learning in group in their daily lives.

Finally, a variation on the theme of mindful walking was also used whenever possible (for example, during break times) and helped us to reinforce the idea that being mindful means paying attention to where we are going and what is around us. Sometimes the children were challenged to walk on only the dark squares of a multicolored and multitextured floor. As the tiles were smaller than their feet, the children had to mindfully observe exactly where they were going and where they were placing their feet. The children began to talk about the subtle shade differences on the floor tiles and they noticed the bumps and grooves in the tile. Until they were encouraged to notice what they were walking on, they had not made these observations. This simple exercise then led into other group discussions concerning other things that we miss when we are not paying attention in the moment. With one group of youths, we provided journals and encouraged them to record their daily intentions, for example, "Today will be a good day." In group, they discussed whether their intentions had any effect on how their day actually progressed and how they felt, and why or why not. Brief meditations and guided imagery activities are also used with the children, and an arts-based activity often follows the meditation; for example, they might learn how to do a body scan and then construct a collage of what their feelings look like or listen to a guided imagery of an underwater world and then sculpt out of clay the creatures they saw in their imaginations.

A Brief Summary of Findings

Adults generally have the ability to articulate how what they have learned in a group has helped them improve their self-awareness and self-esteem. For children and some youths, this is often beyond their capabilities. Therefore, during the post-group individual interviews, we learned to include foster parents and/or child-care workers in order to gain as much feedback as possible. The summary of results presented here is based on the grounded theory analysis of the transcriptions of the group sessions and the post-group individual interviews. While we have not had control groups with which to compare the findings, we have facilitated the six-week program a total of seventeen times over a period of three years, and the results have consistently been the same. First, the children really enjoy participating in the group and express a desire to continue in the program. Second, reports from the children's child-care workers and foster parents are also very positive. "More kids should be referred to stuff like this" is a typical comment made by the foster parents. Third, foster parents, child-care workers, and the children all provide specific examples of how the group helped the children develop self-awareness and self-esteem. Examples included standing up for oneself at school with a bully and feeling happier and more confident. Also reported were feelings of greater comfort in one's body, improved familial relationships, and understanding that sometimes choices exist. Indeed, rather than feeling controlled by certain feelings, most of the children now felt that they could better understand their feelings, and this awareness helped them feel more in control of life situations. Some children also reported that they learned to use their imagination to help themselves achieve tasks and goals outside of the group. Fourth, most of the older children explained that the meditations and guided imagery activities were useful in helping them relax and become more mindful: "I never thought I could get that relaxed because I'm always moving and going and doing something. . . . Being able to take that ten minutes . . . just to sort of relax and settle myself down. . . . [is] something that stood out." Several reported that they used mindfulness meditation to help them relax before sleeping. As one youth expressed, "School is going pretty good, my marks are getting better and all that . . . and I'm sleeping better."

Conclusion

Based on our preliminary research, mindfulness-based activities with children and youths with complex difficulties are effective, but we must take several important considerations into account when delivering such programs. We had originally thought that each group would begin with approximately eight participants, that we would experience attrition, and that we would offer six group sessions. In fact, we have had almost no attrition, and furthermore, the participants wish to keep attending the group beyond the initial six sessions. This being said, we have also found our work with this population to be more challenging than we had originally anticipated. Consequently, we have learned that six sessions just do not provide enough time for these children to explore and develop their self-awareness and, ideally, to learn to incorporate some of the group techniques into their lives. Given both their desire to keep attending group and the need for additional sessions, we have moved to a twelve-week model. We have noticed a dramatic difference in the children's ability to pay attention and be mindful after they completed twelve sessions compared to the first six sessions.

Also, we now believe that an optimal number of group participants is four. While this may seem to be a small number, these children are a challenging population with significant needs, and this number allows the group facilitators to attend to all the participants, to manage the group discussion and interactions, and to engage all the members in activity and discussion. The children and youths who had attended two groups also agreed that a smaller number of participants works better because participants aren't "trying to talk over each other all the time. . . . There wasn't competing against each other . . . and people were more on task."

One of the benefits of a group such as ours is that it may be less threatening for the children; that is, it is not presented as a therapy group where painful experiences have to be discussed and processed. Rather, it is presented as a group that might help them improve their self-esteem and in which they are encouraged to be creative and enjoy themselves. While they are having fun and engaging in a helping process, they are also learning about themselves and others and are developing important skills. Moreover, this type of experience may help some children connect with their feelings and experiences, opening them up to the possibility of talking about their pain so they can heal. In this manner, the group may be a good foundation or catalyst for more in-depth counseling (for children who require this level of assistance).

Mindfulness-based practices can be much more than learning how to meditate. As Berger (2005) explains, arts-based activities and journaling, reading, music, and meditation all help people open up to their experience and process their feelings. This is an important point to keep in mind, particularly when one is working with children and youths, who may have difficulty processing abstract concepts, sitting quietly, and focusing on their breath. Working with children in care adds another layer of complexity to the overall process of facilitating and teaching mindfulness practices. However, we have found our work with this population highly stimulating and rewarding. It has certainly encouraged us to further develop our own creativity, patience, and mindfulness-based practices. The mindfulness practices add a joyful, creative, rich, and holistic dimension to social work practice. Importantly, these practices can be sustained by the clients in their lives outside of group, and hopefully long after our work together ends.

References

Berger, J. (2005). *Emotional fitness, discovering our natural healing power.* Toronto, Ontario, Canada: Penguin.

Birnbaum, L. (2005a). Adolescent aggression and differentiation of self: Guided mindfulness meditation in the service of individuation. *Scientific World Journal, 5,* 478–489.

Birnbaum, L. (2005b). Connecting to inner guidance: Mindfulness meditation and transformation of professional self-concept in social work students. *Critical Social Work, 6*(2). Retrieved from http://www.uwindsor.ca/units/social work/critical.nsf/EditDoNotShowInTOC/EF84B5D985393C9285257017001 BBEC6

Birnbaum, L., & Birnbaum, A. (2004). In search of inner wisdom: Guided mindfulness meditation in the context of suicide. *Scientific World Journal, 4,* 216–227.

Bishop, S., Lau, M., Shapiro, S., Carlson, L., Anderson, N. D., & Carmody, J. (2004). Mindfulness: A proposed operational definition. *Clinical Psychology: Science and Practice, 11*(3), 230–241.

Boyd Webb, N. (2006a). The impact of trauma on youth and families in the child welfare system. In N. Boyd Webb (Ed.), *Working with traumatized youth in child welfare* (pp. 13–26). New York: Guilford Press.

Boyd Webb, N. (2006b). Selected treatment approaches for helping traumatized youth. In N. Boyd Webb (Ed.), *Working with traumatized youth in child welfare* (pp. 93–112). New York: Guilford Press.

Brown, K. W., & Ryan, R. M. (2003). The benefits of being present: Mindfulness and its role in psychological well-being. *Journal of Personality and Social Psychology, 84*(4), 822–849.

Charles, G., & Matheson, J. (1991). Suicide prevention and intervention with young people in foster care in Canada. *Child Welfare, 70*(2), 185–191.

Coholic, D. (2005). The helpfulness of spiritually influenced group work in developing self-awareness and self-esteem: A preliminary investigation. *Scientific World Journal, 5,* 789–802.

Coholic, D. (2006). Mindfulness meditation practice in spiritually influenced group work. *Aretê, 30*(1), 90–100.

Coholic, D., Lougheed, S., & LeBreton, J. (in press). The helpfulness of holistic arts-based group work with children living in foster care. *Social Work with Groups, 32.*

Dumas, J. E. (2005). Mindfulness-based parent training: Strategies to lessen the grip of automaticity in families with disruptive children. *Journal of Clinical Child and Adolescent Psychology, 34*(4), 779–791.

Fontana, D., & Slack, I. (2002). *Teaching meditation to children.* London: Thorsons.

France, H. (2002). *Nexus, transpersonal approach to groups.* Calgary, Alberta, Canada: Detselig Enterprises.

Frattaroli, E. (2001). *Healing the soul in the age of the brain: Becoming conscious in an unconscious world.* New York: Viking.

Goldin, P., & Saltzman, A. (2007). *Child-parent mindfulness-based stress reduction.* Retrieved June 3, 2007, from http://www-psych.stanford.edu/~caan/current_research_child ...parent.html

Goodman, T. (2005). Working with children: Beginner's mind. In C. Germer, R. Siegel, & P. Fulton (Eds.), *Mindfulness and psychotherapy* (pp. 197–219). New York: Guilford Press.

Jenkins, P. (1996). *The joyful child: A sourcebook of activities and ideas for releasing children's natural joy.* Santa Rosa, CA: Aslan.

Kabat-Zinn, J. (1990). *Full catastrophe living: Using the wisdom of your body and mind to face stress, pain, and illness.* New York: Delta.

Kabat-Zinn, J. (2003). Mindfulness-based interventions in context: Past, present, and future. *Clinical Psychology: Science and Practice, 10*(2), 144–156.

MacLean, K. (2004). *Peaceful piggy meditation.* Morton Grove, IL: Albert Whitman.

Morgan, W., & Morgan, S. (2005). Cultivating attention and empathy. In C. Germer, R. Siegel, & P. Fulton (Eds.), *Mindfulness and psychotherapy* (pp. 73–90). New York: Guilford Press.

Napoli, M. (2005). Mindfulness training for elementary school students: The attention academy. *Journal of Applied School Psychology, 21*(1), 99–125.

Neff, K. (2003). Development and validation of a scale to measure self-compassion. *Self and Identity, 2,* 223–250.

Neff, K. (n.d.). *Self-compassion versus self-esteem.* Retrieved April 9, 2009, from http://www.self-compassion.org/self-compassion_versus_self-es teem.html

O'Brien, E., & Epstein, S. (1988). *MSEI: The multidimensional self-esteem inventory, professional manual.* Lutz, FL: Psychological Assessment Resources.

Olendzki, A. (2005). The roots of mindfulness. In C. Germer, R. Siegel, & P. Fulton (Eds.), *Mindfulness and psychotherapy* (pp. 241–261). New York: Guilford Press.

Ott, M. (2002). Mindfulness meditation in pediatric clinical practice. *Pediatric Nursing, 28*(5), 487–490.

Piers, E. V., Harris, D., & Herzberg, D. (2005). *Piers-Harris children's self-concept scale* (2nd ed.). Los Angeles: Western Psychological Services.

Racusin, R., Maerlender, A., Sengupta, A., Isquith, P., & Straus, M. (2005). Psychosocial treatment of children in foster care: A review. *Community Mental Health Journal, 41*(2), 199–221.

Sadao, K., & Walker, W. (2002). Emancipation for youth with behavior disorders and emotional disturbance: A study of student perceptions. *Preventing School Failure, 46*(3), 119–125.

Schiraldi, G. (2001). *The self-esteem workbook*. Oakland, CA: New Harbinger.

Semple, R., Reid, E., & Miller, L. (2005). Treating anxiety with mindfulness: An open trial of mindfulness training for anxious children. *Journal of Cognitive Psychotherapy: An International Quarterly, 19*(4), 379–392.

Silvia, P., & O'Brien, M. (2004). Self-awareness and constructive functioning: Revisiting "the human dilemma." *Journal of Social and Clinical Psychology, 23*(4), 475–489.

Simmons, J., & Weinman, M. (1991). Self-esteem, adjustment, and locus of control among youth in an emergency shelter. *Journal of Community Psychology, 19,* 277–280.

Singh, N. N., Lancinoi, G., Winton, A., Fisher, B., Wahler, R., & McAleavy, K. (2006). Mindful parenting decreases aggression, noncompliance, and self-injury in children with autism. *Journal of Emotional & Behavioral Disorders, 14*(3), 169–177.

Smith, A. (2004). Clinical uses of mindfulness training for older people. *Behavioural and Cognitive Psychotherapy, 32,* 423–430.

Stewart, T. (2004). Light on body image treatment: Acceptance through mindfulness. *Behavior Modification, 28*(6), 783–811.

Tilly, N., & Caye, J. (2004). Using writing and poetry to achieve focus and depth in a group of women parenting sexually abused children. *Social Work with Groups, 27*(2–3), 129–142.

Viegas, M. (2004). *Relax kids: Aladdin's magic carpet and other fairytale meditations for children.* New York: O Books.

Wall, R. B. (2005). Tai chi and mindfulness-based stress reduction in a Boston public middle school. *Journal of Pediatric Health Care, 19*(4), 230–237.

Whitaker, D. (1975). Some conditions for effective work with groups. *British Journal of Social Work, 5*(4), 421–439.

Wilner, K. (2001). Core energetic couples therapy: An integrated approach. *Journal of Couples Therapy, 10*(2), 25–34.

Zylowska, L., & Smalley, S. (2008). *Mindful awareness research centre.* Retrieved July 8, 2008, from http://marc.ucla.edu/

CHAPTER NINE

Integrating Affect Regulation with Mindfulness in Family Therapy

Ellen Katz

This chapter will discuss both theoretical and practice applications of mindfulness to family therapy from the perspective of affect regulation. I see affect regulation and mindfulness as overlapping concepts that can be used in family therapy and are implicitly central to family therapy even when not explicitly discussed and crafted into interventions. Before defining affect regulation and mindfulness, I will situate social work theoretically in the discussion. My aim in this chapter is to demonstrate how social work's unique focus on the individual within both a family context and a larger societal context fits well with the use of mindfulness in family therapy.

I incorporate earlier chapters' definitions of mindfulness and define affect regulation in order to discuss the theoretical foundations of an integrated concept of mindfulness and affect regulation, subsequently demonstrating how such an intervention can be used in the practice of family therapy. Interventions can be designed in work with single families, with couples, or with multi-family groups. I will examine the impact of mindfulness on affect regulation in families and will illustrate how social work is in a unique position to incorporate mindfulness into family therapy.

My interest lies in the use of mindfulness in family therapy both from the vantage point of clinical work and from the theoretical perspectives that include social work's own theory and position in relation to other helping professions. The final portion of the chapter will discuss why these interventions are so useful at this point in time in work with families and will reevaluate the theoretical basis from which mindful family therapy fosters affect regulation in families.

Mindfulness and Affect Regulation

In order for readers to understand the discussion in this chapter, definitions of the central concepts are necessary. Mindfulness was defined in the first chapter of this book and that definition is followed in this chapter.

The definitions of the concepts of affect and emotion are not straightforward. Psychodynamic theory often talks about affect as a complex psycho-physiological state in which emotions are seen as outwardly visible expressions of internally experienced feeling states (Applegate & Shapiro, 2005). Neuroscience provides many different definitions of the terms. Zelazo and Cunningham (2007) define emotion as "an aspect of human information processing that manifests itself in multiple dimensions: subjective experience, observable behaviour and physiological activity" (p. 136). This encompasses both emotions and feelings, according to the psychodynamic definition, leaving affect unmentioned. Lewis (2005) and Panksepp (1998) define emotions in the context of the many different definitions of the terms *affect, emotions,* and *feelings,* stating that the field of neuroscience is challenged to agree upon definitions for these terms. In this chapter, the psychodynamic definition of the terms will be used.

Affect regulation is a concept that is useful in working with families. It refers to the dynamic process, both within an individual and between people, in which the dimensions of subjective experience, observable behavior, and physiological activity are adjusted to create a balance among emotion, feelings, thought, and action. In this way, all the dimensions of human life experience are integrated, creating a person who can manage emotions, thoughts, feelings, and actions. Research demonstrates that the manner in which emotions are communicated and handled in families is predictive of the quality of life and mental health of the individual members as well as of the family as a whole (Doane & Diamond, 1994). When families struggle to manage their emotional lives, they are often grappling with affect regulation. Regulation occurs as individuals communicate their emotional states to one another. An important aim is for each person's emotional state to become regulated in the process of interacting with the other (Fonagy, Gergely, Jurist, & Target, 2002). Helping families increase their ability to regulate emotions is often a central goal in family therapy because many of the families encounter difficulties managing the affective states of their members. In this way, affect regulation and emotional arousal are inextricably linked (Aron, 1998; Chodorow, 1999; Fonagy, 1998; Fonagy et al., 2002; Saari, 1991; Safran & Greenberg, 1998; Stern, 2004).

As stated in the introduction, mindfulness and affect regulation are concepts that are implicitly linked. I will illustrate below how both neuroscience and the psychological disciplines are addressing the integration of these two areas.

Integrating Mindfulness and Affect Regulation

Current literature in both neuroscience and the psychological disciplines (social work, psychology, and psychoanalysis) highlights the central role of emotion in general, and affect regulation in particular, as pivotal elements in the achievement and maintenance of optimal mental health. Neuroscience focuses on the physical basis for emotion's development within the brain and its neural networks. The psychological disciplines locate affect and emotion regulation as developing and being maintained within interactions between people. Affect regulation is a process that may unfold optimally or may be hindered due to problems. Examples of such problems include traumatic experiences as a result of living in a war zone or being sexually abused, or brain damage incurred as a result of the effects of alcoholism.

Research in neuroscience is focused on the role of the brain's neural networks in processing dominant nonconscious emotional reactions and in integrating these reactions with thoughts and actions (Bradley, 2000; Cozolino, 2002; Damasio, 2003; LeDoux, 1996; Schore, 1994; Siegel, 1999). The three main variables involved in this discussion are the traditional variables of emotion, behavior, and cognition, which are inextricably linked. It is the integration of these processes, acknowledging the primacy of emotion in the brain's neural networks, that fosters affect regulation.

The psychological disciplines have approached emotion from the perspective of human interactions. The focus is on the development of affect and emotion regulation within relationships. Research (Aron, 1998; Chodorow, 1999; Doane & Diamond, 1994; Fonagy, 1998; Fonagy et al., 2002; Saari, 1986, 1991; Safran & Greenberg, 1998; Stern, 2004) consistently documents the physiologic base of emotion and its fundamental function of "regulating the interpsychic space between people" (Saari, 1986, p. 72). A primary developmental process is learning to regulate one's own emotional state, learning that begins at birth. Fonagy et al. (2002) describe how parents facilitate their infants' abilities to be aware of, process, and label their own emotions. Safran and Greenberg (1998) describe an "integrative model of emotional processing" similar to the neuroscientific findings that emotions, cognitions, and actions are integrated, with emotion as the area of primacy in human motivation. Related literature in psychodynamics in the last ten years or so focuses on processes of awareness and attention (Aron, 1998) and a reclaiming of a body based in breath and awareness (Dimen, 1998). Awareness and attention are also concepts integral to mindfulness.

Doane and Diamond (1994), in the Yale Psychiatric Institute Family Study, document how affect, in the context of emotion style and expressed emotion, is predictive of families' mental health states, both positive and negative. They cite a large body of carefully controlled studies showing family emotional climate to be influential in the course and treatment of emotional disorders, bipolar disorder, obesity, anorexia nervosa, and diabetes as well as other medical disorders. Stormshak and Dishion (2002) agree with Doane and Diamond's research findings on the influence of emotion in families on mental health. They discuss treatment for severe adolescent problem behavior and target affect and emotion regulation in families.

There has long been an interest among the psychological disciplines in mindfulness, meditation, and Buddhism, as discussed by Steven Hick in chapter 1. Literature in social work (O'Hanlon & Weiner-Davis, 1989), psychology (Bennett-Goleman, 2001; Safran & Muran, 2000), and psychoanalysis (Safran, 2003) documents this interest. Conferences that integrate these areas also occur.

Kabat-Zinn (2005b), Goleman (1997), and Boyce (2005a) document how medical patients make use of mindfulness to improve healing of their physical ailments. These authors also document the effects of mindfulness on the mind and the brain (see Goleman, 2003; Boyce, 2005b). As Goleman (1997, 2003) describes, mindfulness shifts brain activity. It alters brain activity in the same way as the psychological and neurobiological mechanisms do when aimed at increasing the brain's ability to regulate emotion. The literature in neuroscience, psychology, and mindfulness documents an increased integration of neural functioning, the result of which is an increased experience of equanimity, a mind that is active but not unsettled by the processing of a variety of feeling states. Hence, affect regulation and mindfulness are integrated in their focus on the goal of increasing the ability to regulate emotion.

Meditation, then, is a means to contain and manage, not eliminate, emotions and feelings (C. Brazier, 2003; D. Brazier, 2001; Epstein, 1995, 2005). Containment influences actions that result from this process. And it is mindfulness that is the catalyst for change. Mindfulness allows a "stilling" of the mind (Khema, 1997) in its focus during meditation. A stilled mind that develops in the process of mindfulness meditation is a mind that regulates its affective experience. Meditation fosters a mind that is both "open and responsive, but not unsettled . . . a poised mind, bright and clear but without reactivity" (C. Brazier, 2003, p. 101). Neuroscience, the psychological disciplines, and mindfulness all document increased integration of emotion, cognition, and behavior. They label this affect regulation, or emotion regulation, and describe it as an integral component of optimal mental health.

Research on Mindfulness and Family Therapy

Affect regulation appears to be a key component of both individual and family well-being. In addition, it is possible to link affect regulation with mindfulness. It would appear, then, that integrating mindfulness, which implicitly fosters affect regulation, into family therapy would be useful. Families practicing mindfulness could increase their ability to self-regulate. Yet there is a lack of work in this area. Research into the effect of mindfulness on children and families' use of mindfulness is scarce. In an unpublished doctoral dissertation, Semple (2005) documented fewer attention problems in children who participated in a mindfulness group as part of a remedial reading program. Semple, Lee, and Miller (2006) document preliminary support for the treatment of childhood anxiety through the use of mindfulness groups for children. Wagner, Rathus, and Miller (2006) report on their own work using an adapted version of dialectical behavior therapy, which makes use of mindfulness, for use with adolescents who have borderline features or meet the criteria for a diagnosis of borderline personality disorder. They also report the results of three other studies, all of which determined dialectical behavior therapy to be a promising treatment. Harrison, Manocha, and Rubia (2004) developed and tested a family treatment program using mindfulness to address attention-deficit/hyperactivity disorder and found reduced symptoms of ADHD. Though their study was not focused on issues of affect regulation, they refer to families' increased ability to maintain a calmer home environment. To date there are no interventions specifically targeting the ability of families to increase their abilities to self-regulate. It is possible, though, to adapt the above and other existing interventions for use either with individual families or with multi-family groups.

Intervention: Creating a Mindful Family Therapy to Foster Family Affect Regulation

To date, I have used mindfulness interventions with individual families and couples and have recently begun to work with family groups. In my work with individual families, I have integrated aspects of Terry Orlick's (1998) work into family therapy. Orlick provides relaxation, breath-focused, and reflective activities both in his book and on a CD that can be used in family therapy sessions with children of varying ages. His exercises, such as learning to relax and wiggle "spaghetti toes," foster a family focus on thoughts and enhance family ability to "change the channel." The exercises make use of images and popular media familiar to children today. Admittedly, the exercises are not explicitly mindfulness based and may, in fact, be more cognitive behavioral. The reason I make this statement is that there is an effort to "change the channel" to focus on positive thoughts, a cognitive behavioral position, rather than to simply notice and be aware of whatever thoughts are occurring, a meditative position. However, the exercises are related to mindfulness exercises and can be adapted by way of a shift from actively seeking change to a simple focus on awareness and attention to thoughts, feelings, and behavior. Material that is more related to cognitive behavioral therapy can be modified or omitted.

Children attending family therapy sessions can find the need to talk in sessions challenging. Engaging in an experiential activity with parents present and participating has the potential to create an empirical shift in the family experience. Informal feedback from families who have participated in these kinds of family therapy sessions has been positive. I recognize that the evidence from the work I have done to date is anecdotal and see it as preliminary steps to the beginning of building an evidence-based practice in using mindfulness in family therapy.

I have had the same experience incorporating mindfulness into couples therapy. I have integrated Jon Kabat-Zinn's (1990) raisin and breath-focused exercises with John Gottman's (1999) self-soothing and other-soothing material to allow individuals to increase their awareness of themselves and their spouse, to focus on breath, and to be able to calm themselves and their spouse. Couples using this integrated approach have commented on their own increased calmness as well as their increased ability to regulate conflict in the marriage. They have been able to shift marital dynamics to a more positive state. Again, there is no research evidence yet to report. These are early and preliminary attempts to begin to incorporate mindfulness into different aspects of work with family systems.

I have recently begun a multi-family mindfulness group intervention based on an integration of the literature already described.[1] The group intervention has adapted and combined features of groups already in

1. My colleague Christie Hayos is working with me on this new endeavor at the Hincks-Dellcrest Centre in Toronto.

existence that use mindfulness to improve mental health for both adults (Kabat-Zinn, 1990; Segal, Williams, & Teasdale, 2002) and children (Harrison et al., 2004; Semple, 2005; Semple et al., 2006). I have also incorporated Thorngren and Kleist's (2002) work in multi-family therapy, specifically their use of a narrative reflecting team. My own work in using multi-family therapy has demonstrated the power of families working together to both support and challenge each other (Katz & Psenicka, 2000). I am particularly interested in Thorngren and Kleist's use of a reflecting team with groups of families. The narrative concept of reflecting teams provides the concept of reflection, which is also integral to mindfulness in its ability to foster awareness and attention. I think the power of families attending to and aware of themselves and other families builds on breath-based mindfulness interventions. A group of families together in a state of reflection, receiving and providing reflections on their experiences of being with other families, could potentially provide the support needed for families to make changes that they might be less likely to make in work with a single therapist.

Given the presence of children in a multi-family mindfulness group, I follow Harrison et al.'s (2004) design of a shorter group (one-and-a-half hours) than would be the case if the group were for adults only. To compensate for the length of the group, it is ideal to schedule, as did Harrison et al., a group that meets twice weekly for twelve weeks. I believe that the twice-weekly sessions and the longer overall length of the group allow for more time to receive support from other families and more time to practice the breathing. In my ten years leading adult psychoeducational groups, I found that meeting more frequently over a longer period of time allowed for better learning. Again, I admit that this is anecdotal information that is not supported by formal research. I also admit that it may be challenging to contract with families to attend a group twice weekly and to attend for twelve weeks due to families' busyness. However, Greene (2004), in an unpublished dissertation, documents that mindfulness is best fostered by ongoing regular practice.

I plan to build in booster sessions between groups. This will allow families from previous groups to attend subsequent sessions to tune up their skills and keep their practice current. It is my hope that such an intervention could be part of an ongoing family support network for mindfulness practice. Building a community of families practicing mindfulness will increase social support as well as support their practice. Supporting their practice involves both ensuring that their practice is effective by monitoring to make sure that it is being done as effectively as possible and building opportunities to practice in groups. Such booster sessions are modeled on group practice of mindfulness and on meditative and/or Buddhist communities. It is my hope that a mindful family support group could eventually grow from these booster sessions. Should such an intervention be successful, a weekly family meditation group could be held apart from the ongoing mindful family groups. Families at any stage of participation, both current and former participants in family mindfulness groups, could attend these weekly sessions.

Each session of the multi-family mindfulness group based on elements of the groups cited above includes the following elements: (1) mindfulness instruction; (2) five to ten minutes of mindfulness practice; (3) one mindfulness exercise, such as mindful eating, listening, talking, or walking, yoga, tai chi, or body relaxation; (4) a family exercise, examples of which could be family artwork or sculpting the family's present and future interactions to facilitate intrafamily discussion of regulating emotions; (5) reflection by the families in a group on the individual family exercise; and (6) provision and debriefing of the homework exercise through discussion of each family's homework notebook. The homework notebook is used for the purpose of recording the specific mindfulness exercise assigned as homework, the family's record of their daily practice, and family reflections or comments on the progress of daily practice.

Based on the above literature, it is my hope that from the group will develop an increased ability, using mindfulness, to regulate affect and therefore improve mental health. Research is an integral component of an emerging multi-family mindfulness group so that we can study the process with the goal of further developing it. A component of the research may be determining whether the format outlined above is realistic or requires modification.

The Impacts of Family Mindfulness Interventions on Family Affect Regulation

It is reasonable to ask how interventions making use of mindfulness will assist families in increasing their ability to regulate emotions and feelings. As stated above, affect regulation is an interpersonal process in which the state of emotional arousal is shared within a group of people. In this case, the group is the family. Family therapy is generally targeted at specific issues often classified according to the behavior of the children. Such behavior is grouped according to whether it constitutes externalizing or internalizing actions. Externalizing issues include acting-out and antisocial behaviors and threatening and assaulting peers. Internalizing issues include anxiety, depression, and suicidal ideation. As well, some of the many other reasons for families presenting in family therapy include separation and divorce, children in the care of the Children's Aid Society, parents' lack of ability to establish any position as parents within families in which children are in charge of decision making, grandparents raising their grandchildren, and children who are not attending school. However, in a study of empirically supported research related to emotion, Westen, Novotny, and Thompson-Brenner (2004) advocate the development of treatment for general issues of negative emotion and emotional dysregulation rather than an exclusive focus on specific psychiatric syndromes. A model of family therapy with a focus on mindfulness will do just this and will promote the ability to contain, rather than eliminate, emotion. A family working together as a group on this goal of containing affect will be able to interact with a greater ability to reflect on family life and will be able to both support and challenge members. It is my experience that unregulated affect is often implicitly the problem in families seen in therapy. When emotions are the explicit focus of therapy, an underlying cause can become the focus of treatment.

Social Work's Incorporation of Mindfulness into Family Therapy

Mindfulness can be incorporated into family therapy from the perspective of social work's unique focus on the individual within both a family context and a larger societal context. The above section focused on the integration of the concept of affect regulation into family therapy. The integration is useful precisely because the individual exists within a social environment. Affect regulation provides concepts that explain how a family becomes aware of, labels, communicates, manages, and expresses emotions and feelings as a group. These concepts relate to systems theory on two levels. The first level pertains to two main concepts: (1) the whole is more than the sum of its parts, and (2) a change in any one component affects the whole system. The second level extends these concepts more broadly: whole entities themselves are also parts of larger wholes in the sense that the individual is part of a family, which is part of a larger extended family, which is part of a community, which is part of a society, and this can be extended further (Bertalanffy, 1968). In family therapy, these systems concepts belong to modernist thinking. Such modernist thinking includes Minuchin's structural family therapy, among other family therapies. Currently, Minuchin's ideas are not discussed as much as is the narrative therapy developed by Michael White and David Epson (1990).

Yet the concept of affect regulation is systemic and the discussion of affect regulation above translates easily into family therapy. When a member of a family is challenged in any area related to emotion and feeling, the whole family is affected. Should one family member experience either externalizing or internalizing emotional challenges, the whole family shifts to support and/or challenge him or her. Increased emotional closeness and distance in the family are subtly negotiated as family relationships shift amid the struggles of relating to each other. A common example is that of the family negotiating separation and divorce. Literature documenting the effects of divorce on families discusses how all family members are affected by the decision of the adults in a family to divorce (Wallerstein, 1990). Conversely, if a family is able to positively regulate, or manage, their emotions, and if family members are able to calm themselves and each other, then family interactions can become more positive and family life can become more positive. Families can learn how to work through their difficulties, to enjoy each other, and to regulate conflict. Mindfulness is an intervention with the power to provide such tools to families.

As well, social work's focus on the individual within a larger context is similar to the focus of mindfulness. Kabat-Zinn's (1990, 2005a) work was developed to be taught within a group format, and initially supported within a group format. Mindfulness as practiced in Buddhism is practiced within a community of practitioners, a *sangha*. Buddhist teachers explicitly state the need to practice within a community in order to maintain one's practice. The support of the group is said to increase each individual's ability to be mindful on an ongoing basis, as well as the whole group's ability to be mindful. This is an empirical illustration of the theoretical dynamics, discussed above, of a system in action. The individual is inextricably linked to the group. Maintaining one's practice involves the ongoing attempt to hone one's ability to attend to, be aware of, and recognize lived experiences from moment to moment. Such ongoing practice allows the mind to experience with reduced reactivity and to participate wholly in these continual lived experiences, thereby containing and regulating emotion. Two practitioners, one of whom identifies himself as a social worker, integrate mindfulness and therapy, thus explicitly supporting the need to practice within a community of practitioners (C. Brazier, 2003; D. Brazier, 2001).

My own work in multi-family group therapy supported the need to integrate the individual into a larger group (Katz & Psenicka, 2000). My experience of working with families in multi-family groups has been one in which the therapy was made more effective by the work of families together. Working with individual families and bringing families together in therapy counters the isolation of individualist North American society, which can potentially be replicated when individuals are seen on their own or when families are seen one at a time. Again, this is not to say that individual therapy and individual family therapy are not effective. However, the ability to work with the individual and the family within a larger context is a unique focus of social work. As such, it is one that we should consider making use of more often. My aim in fostering ongoing family support through the use of booster sessions between family mindfulness groups is aimed at decreasing isolation, building support, and fostering community.

I do find it ironic that this kind of social work focus harkens back to modernism's systemic tenets. However, the ability to incorporate a component of reflection integrates narrative reflection and postmodernism into this modern theory and practice. Mindfulness's focus on reflection can bridge the modern systemic and postmodern narrative therapies to support a reflective communal practice that recognizes the power of the group to regulate and heal the individual in a context of silent attention to and awareness of lived experience.

Conclusion

I have discussed how theoretical perspectives on affect regulation can be incorporated into clinical interventions using mindfulness in family therapy. In order to do this, I have drawn from psychodynamic concepts of affect regulation and recent shifts in psychodynamics regarding attention and awareness. I have shown how affect regulation is foundational to productive family life. I have also drawn from social work's theoretical concepts of systemic and narrative therapies. Systemic therapy provides a base for the individual's intrinsic connection to a larger social and societal system. Narrative therapy supports this and adds the concept of reflection. Both psychodynamics and narrative therapy contribute to this concept of reflection, which is based in attention and awareness. Mindfulness, of course, is grounded in these concepts as well. It is possible to see the theoretical integration. Mindfulness also supports social work's interest in community, and mindfulness has been developed within group settings. This is drawn from its base in meditation, also practiced within the community in group settings. Mindfulness contributes the experience of silence, which, we have seen, is both challenging in current society and of growing interest, as demonstrated by the increase in number and kinds of mindfulness groups. I have integrated these theoretical concepts to create a clinical mindful family therapy based on a theoretical foundation in mindful affect regulation, as well as the potential for a mindful community of families practicing together. Mindfulness is seen to be the foundational concept.

I described clinical interventions based in mindfulness to be used in family therapy with individual families, with couples, and with multi-family groups. I described how these interventions can assist families in increasing their ability to regulate their emotions and feelings and, in so doing, increase their ability to enjoy each other and live together in a calm environment. In so doing, I have advocated a theoretical integration of systemic, psychodynamic, and narrative concepts based in mindfulness. Family therapy has seen debates about which theoretical concepts are productive, useful, useless, and/or outdated. Rather than engage in this kind of discussion, I prefer to adopt a perspective from which mindfulness originates. Mindfulness pulls from Buddhist concepts of oneness, wholeness, and healing. The word *wholeness* is derived from the Old English word from which the current English word for *health* is drawn (Little, Fowler, & Coulson, 1972). Health and wholeness, attention and awareness, are certainly goals that therapists and families strive to achieve in therapy. If the incorporation of mindfulness into family therapy can create any kind of healing experience, this would be an experience worth awareness, attention, and cultivation.

References

Applegate, J. S., & Shapiro, J. R. (2005). *Neurobiology for clinical social work.* New York: Norton.

Aron, L. (1998). The clinical body and the reflexive mind. In L. Aron & F. S. Anderson (Eds.), *Relational perspectives on the body* (pp. 3–38). Hillsdale, NJ: Analytic Press.

Bennett-Goleman, T. (2001). *Emotional alchemy: How the mind can heal the heart.* New York: Harmony Books.

Bertalanffy, L. von. (1968). *General system theory: Foundations, development, applications.* New York: George Braziller.

Boyce, B. (2005a, May). The man who prescribes the medicine of the moment. *Shambhala Sun*, 29–34, 72–75.

Boyce, B. (2005b, September). Two sciences of mind. *Shambhala Sun*, 34–43, 93–96.

Bradley, S. J. (2000). *Affect regulation and the development of psychopathology.* New York: Guilford Press.

Brazier, C. (2003). *Buddhism on the couch: From analysis to awakening using Buddhist psychology.* Berkeley, CA: Ulysses Press.

Brazier, D. (2001). *The feeling Buddha: An introduction to Buddhism.* London: Robinson.

Chodorow, N. (1999). *The power of feelings: Personal meaning in psychoanalysis, gender and culture.* New Haven, CT: Yale University Press.

Cozolino, L. J. (2002). *The neuroscience of psychotherapy: Building and rebuilding the human brain.* New York: Norton.

Damasio, A. (2003). *Looking for Spinoza: Joy, sorrow, and the feeling brain.* Orlando: Harcourt.

Dimen, M. (1998). Polyglot bodies: Thinking through the relational. In L. Aron & F. S. Anderson (Eds.), *Relational perspectives on the body* (pp. 65–93). Hillsdale, NJ: Analytic Press.

Doane, J., & Diamond, D. (1994). *Affect and attachment in the family: A family-based treatment of major psychiatric disorder.* New York: Basic Books.

Epstein, M. (1995). *Thoughts without a thinker: Psychotherapy from a Buddhist perspective.* New York: Basic Books.

Epstein, M. (2005). *Open to desire: Embracing a lust for life. Insights from Buddhism and psychotherapy.* New York: Gotham Books.

Fonagy, P. (1998). Moments of change in psychoanalytic theory: Discussion of a new theory of psychic change. *Infant Mental Health Journal, 19*(3), 346–353.

Fonagy, P., Gergely, G., Jurist, E., & Target, M. (2002). *Affect regulation and the development of the self.* New York: Other Press.

Goleman, D. (1997). *Healing emotions: Conversations with the Dalai Lama on mindfulness, emotions and health.* Boston: Shambhala.

Goleman, D. (2003). *Destructive emotions: How can we overcome them?* New York: Bantam Books.

Gottman, J. M. (1999). *The marriage clinic: A scientifically based marital therapy.* New York: Norton.

Greene, P. B (2004). *Stress reactivity, health and meditation: A path analytic approach.* Unpublished doctoral dissertation, Boston University.

Harrison, L. J., Manocha, R., & Rubia, K. (2004). Sahaha yoga meditation as a family treatment programme for children with attention deficit hyperactivity disorder. *Clinical Child Psychology and Psychiatry, 9*(4), 479–497.

Kabat-Zinn, J. (1990). *Full catastrophe living: Using the wisdom of your mind and body to face stress, pain and illness.* New York: Dell.

Kabat-Zinn, J. (2005a). *Coming to our senses: Healing ourselves and the world through mindfulness.* New York: Hyperion.

Kabat-Zinn, J. (2005b). Healing mind, healing body. *Tricycle, 55,* 52–55.

Katz, E., & Psenicka, L. (2000, October). *Building connections for children and families: The use of mutual aid groups to increase family therapy effectiveness with clients.* Paper presented at twenty-second annual international symposium of the Advancement of Social Work with Groups, Toronto.

Khema, A. (1997). *Who is my self? A guide to Buddhist meditation.* Boston: Wisdom.

LeDoux, J. (1996). *The emotional brain: The mysterious underpinnings of emotional life.* New York: Touchstone.

Lewis, M. D. (2005). Bridging emotion theory and neurobiology through dynamic systems modeling. *Behavioural and Brain Sciences, 28,* 169–245.

Little, W., Fowler, H. W., & Coulson, J. (1972). *Shorter Oxford English dictionary on historical principles.* Oxford: Clarendon Press.

O'Hanlon, W. H., & Weiner-Davis, M. (1989). *In search of solutions: A new direction in psychotherapy.* New York: Norton.

Orlick, T. (1998). *Feeling great: Teaching children to excel at living.* Carp, Canada: Creative Bound.

Panksepp, J. (1998). *Affective neuroscience: The foundations of human and animal emotions.* Oxford: Oxford University Press.

Saari, C. (1986). *Clinical social work treatment: How does it work?* New York: Gardner Press.

Saari, C. (1991). *The creation of meaning in clinical social work.* New York: Guilford Press.

Safran, J. (Ed.). (2003). *Psychoanalysis and Buddhism: An unfolding dialogue.* Boston: Wisdom.

Safran, J., & Greenberg, L. (1998). Hot cognition and psychotherapy process: An information-processing/ecological approach. In J. Safran (Ed.), *Widening the scope of cognitive therapy: The therapeutic relationship, emotion and the process of change* (pp. 107–144). Northvale, NJ: Jason Aronson.

Safran, J., & Muran, C. J. (2000). *Negotiating the therapeutic alliance: A relational treatment guide.* New York: Guilford Press.

Schore, A. N. (1994). *Affect regulation and the origin of the self: The neurobiology of emotional development.* Hillsdale, NJ: Lawrence Erlbaum Associates.

Segal, Z. J., Williams, M. G., & Teasdale, J. D. (2002). *Mindfulness-based cognitive therapy for depression.* New York: Guilford Press.

Semple, R. J. (2005). *Mindfulness-based cognitive therapy for children: A randomized group psychotherapy trial developed to enhance attention and reduce anxiety.* Unpublished doctoral dissertation, Columbia University, New York.

Semple, R. J., Lee, J., & Miller, L. F. (2006). Mindfulness-based cognitive therapy for children. In R. Baer (Ed.), *Mindfulness-based treatment approaches: Clinician's guide to evidence base and applications* (pp. 143–166). Amsterdam: Elsevier.

Siegel, D. J. (1999). *The developing mind: Toward a neurobiology of interpersonal experience.* New York: Guilford Press.

Stern, D. (2004). *The present moment in psychotherapy and everyday life.* New York: Norton.

Stormshak, E. A., & Dishion, T. J. (2002). An ecological approach to child and family clinical and counselling psychology. *Clinical Child and Family Psychology Review, 5*(3), 197–215.

Thorngren, J. M., & Kleist, D. M. (2002). Multiple family group therapy: An interpersonal/postmodern approach. *Family Journal: Counselling and Therapy for Couples and Families, 10*(2), 167–176.

Wagner, E. E., Rathus, J. H., & Miller, A. L. (2006). Mindfulness in dialectical behaviour therapy (DBT) for adolescents. In R. Baer (Ed.), *Mindfulness-treatment approaches: Clinician's guide to evidence base and applications* (pp. 167–189). Amsterdam: Elsevier.

Wallerstein, J. S. (1990). *Second chances: Men, women, and children a decade after divorce.* New York: Ticknor and Fields.

Westen, D., Novotny, C. M., & Thompson-Brenner, H. (2004). The empirical status of empirically supported psychotherapies: Assumptions, findings, and reporting in controlled clinical trials. *Psychological Bulletin, 130*(4), 631–663.

White, M., & Epson, D. (1990). *Narrative means to therapeutic ends.* New York: Norton.

Zelazo, P. D., & Cunningham, W. A. (2007). Executive function: Mechanisms underlying emotion regulation. In J. Gross (Ed.), *Handbook of emotion regulation* (pp. 135–158). New York: Guilford Press.

CHAPTER TEN

Mindfulness-Influenced Social Work Practice with Immigrants

Miriam George

When I first met Ms. Nair, I expected my session with her to be no different from those with my other clients. Instead, it turned out to be one of the greatest learning experiences of my life. Ms. Nair came from India and had been physically abused by her husband before and after her migration to Canada and was also adjusting to her new life in this new country. She had recently been involved in a workplace accident and was receiving mental health support. Neither my personal experience as an immigrant nor my professional knowledge as a clinical social worker prepared me for this unusual therapy session.

Ms. Nair came to my office with a calm smile and greeted me. She informed me that she would like to begin the session with a short silent prayer. She clasped her hands together and bowed her head, eyes closed, and a few minutes of silence passed. As I watched her pray, I found myself struggling with growing feelings of impatience. I started wondering why she was wasting my time. Then a feeling of insecurity came over me as I pondered my ability to deal with this client's unexpected behavior. At one point she asked me to chant with her. I decided to join her. The words she spoke made no sense to me. I felt very uncomfortable and could sense beads of perspiration forming on my brow. Suddenly, she stopped praying, looked at me, and said, "I am ready to begin." Dismayed and full of the curiosity a child often displays when observing something for the first time, I could not believe how peaceful and calm she appeared. As an observer, I realized that her silent prayer had helped her steady her mind before she began talking to me. I, on the other hand, had felt anxious and disoriented at the beginning of the prayer, but I was able to steady my mind and work with her during the session. At the closing of our session, Ms. Nair once again asked if she could pray. As she repeated the same prayer, I noticed her facial muscles relaxing and a sense of peacefulness come over her and me. I decided to give silent prayer a try before starting my work, and to my surprise, it actually did help me relax and also increased my focus during sessions. More importantly, it helped me realize the significance of being mindful and the powerful therapeutic benefits that mindfulness practice can have for clients in a clinical setting. In Ms. Nair's case, the peace, calm, and optimism that mindfulness brought her affected me and allowed me to notice her change and her ability to focus on issues and navigate through painful feelings in order to access and benefit from therapeutic inner experience.

Mindfulness in the context of social work practice is based on a trust in our own capacity to be fully present, fully awake, and fully active in meeting immigrant clients' needs (Kabat-Zinn, 1994). The self-reflective work often associated with mindfulness practice might be of benefit to many clients, those who have experienced trauma in particular. By making the intentional commitment to be mindful of the needs of immigrant clients, social workers can discover deeper forms of intelligence within themselves that might be useful, especially in those moments when they are overwhelmed by the challenge and task of intervening with an immigrant client.

In recent years, the demographic profile of Western countries has become more diverse due to a huge influx of immigrants from countries all over the globe. Social workers must constantly change in order to adapt to the different beliefs and traditions these immigrants bring with them. Canada has become a hub of multiculturalism. This chapter will explore how social work interactions with immigrants might be influenced by mindfulness practice. The first section provides an overview of immigration in Canada and its implications for social work practice and introduces the concept of mindfulness-based culturally competent social work practice. The following section provides a mindfulness-based social work framework that can be used by social workers to facilitate a holistic social work interaction with an immigrant client. Major themes discussed in this framework are self-awareness and nonjudgment, empathy and trust, communication and interconnectedness, experience and compassion, and acceptance and new beginnings. The chapter ends with suggestions for practicing mindfulness-based social work.

Immigration and Implications for Service Delivery

Upon entering a new country, immigrants often experience considerable challenges that adversely affect their health. In the United States, Canada, and Australia, the healthy immigrant effect is a major concern (Donovan, d'Espaignet, Merton, & van Ommeren, 1992; Hyman, 2001; Hyman, Noh, & Fenta, 2004; Stephen, Foote, Hendershot, & Shoenborn, 1994). The *healthy immigrant effect* refers to the observation that immigrants often are in superior health compared to the native-born population when they first arrive in a new country but lose this health advantage over time (Chen & Wilkins, 1996; Perez, 2002). It has been suggested that resettlement issues strongly influence immigrant health (Fowler, 1998; Srivastava, 2007). Fowler also asserts that cultural differences in information-seeking patterns and communication styles have an impact on immigrants' health. One of the major issues facing immigrants during their resettlement period is accessing and utilizing health and social services. Providing effective and improved care to immigrants requires an understanding of their health from their own perspective and should reflect how their lives influence their physical and mental well-being. Review of the health care literature reveals that immigrants not only have fewer contacts with service providers but also tend to under-use mental health services (Hyman & Guruge, 2002; Kirmayer, Galbaud du Fort, Young, Weinfeld, & Lasry, 1996; Mulvihill, Mailloux, & Atkin, 2001; Simms, 1999). The services provided are not relevant to or reflective of immigrant needs; the absence of culturally relevant service delivery presents the most significant barrier to service utilization. Therefore the biggest reason for immigrants' underutilization of the available assistance is the lack of services that accommodate their diverse social, cultural, and religious backgrounds. This justifies the need for greater emphasis on culturally competent practice. Health care providers have taken the initiative to adopt culturally competent service models to productively deal with immigrants. However, mindfulness-based social work interactions during clinical interventions with an immigrant client can create the quality of gentle, nonjudging curiosity on the part of the social worker, which fosters an inviting and holistic atmosphere for the client (Wheat, 2005). Social work practice with mindfulness produces the nonjudgmental, collaborative, cooperative, and client-centered environment that so many immigrants need. Mindfulness-based social work will not fix all problems. All the normal difficulties that social workers face during their everyday clinical interventions will still be present when they work with immigrants. But awareness of these mindfulness concepts will help social workers navigate much more effectively through these problems and help them to make wiser use of the full range of human emotions.

Cultural Competence and Anti-racism

Cultural competence describes the ability of systems to provide care to clients with diverse values and beliefs and of various races and ethnicities, including tailoring delivery to meet clients' social, cultural, and linguistic needs (Betancourt, Green, & Carrillo, 2002). Cultural competence is characterized by "recognition of, and respect for, difference and an ongoing effort toward working with diversity" (Srivastava, 2007, p. 18). Underpinning the concept of cultural competence is the assumption that competence transforms knowledge and understanding into effective responses or interventions. It is important to note that cultural competence is a lifelong learning process that incorporates attitude (i.e., awareness) as well as knowledge (Srivastava, 2007). The attitude and engagement that a practitioner brings to the clinician-client interaction are as important as cross-cultural knowledge in facilitating culturally sensitive—indeed, culturally comprehensible—care (Wheat, 2005). To achieve this type of clinician–immigrant client interaction, social workers need to understand their own limitations, valuing diversity and managing potential dynamics of systemic bias, racism, prejudice, and exclusion within client–service provider relationships (Srivastava, 2007).

The relevance of understanding race and culture in a therapeutic intervention cannot be overestimated. Achieving awareness of differences in identity is hampered by the trap of seeing differences in individuals as singular and unitary. This mind-set was prevalent before the 1960s. However, during the heady days of the 1960s, new social movements began to resist the idea that the one-size-fits-all model of social services provision could meet the needs of people facing structural inequalities that were rooted in the way that contemporary social relations had been organized to prevent people from different racial and ethnic groups, people with disabilities, and non-heterosexuals from accessing required services, while privileging others (Dominelli, 1988). Unfortunately, this popular movement gave rise to various forms of identity politics that sought to expose the links between the personal hardships experienced by individuals from particular social groups, and their specific social locations. Eventually, as a result of this, many groups returned during the 1980s to the pre-1960s mind-set of focusing on a single dimension of identity (e.g., gender, race, ethnicity, ability/disability, sexual orientation). Social movements have recently begun to embrace the concepts that originated during the 1960s, espousing the need to address the diverse nature of individual identity, and promoting the idea that every person is different in terms of his or her unique cultural, ethnic, racial, and linguistic background (Dominelli, 1996). Dominelli asserts that this change in philosophy came about as marginalized groups eventually started challenging the single-identity treatment they were receiving. They found their own voices and began influencing prevailing discourses in the fields of social work, health, and education (Dominelli, 1996). These voices from below became a significant force for change in the theories used to understand the world and the practices utilized to intervene in people's lives (Dominelli, 2002). During clinical intervention with immigrant clients, social workers may be unsure about how to address differences in values, beliefs, race, culture, and expectations and worry that whatever approach is taken will lead to miscommunication. Social workers may struggle to find the right language and method to effectively address issues of diversity when they encounter immigrants (Srivastava, 2007). This is where the incorporation of mindfulness insights, which can be formed from both the clinician's and client's perspectives, into the immigrant client–social worker interaction can be helpful in overcoming the clinician's and client's differences through self-awareness, communication, compassion, and interconnectedness. Society is looking for various ways to deal with the needs of various populations. Mindfulness has the potential to help social workers realize that there are many different experiences that shape individuals' lives, and the more aware they are of this, the more tolerant they will become of differences and diversity (Langer & Moldoveanu, 2000). Mindful practitioners attend in a nonjudgmental way to their own physical and mental processes, no matter what task they are performing. This critical self-reflection enables them to listen attentively to clients' distress, recognize their own errors, refine their technical approach, make evidence-based decisions, and clarify their values so that they can act with compassion, competence, presence, and insight (Epstein, 1999).

As we will see in this chapter, mindfulness social work practice can work to facilitate an interaction with mindful understanding. When a client experiences a social worker who is present in their interactions, then he or she will feel safer, and perhaps more willing to disclose symptoms or interpretations that the social worker might not even realize (Wheat, 2005). We must listen to their stories rather than impose our own. Each client comes with diverse experiences, especially immigrant clients, who come with their pre-migration, migration, and post-migration struggles. These may include settlement difficulties like unemployment, acculturation difficulties, and culture shock. However, each of these experiences will be different for each client. By focusing their attention on the present moment of client interaction and reserving judgment on clients' diverse cultures, races, experiences, practices, beliefs, and values, social workers can make a lasting connection with their immigrant clients.

Mindfulness-Influenced Social Work Framework for Working with Immigrants

The aim of this proposed mindfulness-influenced social work framework is to provide social workers with a way of understanding and working with immigrant clients. I have integrated mindfulness insights with cultural competence principles in a way that creates increased awareness for social workers during each moment of intervention. When social workers are more present in those moments, a whole new universe opens up, and we see things that we never saw before, both within ourselves and within our clients. Differentials in power and status often determine diagnostic labels (Langer & Moldoveanu, 2000). This framework, which I use in my professional practice, enables me to practice in an intensely self-reflective way that promotes the application of a number of different perspectives and approaches—applied in ways that meet the direct needs of my clients—in ways that are culturally responsive and supportive. It helps clients feel that I am totally present for them, allowing me to cultivate new ways of knowing and understanding, and helping me facilitate the healing of deep wounds. Developing this method of viewing things may help social workers realize the diversity of immigrants (including their needs, their identities, and their uniqueness in being), each of whom has had his or her own experiences, and to see how very different the issues that each has had to face are (Dominelli, 1988). Dealing with diverse individual needs can pose considerable struggles for the social work practitioner. However, as a result of these challenges, opportunities for new ways of thinking and knowing can develop. In the model I have designed (figure 10.1), there are five basic themes that social workers should maintain as the central focus during their encounters with immigrant clients: (1) self-awareness and nonjudgment, (2) empathy and trust, (3) communication and interconnectedness, (4) experience and compassion, and (5) acceptance and new beginnings. Productive application of these concepts will help social workers understand immigrant clients mindfully.

SELF-AWARENESS AND NONJUDGMENT

Mindfulness is a certain way of consciously paying attention. Mindfulness is understood as performing all activities with full awareness (Wheat, 2005). By being consciously attentive, social work practitioners can pay attention to the present moment and be nonjudgmental. As Steven Hick outlines in chapter 1, mindfulness is about being present to ourselves and learning what is going on in our bodies, including our feelings and thoughts. Becoming connected to our bodies and to our innermost feelings and functions can allow the social work practitioner

Immigrant Client   Social Worker

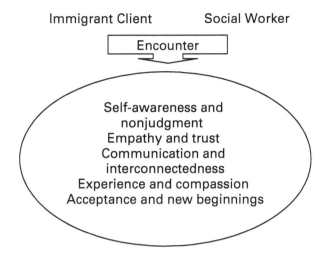

FIGURE 10.1   *Social Worker–Immigrant Client Interaction Model*

to pay attention nonjudgmentally and better identify and understand others' inner experiences. Expanding this concept by using a more sociological definition permits an integration of self-reflexive social work practice through the aware lack of judgment of one's own values, beliefs, and biases in relation to the values, beliefs, and biases of immigrant clients. From a sociological point of view, understanding differences involves considering not only culture as the expression of a community's identity, but also the knowledge, rituals, values, and beliefs through which different communities are defined. Recognizing this complex dynamic of differences is crucial with immigrant clients (Camphina-Bacote, 1999). It is important for social workers to check their own biases and realize that everyone has prejudices and subjective interpretations, which are born of different life experiences. Mindfulness supports these skills. Implications of a mindful practice are that social workers will focus on the inner presence of human life, and that the recognition of the inner essence will lead to a deeper awareness.

Accepting immigrants' values does not mean social workers need to fully accept a complete set of new ideals and judgments. It simply means they must respect the choices of others. Interpersonal awareness helps the mindful social worker be ever conscious of clients' rights, strengths, limitations, and sources of satisfaction. Langer and Moldoveanu (2000) put forth the idea of considering functional diversity as a way of accomplishing this task through relating to differences among people. If we assume that people behaving differently from ourselves are not different but rather are viewing the same stimulus differently, we can take advantage of the different perspectives they offer. This is how differences can become a source of strength. It is necessary to understand the differences' demand for recognition on the basis of the grounds on which recognition has been denied. Understanding the dynamics of differences in culture, race, and language is vital to minimize the lack of interconnection in dealing with immigrant clients. Without recognizing and respecting differences, social workers may develop anxiety or fear of losing control over clients or of their expert status in the client–social worker interaction. The fear of losing authority can create a judgmental attitude toward clients.

Our minds are constantly evaluating our experiences, comparing them with previous experiences, or holding them up against expectations and standards that we've created, often out of fear. If our thinking is not clear and unclouded, we may develop an inaccurate picture of the immigrant client's situation, circumstances, and resourcefulness by minimizing the client's fears, barriers, or strengths, or by exacerbating problems by misinterpreting issues and developing ineffective/unresponsive interventions. When social workers are aware of their thoughts and feelings, they are less likely to judge their clients, which leads to the awakening of their minds into a deeper awareness. If something happens outside of normalcy in a therapy session with an immigrant client, social workers should realize that the different values and customs brought by immigrant clients can be a new experience and a learning opportunity. This will motivate social workers to maintain a nonjudgmental attitude. As social workers, we need to be aware of when our thoughts pull us away so we can make a conscious commitment to being present (Wheat, 2005). Nonjudgment and acceptance are about a willingness to be fully in the present with what is arising. This can refer to both inner experience (i.e., thoughts) and external experience (i.e., behavior of others). This allows us as social workers to notice our reactions to behaviors that may seem out of the ordinary. Being present also means not allowing ourselves to get caught up in the past, by regretting things we have left unfinished or unattempted, or the future (e.g., anxieties about what has not yet occurred). The social worker's engagement in mindfulness practice offers clients highly effective tools for managing anxieties that are often associated with immigration issues like unemployment, acculturation issues, and language difficulties.

In today's society, people are judged based on standards of normalcy and adequate performance in society. Standards of normalcy are created by cultural imperialism, which supports people who do not identify as different in terms of their values, languages, culture, race, and experiences. Recognizing differences also helps social workers consider the values and choices that immigrant clients bring to their interactions and ensure these values and choices are not ignored or excluded if they don't fit with the social worker's conception of normalcy. For example, immigrants from some Asian countries sometimes see health care providers as authority figures and tend to answer yes to all questions simply as a sign of respect. Social workers can manage the potential impact of authority by using open-ended questions to elicit clients' true thoughts and feelings in a nonjudgmental manner. By making concerted efforts to acknowledge clients' underlying thoughts and feelings, mindful social workers can demonstrate genuine caring and concern for immigrant clients, thereby developing the respectful, trusting relationship many immigrant clients seek from helping professionals.

When social workers intervene with immigrants, unexpected things like the practicing of religious rituals, unusual behaviors and actions, lack of English-language skills, or resistance to Western medicine may occur. Recognizing and viewing these unexpected occurrences in a nonjudgmental way or perhaps seeing them as normal to the culture or normal responses to the circumstances experienced by immigrants will create more interconnectedness with immigrant clients. Failure to cultivate awareness and a nonjudgmental attitude will prevent social workers from seeing immigrant clients as they actually are and mobilizing clients' true potential.

One important way social workers limit their interventions is by attributing all of clients' difficulties to a single cause. For example, believing clients' cultural differences are the main reason for their settlement troubles diverts social workers from seeing the various other reasons that may also contribute to their settlement struggles. In the case of immigrant clients, paying too much attention to, and having a judgmental attitude toward, clients' differences instead of accepting them as they are will limit or reduce the range of solutions that social workers might seek (Langer, 1989).

EMPATHY AND TRUST

The process of building empathy for an immigrant client involves acknowledging the immigrant client's struggles and supporting the client to empower him- or herself. Having empathy for an immigrant client is the ability to put oneself in the shoes of that person and understand what he or she must deal with in daily life. Empathy building can also help social workers understand and respect the differences among immigrants. It is not only very important to understand that immigrants have different issues and needs than the mainstream population, but also necessary to recognize that there is diversity within the immigrant population. If social workers do not recognize there are differences among individual immigrants, they may design a single intervention for all immigrants. Social workers need to respect the diverse individual, cultural, social, racial, and political experiences beneath the single identity of being an immigrant.

A mindful social worker–immigrant client relationship can develop empathy building. In order to strengthen this relationship, both social worker and client need to hear each other and value each other's experiences and contributions. The goal of mindfulness-influenced social work practice is to become more aware of one's own mental processes that may impede or promote empathy. This will encourage social workers and their immigrant clients to reconcile their differences and create a connection. Mindfulness practice challenges social workers to identify, expose, and challenge internal biases and fears surrounding control/power (i.e., being challenged by clients). These issues can be overcome through diligent mindfulness practices like creating new and deeper awareness, welcoming new information, and recognizing and accepting more than one view.

Building empathy for clients starts with a trusting heart and self-empathy. It is my experience that social workers' empathy for others is often blocked when the social workers themselves have unmet needs as victims in their own personal lives. This can happen to immigrant social workers who experience rejection and disappointment when they seek services. For example, if an immigrant social worker feels that he or she was not welcomed by immigrant communities, this hurt may preclude his or her ability to empathize with immigrant clients. It is very important for social workers to examine deeply what they can trust in themselves and try to empathize with their own significant losses or pain.

Social workers must first develop self-awareness and accept their own challenges, which will lead them to explore more deeply clients' experiences and give value to them. Without fully experiencing trust and empathy for themselves—which will create a healthy processing of emotional feelings—social workers won't be able to understand and feel empathy for their immigrant clients. Self-empathy enables us to consider the question "What did I want most in this situation?" We may not always understand what is happening to ourselves or to others or what is occurring in a particular situation with our client. But if we trust in this process, we can find a powerful stabilizing element that embraces balance and openness within the relationship (Kabat-Zinn, 1994). Only if social workers can trust their ability to observe, be attentive to, and reflect upon immigrant client experiences can they learn to respect the differences among immigrants and respond to their needs mindfully. Most of us would like to be treated with kindness, compassion, understanding, and respect. All of these depend on the ability to empathize (Kabat-Zinn, 1994). Spiritual realization in the ability to see clearly that what immigrant clients perceive, experience, think, or feel beyond their appearance is one of the central points of mindfulness. Empathy is a basic skill that most social workers believe they possess. Spiritual realization helps social workers develop empathy, which encourages them to recognize the dimension of being more familiar with immigrant clients' worlds.

Social workers can develop empathy for immigrants by carefully listening to what they say. Immigrants from Eastern countries often communicate through life stories that detail their lives, losses, and experiences. Stories are often seen as mental fabrications based on past conditioning when they are not viewed from a mindfulness perspective. Memories underneath these stories are a sense of self. Stories often consist of mental and emotional memory. Stories help social workers learn of the emotional and mental baggage that is affecting clients' lives. Most often the instruction is to let go of the story, as it is not our own. In working with immigrants or in working cross-culturally, stories may be the window to a holistic understanding. The key here is for social workers to allow themselves to be moved by these stories. Social workers should enter their clients' worlds by imagining what their clients' lives must have been like (Shulman, 1987). It should be remembered that telling these stories can be extremely traumatic for immigrant clients, especially if they are coming from countries torn apart by war or natural disasters. Therefore it is absolutely crucial to acknowledge their experiences during this process.

It is hard to empathize when clients' interests or views seem to conflict with our own, and so our ability to empathize in a broader range of situations takes intentional cultivation. Intentional cultivation means that there should be a continuous attempt on our part to develop awareness of clients' life experiences. We need to understand that immigrants come from environments that are different from the ones in which we were likely born and brought up. When we cultivate empathy, we are able to see things from our clients' points of view. To reach this level, we need to use mindful understanding as a powerful inner resource to connect with our immigrant clients. Self-reflection accomplished through mindfulness practice frees social workers from their own constraints to better focus on and connect with client challenges.

As social workers, it is our continuing duty to build the relationship and maintain the connection with our clients. At times, our personal circumstances may cloud or limit our ability to fully focus or concentrate on our clients' needs. Mindfulness practice helps ground us, and this grounding can facilitate social work practice that is continually client centered and client focused. Through conscious practice of mindfulness, we can express moment-to-moment sensitivity to clients' needs. Continual restoring of empathy is the foundation of mindfulness-based social work practice. Seeing things from our clients' points of view, no matter how different they may be from our own, will guide us in the choices we make and help us bring an empathetic presence at all times.

COMMUNICATION AND INTERCONNECTEDNESS

> I would ask you to remember only this one thing. The stories people tell have a way of taking care of them. If stories come to you, care for them. And learn to give them away where they are needed. Sometimes a person needs a story more than food to stay alive. (Lopez, 1992, p. 14)

Communication with curiosity and openness and devoid of judgment allows a mindful social worker to create interconnection. The role of mindfulness with respect to social interactions is centered on avoiding stereotyping and other biased social information, and reducing conflict and intercultural misunderstandings (Burgoon, Berger, & Waldron, 2000). Social workers need to be aware of the feelings and needs underlying client stories. Communication encompasses not only what is said, but also how it is said, to whom it is said, and what remains unsaid (Srivastava, 2007). Communication skills are critical when social workers deal with immigrant clients. They greatly facilitate interactions with clients, who feel heard, and give us an opportunity to gauge whether our sense of their feelings and needs is correct (Wheat, 2005). They allow their sorrows to resonate with us because we are interconnected (Kabat-Zinn, 1994).

Without effective communication, developing interconnectedness through therapeutic relationships would not be possible. Research has shown that communication in a health care context centers around the health care provider rather than the client (Rottman, Godard, Rogers, & Smith, 2005; Suarez-Almazor, 2004). Social workers are in a position to show love and compassion through effective communication in the therapeutic moment. This compassion and love benefit their clients, who will spread these virtues to the other people with whom they interact. Ineffective communication, on the other hand, can lead to feelings of neglect and sadness in clients, which can just as easily spread to others in their social and support networks. Social workers should develop a commitment to listen to client voices, even if it requires deviation from their usual therapy approach. Making this commitment shows that they recognize and value their immigrant clients and appreciate the diverse backgrounds each one comes from. When book knowledge and clinical experience are insufficient, mindful social workers must rely on their personal knowledge of the client (Epstein, 1999).

Mindful communication skills encourage us to focus on what we and others are observing, how and why we are each feeling as we do, what our underlying needs are, and what each of us would like to have happen. These skills emphasize personal responsibility for our actions and the choices we make when we respond to others. The tone of the communication should be sincere, polite, and nonjudgmental. Immigrants from Asian countries often see health care professionals as people of power. Clinicians need to be aware of their own verbal and nonverbal communication, ensuring that they express compassion for clients during clinical intervention (Rosenberg, 2003). Social workers should convey awareness of, interest in, and respect for the diverse social, cultural, and political backgrounds of their immigrant clients. Relationships with clients are not always simple and linear (Kabat-Zinn, 1994). The social worker–immigrant client interaction must be bidirectional, with equal give-and-take, in order to produce shared decision making. Each immigrant client's experiences can lead to new information and awareness of more than one perspective.

Developing two-way dialogue with immigrant clients is key to ensuring they feel their concerns are being taken seriously and are not being marginalized. Mindfulness-based two-way dialogue gives us more choices in how to respond by helping us to understand that other people may not be so different, which creates empathy and enlarges social workers' range of responses. Suarez-Almazor (2004) asserts that health care providers typically dominate conversations with immigrant clients, use closed-ended questions, and constantly interrupt or dismiss client questions. This may be due to insecurities resulting from their lack of understanding of the different backgrounds of immigrant clients. Cultural dissimilarity has been identified as a leading cause of ineffective communication between health care provider and client (Coffman, 2004). If social workers do not change the way they respond to immigrant clients, these clients will no longer respond to social workers due to fear of authority or a desire not to be judged or ignored.

We should always be open to new information, even if it is different from our normal way of thinking. Mindfulness-based social workers can be receptive of the new information and balance their thinking. Behavior generated from mindful listening or watching, or from an expanding, increasingly differentiated information base, is likely to be more effective. Through mindful communication, social workers can create threads of interconnectedness. Mindfulness training will motivate clinicians to experience openness, reflexivity, and spiritual awareness between themselves and immigrant clients that they were not able to experience previously. At some point, we may even come to realize that we are no longer the ones doing the threading. Shifting of power can be accomplished as an outcome of mindfulness practice. Through mindful thinking, social workers can learn to recognize the voice of power and control that can harm their interconnectedness with immigrant clients. Mindful awareness of the present moment can allow us to let go of the negative emotions of power and leads us to guide our interventions with love and a compassionate understanding of immigrant clients as they are. Mindfulness is undefended consciousness (Gendlin, 1984). It results in the dismantling of clinicians' efforts to control and fuels the therapeutic process with high energy. When we open up our own inner feelings, we open the gates of self-exploration and discovery.

Nevertheless, social workers have to consciously and continuously foster this connection through their communication with clients. Mindfulness can help social workers to create active and fluid information processing, sensitivity to context, multiple perspectives, and a fresh and unbiased understanding (Langer, 1989). Mindfulness gives social workers an awakening to views other than their own, and social workers start to realize that there are as many different views as there are different observers. Through awareness of many perspectives, clinicians can accept that the opinions of both clinician and client can be right and that they may have different interpretations of things, which leads to different options for interventions.

When a nonjudgmental, open, trustful, and respectful relationship exists, clients are more willing to discuss their deeper experiences. Cultural, racial, social, and political barriers exist with respect to disclosure of personal and intimate information. Prerequisites for disclosure include an element of trust and the establishment of both a relationship and shared values. Clients from some cultures may be uncomfortable during direct questioning or may consider the practice rude and not worthy of a complete response. In these situations, social workers should monitor their own thinking. When we begin to pay close attention to our thought processes, we can consciously create positive thinking (within ourselves and our clients) and cultivate mindful conversations through open and trustful communication.

Listening and silence are also integral components of effective communication, helping clinicians to focus and refocus their minds as necessary. To be good listeners, clinicians should learn to empty their minds of all other concerns and find the state of tranquility that comes from being fully present in the communication. Clinicians should make every effort to let immigrant clients know that their primary focus is empowering them to deal with their life events. Eventually, clients will lead us in the healing process and social workers will be able to support immigrant clients during the clinical intervention. Learning to listen and be silent begins with mindfully changing one's attitude about what it means to be a good listener. Training in mindfulness will encourage social workers to enhance their ability to observe and listen nonjudg-mentally, a process important for all interactions and particularly essential in cross-cultural encounters (Wheat, 2005).

EXPERIENCE AND COMPASSION

Experience and compassion are interconnected, especially when clini-cians deal with immigrants coming from backgrounds very different from their own. The self-investigation aspect of mindfulness practice can enable social workers to feel these experiences fully without reject-ing them (Sankar, Moran, Merz, & Jones, 2003). Clinicians who are able to mindfully accept their own experiences are able to fully accept and listen to their clients' diverse experiences holistically. Clinicians' resis-tance to their own difficult experiences can make some situations very painful, often more than the experience itself. For example, an immi-grant social worker who went through painful resettlement experiences may see him- or herself in the client's resettlement situation and pro-vide suggestions that may be useful only to the social worker him- or herself. Staying with our own experience as it unfolds, moment to moment, can be one of the most difficult challenges to face. In particu-lar, coming to terms with the traumatic experience embedded in the body requires determination and a great deal of courage to acknowl-edge the presence of fear and consideration for one's own pain. Mind-fulness practice marks the point where the clinician's basic rejection of experience meets with his or her compassionate awareness (Fulton, 2005).

Several therapeutic interventions can facilitate the journey to mind-fulness within social work practitioners. Psychotherapy works with the clinician's acknowledgement of his or her client's frozen experiences, thawing them into fluidity through the serene warmth of the clinician's attention (Sankar et al., 2003). By accepting their own experiences, social workers can create an open awareness within themselves that enables them to accept their clients' experiences (Kabat-Zinn, 1994). The key to giving the clinician's own experience the space it needs to exist is to pay attention to it and actually experience it, rather than try-ing to compress, contract, judge, attack, reject, or run away from it. It is vital for the clinician to feel kindness and understanding toward him- or herself, rather than pain and failure (Neff, 2003). Over time, clinicians may discover that it's their resistance to their own experiences that cre-ates their discomfort in dealing with immigrant clients, not the clients' experiences themselves. Understanding their own and their clients' experiences can also help clinicians see individual experiences as part of the larger human experience (Neff, 2003). Clinicians need to learn to be open to their experiences and move with them rather than struggle against them (Sankar et al., 2003). Regardless of how different one's experiences and background may be, being mindful is being fully present in the moment—being aware of a breath in or out, a catch in the throat, a flutter of fear, a tightening in the lower back. This process is also reflective of acceptance of an immigrant client's experience and staying focused on that experience.

The single determining factor in therapy's effectiveness is how well a client is able to stay with his or her own experience (Gendlin, 1984). Sometimes it's very hard for immigrant clients to face a traumatic experience, but skilled clinicians can make it easier for them by connecting with their experiences mindfully. By bringing aspects of mindfulness meditation into the therapeutic process, clinicians tap into the potential to go beyond the different models of therapy and reach the deepest roots of body, mind, and psyche (Sankar et al., 2003). Mindful meditation involves focusing your mind on the present. Being mindful is being aware of your thoughts and actions in the present, without judging yourself. By applying the clarity of awareness to the immigrant client intervention, the clinician can gradually embrace the client's differences with compassion for the suffering involved.

Mindfulness requires that we, as clinicians, have not only awareness of ourselves and our experiences, but also compassion toward our own experiences. This has been described as self-compassion (Neff, 2003). Emotional healing requires a warm and attentive listener—someone who is willing to take in another's experience and feel it fully. In practicing mindfulness, self-compassion is a prerequisite to feeling compassion for others. The power of this "suffering with"—the root origin of the word *compassion*—cannot be overstated (Sankar et al., 2003). It can help unburden immigrant clients of their painful experiences by allowing them to talk about their problems with a mindful social worker. Being fully seen and understood by another, even if that understanding is entirely wordless (as may happen during clinical interventions), can support immigrant clients' understanding of themselves. An unconditional loving presence provides the context for deep emotional healing (Neff, 2003). It creates the space in which the client, as well as the clinician, can grow. When we help clients embrace their pain with compassion and encourage them to stay with their experience as it unfolds in the moment, this compassionate attention will, over time, diminish their restlessness and struggles with the realities of life. This is the ultimate goal of spiritually oriented psychotherapy.

ACCEPTANCE AND NEW BEGINNINGS

Acceptance is one of the cornerstones of mindfulness-based therapeutic relationships. Acceptance is an inner orientation that acknowledges that things are as they are, whether they are the way we want them to be or not, no matter how terrible they may be or seem to be at certain moments (Kabat-Zinn, 1994). Social workers dealing with immigrant clients must be willing to accept the idea that there are social, cultural, political, and behavioral differences among immigrant clients. Immigrant clients, because of their diversity, view the world differently and have developed a different set of perceptions. They have also developed certain ways of communicating in a relationship. Accepting a client's style of communication or allowing clients to determine the way a session proceeds is not an indication of failure on the part of the social worker. Acceptance is a door that, if opened, leads to seeing in new ways and discovering new possibilities (Kabat-Zinn, 1994). In dealing with immigrant clients, social workers need to develop their own awareness and accept every new way of thinking. By mindfully understanding our biases, we will become aware of differences in values, cultures, and communication styles and will be able to embrace these differences as allies in the healing process. Mindfulness is a discipline and a state of mind. It requires critical, informed curiosity and the courage to accept how the world is in order to move toward it (Epstein, 1999).

A recent article by Agrell (2007) on young people in the workforce notes that younger employees are more likely to be overconfident than older employees. The article concludes that members of the younger generation are so sure of themselves that they are less accepting of the opinions and ideas of others. Believing our thoughts and ideas are superior to all others is akin to failing to accept ourselves—who we really are, including all our faults and weaknesses—and creates emotional reductionism by reducing the complex emotions involved with our experiences. Such emotional reductionism is bound to impede a young social worker's ability to establish rapport with immigrant clients and to form the therapeutic alliances that are the foundation of the profession. This is where as little as five minutes of meditation can help us see more clearly. Meditation provides the opportunity to monitor our thoughts and feelings as they arise from moment to moment and to see them as occurrences that do not have to be reacted to (Kabat-Zinn, 1994). In situations where we are having difficulty accepting differences, deep breathing meditation may bring clarity and calmness. Here are some suggested steps for deep breathing meditation:

1. Find a quiet and comfortable place. Sit in a chair or on the floor with your head, neck, and back straight but not stiff.
2. Try to put aside all thoughts of the past and the future and stay in the present.
3. Become aware of your breathing, focusing on the sensation of air moving in and out of your body as you breathe. Feel your belly

rise and fall, the air enter your nostrils and leave your mouth. Pay attention to the way each breath changes and is different.

4. Watch every thought come and go, whether it is a worry, fear, anxiety, or hope. When thoughts come up in your mind, don't ignore or suppress them but simply note them, remain calm, and use your breathing as an anchor.

5. If you find yourself getting carried away in your thoughts, observe where your mind went off to, without judging, and simply return to your breathing. Remember not to be hard on yourself if this happens.

6. As the time comes to a close, sit for a minute or two, becoming aware of where you are. Get up slowly.

It is important for social workers to realize that full acceptance and full awareness are only the beginning when they work with immigrant clients. The process of becoming able to treat an immigrant client is long and ongoing. Social workers may not agree with everything their clients say. Of course, there will always be differences when we are dealing with different people. But it is social workers' mission to cultivate curiosity, reflection, and acceptance of the client as he or she is. This acceptance creates new awareness, new understanding, and a positive interaction. We may have a picture in our heads of how a client interaction should be. However, it's just a picture—a figment of our, or of someone else's, imagination.

Acceptance and awareness complement each other. Just as acceptance leads to awareness, acceptance is possible only when we can bring awareness to those "sticky" moments, especially if we are able to recognize when we are getting caught up in either pursuing or rejecting our own goals (Kabat-Zinn, 1994). Interaction with diverse immigrant clients can help social workers to become aware of who they are, how they learn to follow socially constructed standards of behavior, whether they are happy with what they are doing, and where they truly want to be. All these are questions we might want to ask ourselves during our daily practices.

Suggestions for Practice

The following suggestions are intended to help social workers become more mindful when they intervene with immigrant clients.

1. Realize that being mindful is a never-ending process. Every immigrant client is different in his or her experiences, culture, race, language, and social/political background. Mindfulness requires

moment-to-moment learning for clinicians to connect with immigrant clients.

2. Open your heart like a beginner when you intervene with an immigrant client. A beginner's mind is open to any experience that comes to him or her, whereas experts try to narrow down the possibilities.

3. Keep a journal. Write down your emotions and feelings. Social workers need to attend to their own emotions and feelings, as well as be attentive to those of clients. Especially when dealing with immigrant clients, clinicians experience new thoughts and feelings. Writing them down will help us to become more aware of these thoughts.

4. Take fifteen minutes of time for yourself (for example, mindful eating or mindful driving). You should be in complete awareness of yourself during this time. This will help you to reflect on your experiences with a client. Personally, it helps me to reflect on my sessions with an immigrant client and evaluate how I, as a clinician, accepted or rejected the client's experience.

5. Peer evaluations can be extremely beneficial. Talk to a colleague who is experienced in intervening with immigrant clients. This process may help you to focus on your thoughts and feelings.

6. Try to practice mindful meditation (while sitting or walking) for five minutes before and after each client session. This will lead to new awareness and experience in each session with an immigrant client.

7. Find a mentor. Try to connect with a mentor you can rely on completely to talk about yourself. This will help you gain more self-knowledge. Also, being a mentor to others can help you to reflect on your own thoughts and experiences.

8. See openings in every ending. Consider the different possibilities that exist behind closed doors.

Conclusion

Cultural competence enables social workers to be more sensitive to cultural variables, whatever our knowledge of a particular culture may be. Combined with mindfulness, it allows us to be aware of our reactions, to let them go when they are unhelpful, and to return to the nonjudgmental awareness of communication and interaction that occurs in the present moment (Wheat, 2005). Developing multicultural mindfulness in social workers requires more than attention to race, culture, and ethnicity. It requires us to seek to understand, accept, and respect different cultures and values and recognize how we relate to our clients' needs.

As was discussed in this chapter, with awareness, compassion, and openness, mindfulness has the potential to incline the mind toward curiosity and respect for diverse beliefs and traditions. Mindfulness-inspired social work practice requires social workers to understand their immigrant clients as unique human beings. Mindfulness attunes the social worker to the relationship dynamics occurring in the therapeutic relationship. This is absolutely crucial when one is working with immigrant clients. Successful service delivery depends on effective management of these dynamics. In addition to cultivating a successful social worker–client relationship, mindfulness provides a tremendous opportunity for social workers to learn more about different human experiences from their immigrant clients, as well as from themselves. As we move into an increasingly pluralistic and multicultural society, social workers are among those best equipped to deliver the needed care and to empower people from all backgrounds to lead connected, healthy lives (Cheung & Leung, 2008). Ultimately, mindfulness-influenced social work practice is about seeing our clients clearly, and listening to and trusting our own hearts. It involves a rotation in consciousness to a point where we can appreciate the deep seeing that comes out of present-moment awareness, allowing what is best in us, and also in our clients, to emerge.

References

Agrell, S. (2007, July 12). Thirty something to thirty nothing. *Globe and Mail*, p. 10.

Betancourt, J. R., Green, A. R., & Carrillo, J. E. (2002). *Cultural competence in health care: Emerging frameworks and practical approaches.* New York: Commonwealth Fund.

Burgoon, J., Berger, C., & Waldron, V. (2000). Mindfulness and interpersonal communication. *Journal of Social Sciences, 56*(1), 105–127.

Camphina-Bacote, J. (1999). A model and instrument for addressing cultural competence in health care. *Journal of Nursing Education, 38*(5), 203–207.

Chen, N., & Wilkins, R. (1996). The health of Canada's immigrants in 1994–1995. *Statistics Canada–Health Reports, 7*(4), 33–45.

Cheung, M., & Leung, P. (2008). *Multicultural practice and evaluation: A case approach to evidence-based practice.* Denver, CO: Love.

Coffman, M. (2004). Cultural caring in nursing practice: A meta-synthesis of qualitative research. *Journal of Cultural Diversity, 11*(3), 100–109.

Dominelli, L. (1988). *Anti-racist social work* (2nd ed.). London: Macmillan.

Dominelli, L. (1996). Deprofessionalising social work: Competencies, postmodernism and equal opportunities. *British Journal of Social Work, 26*, 153–175.

Dominelli, L. (2002). *Anti-oppressive social work theory and practice.* London: Palgrave.

Donovan, J., d'Espaignet, E. M., Merton, C., & van Ommeren, M. (1992). *Immigrants in Australia: A health profile.* Canberra: Australian Government Publishing Service.

Epstein, R. M. (1999). Mindful practice. *Journal of American Medical Association,* *282*(9), 833–839.

Fowler, N. (1998). Providing primary health care to immigrants and refugees: The North Hamilton experience. *Canadian Medical Association Journal, 159*(1), 388–391.

Fulton, P. (2005). Mindfulness as clinical training. In C. Germer, R. Siegel, & P. Fulton (Eds.), *Mindfulness and psychotherapy* (pp. 55–72). New York: Guilford Press.

Gendlin, E. T. (1984). Imagery and focusing. *Focusing Connection Newsletter, 1*(1), 4–5.

Hyman, I. (2001). *Immigration and health.* Ottawa: Health Canada.

Hyman, I., & Guruge S. (2002). A review of theory and health promotion strategies for new immigrant women. *Canadian Journal of Public Health, 93*(3), 183–187.

Hyman, I., Noh, S., & Fenta, H. (2004). Determinants of depression among Ethiopian immigrants in Toronto. *Journal of Nervous and Mental Disease, 192*(5), 363–372.

Kabat-Zinn, J. (1994). *Wherever you go, there you are: Mindfulness meditation in everyday life.* New York: Hyperion.

Kirmayer, L. J., Galbaud du Fort, G., Young, A., Weinfeld, M., & Lasry, J. C. (1996). *Pathways and barriers to mental health care in an urban multicultural milieu: An epidemiological and ethnographic study* (Culture and Mental Health Research Unit Report No. 6). Toronto: Culture and Mental Health Research Unit, Sir Mortimer B. Davis Jewish General Hospital.

Langer, E. J. (1989). *Mindfulness.* Cambridge: Perseus Books.

Langer, E. J., & Moldoveanu, M. (2000). Mindfulness research and the future. *Journal of Social Issues, 56*(1), 129–139.

Lopez, B. (1992). *Crow and weasel.* London: Harper Collins.

Mulvihill, M. A., Mailloux, L., & Atkin, W. (2001). *Advancing policy and research responses to immigrant women's health in Canada.* Ottawa: Centres of Excellence in Women's Health, Canadian Women's Health Network.

Neff, K. (2003). Self-compassion: An alternative conceptualization of a healthy attitude toward oneself. *Self and Identity, 2,* 85–101.

Perez, C. E. (2002). Health status and health behaviour among immigrants. *Health Reports–Statistics Canada, 13*(Suppl.), 89–100.

Rosenberg, M. B. (2003). *Nonviolent communication: A language of life* (2nd ed.). Encinitas, CA: Puddle Dancer Press.

Rottman, D. B., Godard, D., Rogers, J. D., & Smith, D. (2005, December). *Immigrants and court: A report from California.* Paper delivered at meeting of the American Society of Criminology, Toronto.

Sankar, P., Moran, S., Merz, J. F., & Jones, N. L. (2003). Patient perspectives of medical confidentiality: A review of the literature. *Journal of General Internal Medicine, 18*(8), 659–669.

Shulman, L. S. (1987). Knowledge and teaching: Foundations of the new reform. *Harvard Educational Review, 57,* 1–22.

Simms, G. (1999). *Aspects of women's health from a minority/diversity perspective.* Ottawa: Health Canada.

Srivastava, R. (2007). *The healthcare professional's guide to clinical cultural compe-tence.* Toronto: Mosby.

Stephen, E. H., Foote, K., Hendershot, G. E., & Shoenborn, C. A. (1994). *Health of the foreign-born population: United States 1989–90* (Advance Data No. 241). Hyattsville, MD: National Center for Health Statistics.

Suarez-Almazor, M. E. (2004). Patient-physician communication. *Current Opinions in Rheumatology, 16,* 91–95.

Wheat, P. (2005). Mindfulness meditation: Promoting cultural competency. In S. C. Caulfield (Ed.), *Spectrum* (pp. 35–37). Boston: Chickering Group.

CHAPTER ELEVEN

Mobilizing Communities for Social Change: Integrating Mindfulness and Passionate Politics

Sarah Todd

Laura Pulido (2003) suggests that political action is not just about changing the external world but is also an "exercise in creating and changing ourselves" (p. 51). For Pulido, the interior includes "such things as our emotions, psychological development, souls and passions, as well as our minds" (47). In this chapter I explore the ways that mindfulness practices can be useful in mobilizing community members and sustaining community change. In particular, I will explore what these practices offer for communities that are negotiating passionate emotions and are attempting to engage others in their activities, and that want to enhance people's ability to listen to each other and want to create sustainable change. Through this integration, I will articulate the possibilities for progressive social change that can be enhanced and sustained by an understanding of how our interior lives shape our external worlds and the possibilities that mindfulness practices have for increasing the transformative potential of this interaction.

The most influential organizers of our time have understood the significance of people's interior lives when mobilizing for social change. Saul Alinsky (1971) saw the role of an organizer as initially "rubbing raw" people's resentments, cultivating hope and desire, and ensuring that

---

Thanks to Purnima Sundar for her comments on an early version of this chapter.

community members enjoy the experience of organizing. He was able to imagine community activists as both rational and emotional, as having the ability to strategically use their emotions and the emotions of those who were in opposition to their cause (Goodwin, Jasper, & Polletta, 2001).

Paulo Freire (1993) suggested that it is only by identifying issues that community members feel strongly about and bringing these to the surface that community educators are able to challenge powerlessness and apathy. He detailed an approach to social change that challenges what he described as the oppressed's "emotional dependence" on the oppressor (p. 47). Freire was concerned with the tendency of oppressed people to suffer and to cause suffering within themselves, their families, and their communities as a result of their submission. He argued that any action for social change must be paired with serious self-reflection so that we can understand the ways in which we reproduce oppressive relations even if we do not occupy particularly powerful social locations.

Community activists were one of the groups that Hochschild (1983) first identified as engaged in "emotional labor." This term describes how community activists manage their feelings and seek to influence the emotional responses of others in order to achieve goals of social change. Such labor is exciting, difficult, and draining; it often involves negotiating emotional norms, practices, and interpretations that are part of broader activist agendas, an individual's personal history, and the local community's expectations (Whittier, 2001).

Two dangers emerge when we engage in the emotional labor of community work. The first is burnout. Invariably, community activists find themselves frustrated, overwhelmed, and in need of a break. The second is the overabundance of emotions in communities that are struggling under the burden of oppressive relations (Chatterton, 2006). Those emotions are experienced not only by community members who are actively trying to create change, but also by those who remain on the sidelines. Such an overabundance of emotions can make it difficult for community workers to pause and find commonalities between themselves and others (Chatterton, 2006). In the rush and intensity of the work, issues are often polarized and boundaries become rigid. We begin to become more antagonistic, frustrated, and judgmental in our work, forgetting that the most valuable strategy might be to use curiosity and compassion to incite interest in others (Chatterton, 2006).

Despite this clearly theorized link between an individual's interior life and social activism (his or her external life), discussions of the interior lives of community members and community activists are only briefly mentioned in contemporary textbooks on community work (see, for example, Brown & Hannis, 2008; Rubin & Rubin, 2001). In this chapter, I argue that a recentering of the interior lives of community members can help us to understand the impact that mindfulness practices can have on community mobilization and sustaining change. I argue that mindfulness practice offers us the possibility to reconnect to our sense of curiosity and compassion and in so doing offers the potential to broaden opportunities for a more centered, self-reflective, and creative approach to community change. Mindfulness practices are particularly valuable when we are negotiating difficult emotions, when we need to increase compassion among community members, and when we need to refine our ability to listen to each other and especially to those with whom we disagree.

Linking Community Work and Social Work

Community organizing and development, which I will group together under the more general term of community work, have always been part of the profession of social work. At the turn of the twentieth century, Jane Addams and the women of Hull House began to practice an applied sociology that would eventually become social work. They carried out extensive research on the problems faced by the poor in the Near West Side of Chicago and then used this research to develop community programs, change social policy, and mobilize communities to organize for change (Deegan, 1988). While community practice is somewhat marginalized in the practice of social work and social work education (Lee, McGrath, Moffatt, & George, 1992; Mizrahi, 2001), it has historically been a means for social work to remain located in an explicit struggle for social justice (Wills, 1992).

These practices have always been believed to have an emotional component. Community workers are often perceived by themselves and others as passionate about their work (Stebner, 1997; Walzer, 2002). Since the early days of the settlement movement, community organizers have understood the importance of friendship and the affective bonds between community members as instrumental to creating social change (Stebner, 1997). What organizers have recognized is that the emotional bonds of friendship provide people with the sense of belonging and companionship we desire but also encourage us to become good citizens (Eliasoph, 1998). It is through conversations that we enhance our sense of caring, expand beyond ourselves, and sometimes develop an understanding of the political world. As we encounter people with compassion rather than judgment, we have more conversations, increase our bonds with others, and become engaged citizens.

Increasing community participation, having community members listen to each other, and showing a genuine interest in one another is key to the practice of community organization and social change.

In the mid-twentieth century, community organizing split into two directions. The first was toward social planning, a clearly technocratic, rational exercise in which emotions were largely ignored or seen as annoying (Goodwin et al., 2001). The second direction was community activism. In this direction were feminist and peace activists, anti-poverty activists, Aboriginal organizers, and anti-racism activists. Here emotions are considered vital but are often represented by the media and those outside the movement as irrational and even dangerous, which has at times created barriers to the building of broader support for change. Emotions have also created problems within groups, where their overabundance has resulted in fragmentation and at times the dissolution of groups.

In the early twenty-first century we see a number of trends in the relationship between community work and social work. On one hand, there is increasing pressure to professionalize and regulate social work, which has the effect of excluding activist practices of community organizing, which are difficult to regulate (Todd, 2004). This push toward a narrow profession is counterbalanced by a broad shift toward deprofessionalizing social services and hiring cheaper labor than that provided by social workers (Mizrahi, 2001). In this context there has been an increasing call to communities to take over the responsibilities previously handled by the state. Communities are increasingly seen as the most cost-effective space in which to respond to social problems (Mizrahi, 2001). These trends leave community activism in a difficult place, as communities are given the opportunity to organize, but without the state support necessary to challenge inequality. As a result, the contradictions and burdens facing many oppressed communities can be overwhelming, leaving community activists on a roller-coaster ride between securing funds for innovative projects and realizing that they lack system support for any significant change. Community activists often feel disconnected from social work, which is often perceived as having moved away from its radical roots (Wills, 1992). This isolation and the sense of being overwhelmed by the inequalities we face contribute to the emotional tenor of community practice as intense—sometimes even destructive.

Key Terms

MINDFULNESS

For the purposes of this chapter, I draw on Mark Lau's definition of mindfulness as a nonelaborative, non-judgmental, present-centered awareness in which each thought, feeling, or sensation that arises in the attentional field is acknowledged and accepted as is (Lau et al., 2006). I also focus on mindfulness as a way of being. In this conceptualization, mindfulness practice can offer an opportunity for community activists to cultivate the ability to *be with* our emotions, to help us to pause and listen, rather than always *working with* our emotions. This cultivation happens most often through various meditative practices that help us remain in the present. It becomes an avenue for getting closer to people's experiences and for shifting away from a continual push for change. Although counterintuitive, easing up on our push for change may, in fact, open up creative alternatives for disadvantaged community members. Mindfulness is the practice through which Freire's passionate ideas about valuing the humanity of all within society are put into practice. Through daily acts of being present; being with our feelings, thoughts, and emotions; and quieting the voices of distraction in our heads, it becomes possible to recognize our humanity.

COMMUNITY MOBILIZATION

When using the phrase *mobilizing community*, I am referring to that middle phase of community work that occurs after organizers have built relationships with community members and have a sense of what issues elicit a strong emotional response in people. By this point in the process, it is likely an organizer has done some type of listening survey—or has listened to what community members describe as issues of importance in their communities—and that some initial collaborative problem definition and analysis have occurred (Hope & Timmel, 1984; Lee, 1999). The reason why I focus most of my discussion on the work that we do in the middle phase of community practice is that this phase of community practice is perceived as relying heavily upon communities' experiences of anger and frustration (Alinsky, 1971; Hercus, 1999). In order to get a community to mobilize for action, the theory goes, we need to find those issues that bring them together in collective outrage. This is considered the spark that is necessary to light the fire of community activism.

While I agree that such negative emotions might help shift a community from apathy to action, fear, anger, and frustration are not sustainable or healthy in the long run. My concern is that over time frustration and anger have a tendency to turn in on themselves, onto other community members, and even onto us. We often see valuable activist groups paralyzed or even torn apart by infighting. We need to ensure that activists and community members develop ways to negotiate the difficult emotions that often serve as the energy behind community mobilization. One way to do so is to increase our capacity to sustain community mobilization through curiosity and compassion. I think that it is possible to pair feelings of frustration and anger with actions that cultivate compassion and create a healthier and more sustainable way to sustain community change.

EMOTIONS

In speaking about emotions, I distinguish between emotions as unconscious and feelings as the conscious expression of our emotions. More specifically, Marcia Cavell (2006) suggests that "emotional processes may be going on of which we are not consciously aware; feelings, however, though we may not know just what the feeling is, are always conscious, that is to say, felt" (p. 127). There is increasing consensus among psychoanalysts that emotions are at the core of our motivation to act (Cavell, 2006; Hogget & Miller, 2000). It logically follows that they are central to any process that relies on community participation. Emotions are the register of what we care about. If we didn't "care about things and people in the world, we would not feel anger, fear, anxiety, pride, or envy or anything else" (Cavell, 2006, p. 136).

The link between caring as the emotional force behind feeling and action is circular, as Nina Eliasoph (1998) argues: "Participation in the public sphere helps cultivate a sense of a community, so that people care more, and think more, about the wider world" (p. 11). Thus the link between participation and emotions is complex, and emotions drive our participation, but our participation in turn helps to cultivate the caring that drives our emotional response to the world.

However, in modern society our feelings can create problems for us, as we have a tendency to think of them as commodities or "particular things, rather than *as ways in which* sequences of an ongoing journey are experienced" (Cavell, 2006, p. 136). By situating feelings in this way, we tend to disconnect them from the emotions that exist in our interior lives and see them solely as a response to the external world. As things, feelings are understood as having permanence and truthfulness; we are inclined to cling to them. The certainty of our feelings tends to become of paramount importance. When others do not share our feelings, we often have trouble building common ground and can even become quite judgmental of and frustrated with our differences.

What mindfulness meditation helps to cultivate is an earlier attention to feelings, and thus emotions, which allows us to consider an emotion before acting on it and to understand the link between opinions, beliefs, and our emotional states (Cavell, 2006). In other words, mindfulness practices provide the opportunity for a pause, which

enables us to increase our awareness of our feelings and to have opportunities to make decisions in a more thoughtful, less reactive fashion. It
opens up the possibility of letting go of our emotions, of seeing them
and valuing them so that they can enter our consciousness, but not
holding onto them and forcing their permanence—rather embracing
them as flowing through and past us (Kabat-Zinn, 2005b). In turn, those
with different feelings can become less often the source of our frustration and instead can be approached with a sense of compassion and
curiosity as someone who can help us enhance our understanding of
ourselves, others, and our world.

The important idea regarding emotions for this discussion is that
emotions are what account for subjectivity (Cavell, 2006). Emotions are
the mechanism through which we perceive the world, thus determining
how we are in the world. They are *who* we are in the world. Becoming
more aware and conscious of them opens up the possibility of being in
the world in new and creative ways. As Paulo Freire (1993) argues, the
world is a subjective experience, which is why people can change the
world by changing how they perceive themselves in the world. Mindfulness practices ask us reconsider the idea that feelings are solely a
response to the external world, and to open ourselves up to the possibility that our emotions create the world as much as the world creates
our feelings.

Mindfulness and Community Practice

In the past, there has been a reluctance to attend to the interior world
of community activists. This interiority has been largely the terrain of
psychoanalysis. Goodwin et al. (2001) argue that "efforts to bring psychological insight to bear on politics usually reduced the latter to little
more than internal personality dynamics. On the other hand, group
psychology often ignored individual traits altogether. Little was recognized between the individual and the social: no social networks, organizations, shared cultural meanings, processes of negotiation and
interaction" (p. 4). This danger still exists. In a world where individualism is so entrenched in our psyche that it seems all too easy to lose
sight of the collective, the stakes of such a shift are high. In contemporary capitalist societies, organizing communities is an important strategy for getting needs met and stabilizing society. Communities emerge
within societies in which resources are understood as limited and different communities are able to get their needs met in different ways,
depending upon the amount of control they have over the means of
economic and cultural production. The risk of redirecting community

analysis to the interior lives of activists is the devaluation of such collective mechanisms of survival and possibilities for securing justice. If the challenges and solutions regarding social injustice are reframed entirely as issues concerning the interior lives of individuals, then clearly there is a danger of depoliticization and increased isolation.

However, the reason for suggesting an integration of mindfulness practices into community work is Freire's (1993) belief that overcoming oppression requires internal work to see the interconnectedness of all human beings and to recognize the inherent humanness and value in all of us. This does not necessarily mean that activists have to engage in therapy or understand themselves as the only site of change, but it does suggest that practices of self-reflection that increase our awareness of our internal state can help to challenge the "powerlessness [that] comes from being inattentively caught in the 'web' of human relationships" (Arendt, 1958, p. 183). With active, mindful political participation, we weave reality and a place for ourselves within it (Eliasoph, 1998). From this perspective, the turn toward mindfulness is not toward individualism, but rather a strategy of reconnection or a disruption of the idea that the individual is the only practical possibility for understanding humanity.

Jon Kabat-Zinn (2005a) links the practice of mindfulness to a politic of social change. From his perspective, the path of making social change is "neither fixed nor predetermined, which is to say there is no destination, only the journey itself" (p. 2). He also remarks that "we often act as if there were a significant separation between out there and in here, where our experience tells us that it is the thinnest of membranes, really no separation at all" (p. 3). So, a politics that embraces mindfulness is a present-focused practice, where our attention is on how to create justice in every moment. The very moment we are in requires our attention and is not to be missed because we are constantly distracted by an imagined end goal. This is where justice lies, in the valuing of and being present in the present. This is a radical shift in thinking about community change, which is often entirely future focused. There are a number of possibilities that open up when we move away from such a drive to change the future. First, the possibilities for justice in the present are expanded. While these present possibilities are often smaller than the large change that we imagine, mindfulness practitioners suggest that they are cumulative, creating justice as they build on one another.

In addition, our practices of social activism are reframed as deeply connected to our interior lives. The actions of community activists are linked to our perceptions, beliefs, emotions, and feelings. Thus this passionate politics involves learning how to be with and notice our emotions: to see their value and to let them flow through us, rather than clinging to them. This is not a reactive, fast-paced politics, but it is also not just reflection. Mindfulness is about doing, but also being present in the doing, trying to calm the worrying and thinking that we engage in when anticipating and remembering our actions. It is reflection in action, where one attends to the moment. It is a more thoughtful present.

Kabat-Zinn (2005a) also suggests that "When cultivated and refined, mindfulness can function effectively on every level, from the individual to the corporate, the societal, the political and the global. But it does require that we be motivated to realize who we actually are and to live our lives as if they really mattered, not just for ourselves, but for the world" (p. 11). In establishing this link between the internal transformative power of mindfulness practices and creating social change, Kabat-Zinn offers tools for working with communities that allow us to move toward decreasing individual suffering and social suffering. What is so inviting and sustaining about this approach is that it is not an activism constituted through self-sacrifice and self-denial, which I would suggest is unsustainable and even destructive over time. Instead it is about seeing ourselves and our world as if we matter. It is a deeply empowering and self-affirming practice for community activists, particularly those who have lived in oppressive conditions that constantly tell them that they do not matter.

Mindfulness in community practice has a number of concrete forms. First, it can be a practice that is integrated into the daily activities of community activists and as something that becomes part of the way organizers engage and mobilize communities. This relies on a daily practice of meditation. However, even some of the less structured breathing exercises that constitute more informal models of mindfulness could be quite helpful in enhancing the space of community activism (see Nhat Hanh, 1991). In the following sections, I speak to the particular areas of community practice where mindfulness practices can have a significant influence.

RETHINKING REALITY

For some time now, psychoanalysts have argued that our conscious and unconscious tend to shape our understanding of the world and our behavior in it (Lemma, 2003). By doing so, emotions can create the world, which, as I have argued earlier, only exists in our subjective experience of it. For psychoanalysts, the inner world is comprised of feelings, memories, beliefs, and fantasies, which constitute our unconscious (Germer, Siegel, & Fulton, 2005). Freud believed that our unconscious processes are not constrained by reality. Time can collapse, so that an event that happened many years ago can be experienced as though it is happening in the present (Lemma, 2003). The goals of mindfulness practice and psychodynamic counseling are quite close to one another: one of the aims of psychodynamic counseling is to make more of our minds available to conscious awareness, so that we can live our lives more aware of what motivates us and therefore have more freedom and choice in how we act (Cavell, 2006). This is very similar to the impact that mindfulness practices have on our experience in the world.

The first challenge that mindfulness presents to our ideas about reality is the possibility that in our efforts to negotiate our personal pain, "a tremendous disparity is created between inner reality and the circumstances of the external world" (Salzberg, 2002, p. 134). The effect of this lingering pain and the ways it shapes our perceptions of and behaviors in the present are powerfully described in Anne Bishop's book *Becoming an Ally*. In it, Bishop (1994) illustrates how children experience powerlessness in Western societies and are taught not to express emotion, so their pain is often buried in their unconscious, where it becomes like a "gully carved out in our thinking" (p. 50). This gully shapes our present responses. Time collapses as we perceive and respond to present situations, using the perceptions and strategies we developed to cope with our childhood experiences of pain. Thus our perception of the present, and our behavior in it, is as much about our emotions from past experiences as it is a response to the external world. Bishop describes how destructive this can be within activist groups, where these past hurts can foster infighting and the eventual painful dissolution of the group.

Salzberg (2002) suggests that once we recognize and appreciate the disparity between our perceptions and the real world, the opportunity to name injustices and change inequities and hate-filled situations does not fade, but instead we consider the possibility of whether we can work for change without prejudice or fear, without destroying ourselves with our anger and frustration. If we are able to hold less tightly onto our perceptions of reality, it is possible to foster greater connectivity, to respond to difficult and painful situations with more thoughtfulness and compassion, and, in turn, the world can begin to look quite different.

The problem is how to work with community members to validate their experiences and to hear them, yet to encourage group members not to hold too tightly onto their perceptions. Jon Kabat-Zinn (2005a) draws on two statements made by Albert Einstein to introduce this idea: "Reality is merely an illusion, albeit a very persistent one" and "The problems that exist in the world today cannot be solved by the level of thinking that created them" (p. 510). These sentiments resonate with Freire's (1993) argument that reality is fictitious, a subjective experience determined by our perceptions. Such a reorientation is often difficult when people are frustrated by the external conditions that shape their lives. Here Freire and Einstein are not suggesting that what we experience is not real for us, but rather that reality is shaped by what is outside us *and* our internal reaction to that external world. When we shift our view of our reality in this direction, a couple of things become possible. First we begin to see ourselves as having a role in determining our lives; it increases our sense of agency: "We can easily drift away from remembering how much the body politic depends on the agency of all of us, and how much our agency is based on our inner development and understanding of who we are and how we are treating the world, as well as on how the world is treating us; on what we are offering the world as well as what the world is offering us" (Kabat-Zinn, 2005a, p. 560).

Second, the possibility of listening to and valuing other people's definitions of reality increases. This opens up spaces for increased dialogue. Kabat-Zinn (2005a) suggests that such a repositioning might help us develop "a more gracious understanding of others who may not aspire to what we hold to be most important" (p. 13). The contribution that mindfulness makes to our ability to listen to one another will be discussed later in this chapter, but here I focus on the possibilities that are created when we are able to develop a politic that does not require our own experience to be the only truth.

Clearly there are moments in a community's struggle when it is of strategic importance to assert one's reality as a singular and just truth. This does not, however, mean that is the ongoing frame through which a community constitutes itself. To do so is to create rigid boundaries defining individuals as insiders and outsiders, which ultimately limits a community's opportunity to embrace allies and create systemic change. The changes desired by most activists are not those that can be transferred to small collectives but those that speak to the social systems and practices that have broad and deep impacts on society. The creation of such change relies on us reaching out, building alliances, and creating broad movements. This work requires enormous amounts of patience and curiosity because it is about building networks with people who do not necessarily feel as strongly or in the same ways that we do.

BEING WITH OVERABUNDANT EMOTIONS

The problem with community organizing built on passionate politics is that such passion often results in issues becoming polarized. For organizers such as Alinsky, such polarization is desirable for specific moments in the organizing process, but the difficulty with such strategies is that over time they tend to distort the discussion. This was evident for me when I worked in the pro-choice movement. It was very easy when I was involved in this movement to observe how polarization often evolves into a certainty that in itself can become dogmatic (Walzer, 2002). In many ways, the discussion of abortion rights has become so polarized that all middle ground has been lost. This presents challenges, both in terms of the energy it takes to maintain a polarized position and the barriers it presents to engaging women in the movement. Researchers have shown that if people involved in both sides of this debate are brought together in a space where a discussion is facilitated on the foundations of curiosity and compassion, most of us will find that we inhabit a significant middle ground, even though we claim to belong to one side or another (Backer, Chasin, Chasin, Herzig, & Roth, 1995). While such dialogue is not possible at every point in the community mobilization process, it seems important that such opportunities for discussion remain part of a set of tools that activists can use. Such conversations offer an opportunity to decrease the fixed emotions of anger and even hate that can emerge as issues become polarized. Instead activists have the opportunity to develop skills to be with their own and others' emotions, even on issues that evoke strong feelings.

Jon Kabat-Zinn (2005a) makes the point that "when we find ourselves clinging strongly to the certainty that we are right and others are wrong, even if it is true to a large degree and the stakes are very very high (or at least we think they are and are attached to our view of it), then our very lenses of perception can become distorted, and we risk falling into delusion and doing some degree of violence to what is and to the truth of things and of the relationships we are in, far beyond the 'objective' validity of one position of another" (p. 503).

What mindfulness scholars suggest is that we expand our compassion. With compassion we can engage in forceful action, but without anger or aversion. Salzberg (2002) writes of how when a small child reaches for a hot burner, our response is to reach out and pull the child back, but we do not reject or condemn the child. Our work becomes learning how to speak our truth without blame or judgment. Instead of seeing the world as good and bad, right and wrong, we see it as suffering and the end of suffering (Salzberg, 2002). We no longer have to expend a tremendous amount of energy on holding onto our feelings and maintaining positions of righteousness. Instead our work is more purposeful and engaged.

Mindfulness, Kabat-Zinn (2005a) argues, is also not a call to not have opinions and strongly held views. Instead, he suggests that "the closer those views can be to the inter-embeddedness of things, the better our ability to interface with the world and with our work and with our longing and our calling in ways that will contribute to greater wisdom and harmony, as opposed to greater strife and misery and insecurity" (p.

505). Thus the work is to try to minimize our destructive tendencies and to maximize our capacity for "mobilizing and embodying wisdom and compassion in the choices we make from moment to moment about how we need to be living and what we might be doing with our creative energies to heal the body politic" (p. 505).

ENGAGEMENT

The peace activist George Lakey (1987), in his book *Powerful Peacemaking*, speaks of the importance of cultivating a profound respect for people, whether they are ready to take action or are in a place of apathy. He argues that education is an "exercise in real honesty" (p. 51). It is through practices of mindfulness that we are able to foster what Carl Rogers referred to as unconditional positive regard (Mearns, 1998). It is this regard that underpins the trust that George Lakey and Paulo Freire suggest that we need to have with the people with whom we work in communities, and that community activists need to have with each other and those who oppose them. Unconditional positive regard opens up the opportunity to build a movement through engaging others who are outside the small group of people who think the same way we do and share our beliefs. It is about approaching all people with a deep sense of respect and a belief in their capacity to understand and work to end suffering.

When we are mobilizing communities in particularly difficult situations, it seems important to reflect on Jon Kabat-Zinn's (2005a) question of whether we have allowed a situation or topic to become so polarized that it is no longer possible to see and know things as they are or to remember that not knowing a situation also has power. This type of reflection becomes of paramount importance when we are trying to build a broad-based movement that will appeal to the general public. It is equally important to maintain and embrace insiders, who may have doubts or questions or even see the issue differently than we do. Such an openness allows for the opportunity for activists to be congruent. Their moments of not knowing or uncertainty do not have to be denied but are reconstituted as opportunities for creative alternatives and building bridges. Such an approach is difficult to maintain and requires an engagement with a daily practice of trying to slow down and recenter on our own feelings, and letting go of some of our worries about the past or the future. It requires some time to take note of and be in the present.

LISTENING

In order to effectively mobilize community members, we have to be able to listen to the emotional content of the stories people tell about their lives and their communities. This is often difficult to do when we are distracted by our own agendas. In her book, *The Zen of Listening: Mindful Communication in the Age of Distraction*, Rebecca Shafir (2003) highlights how not being self-aware when we are listening results in "assumptions and periods of selective listening" (p. 7), which leads us to miss valuable information. It is not that we need more time to listen; rather, Shafir argues, we need to have a "willingness to see a situation through the eyes of the speaker" (p. 10), which is difficult to do when our scope of listening is narrowed by our own self-interest. Shafir argues that mindfulness practices help us quiet our internal voices so that we are more able to get close to the stories of others and to approach them with curiosity rather than judgment. The ability to really listen to community members and those outside communities strikes me as central to any community mobilization process. Oftentimes, our passionate politics makes it difficult to listen. In an effort to manage our own emotions, we tend to simplify others and their opinions and polarize the issues that we are taking on. We evaluate what people say and decide whether they are friend or foe, rather than putting our agendas aside and approaching them with curiosity. This tends to limit our ability to develop broad-based support for our causes. It also creates fractures within our community groups. I have often sat around a coalition table and found myself no longer listening to another member, instead saying to myself that what he or she is saying is exactly what I would expect from a person who works for a bank, identifies as an anarchist, or runs a religiously based nonprofit. I contain the person and stop listening, thinking that I know the story that he or she is going to tell and that it is of little value. Embracing a more mindful approach to community activism helps to cultivate the space necessary to get inside other people's stories, to approach them with curiosity. When people truly feel heard, they are more likely to want to engage.

Conclusion

I sometimes wonder how different our organizing meetings would be if we were to follow Thich Nhat Hanh's (1991) suggestion that we find gratitude and goodness in the beginning, middle, and end of all that we do. What an interesting practice upon which to build community organizations. The integration of mindfulness practices into a community mobilization process can take many forms. I know of some community houses that have a meditation room, and meditation classes a few times a week. Others offer yoga. I know of some groups that work to integrate breathing and paying attention to the moment into their practices. It does seem that in order to cultivate the compassion and quiet necessary to develop more self-awareness and to engage with our internal and external worlds, we need to carve some time out for such a practice every day. Not all community members will be ready for such a transition. It may require the ideas and practices of mindfulness to be introduced in more subtle and integrated ways. To do so, the organizer herself will need to be committed to a practice so that she can remain aware of the possibilities of integration when they arise.

Mindfulness practices encourage us to attend more to the possibility of acting, of being the activists we want to be, and to do so wisely. Through the use of the ideas of Jon Kabat-Zinn and other mindful practitioners, "the healing of the body politic can evolve without rigid control or direction, through the independent and interdependent agency and efforts of many different people and institutions, with many different and rich perspectives, aims, and interests, but with a common and potentially unifying interest as well, that of the greater well-being of the world. At its best, this is what politics both furthers and protects" (Kabat-Zinn, 2005a, p. 511). This is the recipe for sustainable activism. It is an activism that works against the urge to control and change others but embraces our full humanity in its diversity. In this daily practice, the impassioned justice imagined by people like Paulo Freire comes to the forefront.

References

Alinsky, S. (1971). *Rules for radicals: A pragmatic primer for realistic radicals.* New York: Vintage Books.

Arendt, H. (1958). *The human condition.* Chicago: University of Chicago Press.

Backer, C., Chasin, L., Chasin, R., Herzig, M., & Roth, S. (1995). From stuck debate to new conversation on controversial issues: A report from the public conversations project. In K. Weingarten (Ed.), *Cultural resistance: Challenging beliefs about men, women and therapy* (pp. 143–163). Binghamton, NY: Haworth Press.

Bishop, A. (1994). *Becoming an ally: Breaking the cycle of oppression in people.* Halifax, Nova Scotia: Fernwood.

Brown, J., & Hannis, D. (2008). *Community development in Canada.* Toronto: Pearson.

Cavell, M. (2006). *Becoming a subject: Reflections in philosophy and psychoanalysis.* Oxford: Oxford University Press.

Chatterton, P. (2006). "Give up activism" and change the world in unknown ways: Or learning to walk with others on uncommon ground. *Antipode: A Radical Journal of Geography, 38,* 259–281.

Deegan, M. (1988). *Jane Addams and the men of the Chicago School, 1892–1918.* New Brunswick, NJ: Transaction Books.

Eliasoph, N. (1998). *Avoiding politics: How Americans produce apathy in everyday life*. New York: Cambridge University Press.

Freire, P. (1993). *Pedagogy of the oppressed*. New York: Continuum Press.

Germer, C., Siegel, R., & Fulton, P. (2005). *Mindfulness and psychotherapy*. New York: Guilford Press.

Goodwin, J., Jasper, J., & Polletta, F. (2001). *Passionate politics: Emotions and social movements*. Chicago: University of Chicago Press.

Hercus, C. (1999). Identity, emotion and feminist collective action. *Gender & Society, 13*(1), 34–55.

Hochschild, A. R. (1983). *The managed heart: Commercialization of human feeling*. Berkeley: University of California Press.

Hoggett, P., & Miller, C. (2000). Working with emotions in community organizations. *Community Development Journal, 35*(4), 352–364.

Hope, A., & Timmel, S. (1984). *Training for transformation* (Vol. 1). Gweru, Zimbabwe: Mambo Press.

Kabat-Zinn, J. (2005a). *Coming to our senses: Healing ourselves and the world through mindfulness*. New York: Hyperion.

Kabat-Zinn, J. (2005b). *Full catastrophe living: Using the wisdom of your body and mind to face stress, pain, and illness*. New York: Random House.

Lakey, G. (1987). *Powerful peacemaking: A strategy for a living revolution*. Baltimore, MD: New Society Publishers.

Lau, M. A., Bishop, S. R., Segal, S. V., Buis, T., Anderson, N. D., Carlson, L., et al. (2006). The Toronto Mindfulness Scale: Development and validation. *Journal of Clinical Psychology, 62*(12), 1445–1467.

Lee, B. (1999). *Pragmatics of community organization*. Mississauga, Canada: CommonAct Press.

Lee, B., McGrath, S., Moffatt, K., & George, U. (1992). Community practice education in Canadian schools of social work. *Canadian Social Work Review, 13*(2), 221–236.

Lemma, A. (2003). *Introduction to the practice of psychoanalytic psychotherapy*. Chichester, UK: John Wiley & Sons.

Mearns, D. (1998). *Person-centred counselling training*. New York: Sage.

Mizrahi, T. (2001). The status of community organizing in 2001: Community practice context, complexities, and contributions. *Research on Social Work Practice, 11*(2), 176–189.

Nhat Hanh, T. (1991). *Peace is every step: The path of mindfulness in everyday life*. New York: Bantam Books.

Pulido, L. (2003). The interior life of politics. *Ethics, Place and Environment, 6*(1), 46–52.

Rubin, H., & Rubin, I. (2001). *Community organizing and development* (3rd ed.). Boston: Allyn and Bacon.

Salzberg, S. (2002). *Lovingkindness: The revolutionary art of happiness*. Boston: Shambhala.

Shafir, R. (2003). *The Zen of listening: Mindful communication in the age of distraction*. Wheaton, IL: Quest Books.

Stebner, E. (1997). *The women of Hull House: A study in spirituality, vocation and friendship*. Albany: SUNY Press.

Todd, S. (2004, May). *Professionalizing social work: Implications for community practice*. Paper presented at the annual conference of the Canadian Association of Schools of Social Work, Congress of Humanities and Social Sciences, University of Winnipeg.

Walzer, M. (2002). Passion and politics. *Philosophy and Social Criticism, 28*(6), 617–633.

Whittier, N. (2001). Emotions in the movement against child sexual abuse. In J. Goodwin, J. Jasper, & F. Polletta (Eds.), *Passionate politics: Emotions and social movements* (pp. 233–249). Chicago: University of Chicago Press.

Wills, G. (1992). Values of community practice: Legacy of the radical social gospel. *Canadian Social Work Review, 9*(1), 28–40.

CHAPTER TWELVE

Mindfulness in Activism: Fighting for Justice as a Self-Reflective Emancipatory Practice

Tracy London

I shall lose my usefulness the moment I stifle the still small voice within.

—Mahatma Gandhi (1925)

At this particular moment, I am only seeing one thing—that I am moving in the right direction.

—Wangari Maathai (2000)

Activism is conceptualized as acting as a change agent to transform society through externalized action. As noted by Dorothy E. Smith (2006), "an activist sees the world in terms of what people are doing—what he is or she is doing and what others are doing" (p. 21). However, activism also embodies a transformative and transcendent personal quality of mindful internalized action, variously called conviction, courage, righteousness, or that "still small voice within," as articulated by Mahatma Gandhi, the leader of India's movement for independence from British colonial rule. I see mindfulness as foundational to work devoted to the realization of social justice. An activist's work has the potential to be either poetic and courageous or destructive and blind in its intent and consequences. Therefore, an activist needs to purposively direct her intent in order for her actions to be congruent with social justice aims. The activist who endeavors to integrate her consciousness of self with her awareness of societal injustices maintains her usefulness for realizing fundamental social change. Mindfulness can be seen as a necessary condition for an activist to become mature in her passion and mission to fight for justice.

In this chapter, I examine intersections between the internalized action of self-knowledge and ways of being in the activist's role as a change agent of self, and the externalized acting and doing in her role as a change agent of society. However, this chapter is also about the intensely personal and painful journey for truth that can be at the heart of the choice to be an activist. Mahatma Gandhi's statement that "I shall lose my usefulness the moment I stifle the still small voice within" speaks to the internal struggle to maintain that stillness of mind and integrity to listen to one's own conscience, and to focus one's mindfulness on inner conviction rather than external convention. In chapter 1, Steven Hick notes that mindfulness is not a simple set of techniques that one picks up but is a spiritual and self-revelatory dimension of being. I find that mindfulness in the emancipatory process of self and society is at the heart of a struggle to locate one's own usefulness within a social justice movement, but also core to the struggle to locate one's own still small voice within. I do not set out a singular practice of mindfulness, because I learned in writing this chapter that a mindful activist engages in a Gandhian process of her own unique "experiments with truth" (Gandhi, 1993, p. xxvi) to locate her authentic voice.

Constructing activist strategies and tactics for social change is only a fraction of the struggle of the internal work of finding one's moral and spiritual compass. An activist needs to be conscious of her moral and spiritual compass to impart truth and meaningfulness into the directed actions of activist strategy. It is the still small voice that constantly challenges us as to whether we are replicating or replacing manipulative and coercive social structures within our activist work. It is the still small voice that helps us discern whether we are making fundamental change in the consciousness of those who play a role in the processes of social or environmental exploitation. There are no simple techniques of mindfulness in activism akin to the activist toolkit of tactics that one can strategically employ. It is all too easy to ignore that still small voice, and to lose oneself and one's intent in the managed chaos and reactiveness in the doing and acting of activism.

Wangari Maathai provides an example of extraordinary congruency between the still small voice and activism. Maathai won the 2004 Nobel Prize for her environmental and human rights activist work as founder of the Green Belt movement, a global grassroots organization dedicated to empowering women's groups to plant trees to restore the environment and improve living conditions. She embodies this realization of self through mindful focus in observing that "At this particular moment, I am only seeing one thing—that I am moving in the right direction" (Maathai, 2000). Chapter 3 discusses the self-discipline and mastery of uniting mind with external action that I believe Wangari

Maathai manifests. She is grounded in the strength of her voice and vision of realizing social justice. The activist is always seeking that balance between listening to her doubt and conscience and feeling strength and a peaceful conviction in her heart and soul that she is moving in the right direction.

Chapter 2 discusses the notion of finding the time for wisdom and compassion in everyday moments of meditation and contemplation. Confrontation and conflict with an oppositional force are part of activism, and the mindful activist transforms that conflict into rightful purposeful direction internally and in the world. An activist needs to seek wisdom and compassion in her still small voice and singleness of vision when the time and space for mindfulness with those whom the activist opposes, and even those with whom the activist works in solidarity, are rarely provided. In my experience, it is easy to forget to engage in an activist practice of finding the time and space to be mindful of wisdom and compassion—a right direction—in the push to achieve campaign goals and communications objectives—a willful direction to get power over an adversary.

There is mystery and paradox in the spiritual journey to emancipate oneself, and to actualize compassion through the emancipation of others in a just world. We share fundamental elements of that journey in our common experiences, which are at the essence of our humanity. In chapter 11, Sarah Todd identifies the practices for mindful compassion in community organizing that we all need to employ as activists. In chapter 13, Mishka Lysack sets out a path of environmental compassion in the development of an ecological self, a self essential for humanity and earth's survival, which is universally applicable to activist practice in the environmental movement. The mystery is in finding the beauty of our common humanity. The paradox is in recognizing our multiple inhumanities. When we have the tendency to see the world in black and white, us versus the other, we often miss the banality of evil where acts of inhumanity are committed by ordinary people like ourselves.

I will be looking at those elements of that journey that are sometimes lonely experiments with truth, a rational and soulful process marked by emotional struggle and ethical deliberation. The contemporary German philosopher Jürgen Habermas's concept of the emancipatory interest provides insight into this unity of self and society within reasoned internal and external communication. I then look to the words of Mahatma Gandhi and Wangari Maathai, which I see as exemplifying the fight for justice as a self-reflective emancipatory practice. In conclusion, I scrutinize my own activist practice and tentatively propose a path for experiments with truth. I discuss my personal challenges in locating and trusting my inner voice, and believing in the legitimacy of my experiments with truth. The mystery is finding our own truth, and the paradox is that our truth has always been there for us to find.

Self-Reflection and History: A Dialectical Experience

Jürgen Habermas is a German philosopher and critical social theorist whose formative years in Nazi Germany and after shaped his view of the democratic necessity of ethical and inclusive rational discourse to prevent the repetition of the crimes against humanity that were perpetrated during the "normality of everyday life" in Nazi Germany (Habermas, 1994, p. 35). Habermas contributes significant insight into the self-reflection behind the goal of emancipation in social justice activism.

I will argue here that the activist is engaged in a dialectical experience with history, and it is within this dialectical relationship with history that the activist must seek perspective regarding her contribution to social relations over time and space. Second, in considering Habermas's insights into the role of self-reflection in actualizing the goal of emancipation, I postulate that the activist mediates that dialectical experience with history through ethical and moral rationality in participating in dialogue with others, and through an inner dialogue of self-reflection that enables her to emancipate herself from distorted thinking and the unconscious manifestations of her own actions in maintaining oppression or exploitation.

In general discourse, the activist project is conceptualized according to the liberal and social welfare paradigms of law and democracy. Rights within the Kantian liberal tradition are set out as negative rights against the state, while the competing social welfare paradigm sets out positive rights for substantive social goals (Habermas, 1996). Accordingly, activism is viewed as the fight for freedom from state tyranny, within a liberal paradigm, or as the fight for the state to provide resources and regulatory limits, within a social welfare paradigm.

These liberal and social welfare paradigms are manifested in social work's approaches to activism. The most visible form of activism practiced by the organized social work profession has been in the vein of liberal reform (Abramovitz, 1998), a "great tradition" focused primarily on influencing social welfare policy (Schneider & Netting, 1999). Social work's challenge of the injustices of nineteenth-century industrialization finds its current manifestation in activism concerning global neo-colonial social justice issues such as debt relief for impoverished countries of the Global South (Polack, 2004). Even so, activism is a peripheral activity of social work. As a "child of modernity," the historical development of social work practice has been defined by "care, control and cure" (Howe, 1994, p. 188). Reeser and Epstein (1990) document a marked decrease in service to the poor and political activism as the discipline of social work became increasingly professionalized from the 1970s onward.

I argue that the essence of the activist's emancipatory project is missed when it is defined through the lenses of the liberal and social welfare paradigms. Transcending objectives of negative or positive rights, Habermas takes the determinism of social work's social justice aims beyond social welfare and liberal paradigms. He notes that "the two ideas of human rights and popular sovereignty have determined the normative self-understanding of constitutional democracies to the present day" (Habermas, 1996, p. 94). The conceptual basis for the human rights of self-determination and self-realization has an ethical dimension that is subjective, where the conduct of personal life has significance for political discourses on collective identities such as nation-states. Habermas states that "radicalized interiority is burdened with the task of achieving a self-understanding in which self-knowledge and existential decision interpenetrate" (p. 96). Self-determination has an interiority that is ethical-existential in terms of one's own life history, and an exteriority that is ethical-existential in terms of the political structures that determine the self-determination of all people. In this respect, the emancipatory project of democratic participatory processes and of universalist values is born from self- and collective reflexivity. In applying Habermas's constellation of self-understanding, ethical-political discourses, and democratic pluralism, the emancipatory project encompasses the activist acts of inner mindfulness in seeking self-knowledge, and of outer mindfulness in advocating participatory processes.

Habermas (1971) identifies the "emancipatory power of reflection, which the subject experiences in itself to the extent that it becomes transparent to itself in the history of its genesis" (p. 197). He asserts that "the pursuit of reflection knows itself as a movement of emancipation" (p. 198). Accordingly, the activist's emancipatory project is in equal measure a complex self-reflective process and practice at the historical interface between the individual and society. In response to a need for a revitalized paradigm to invigorate the emancipatory project in social work, incorporating mindfulness in an alternative paradigm would deepen our understanding of our own and the discipline's potential. Habermas inserts self-reflection as the critical element that provides the activist with the rational means to become a change agent in history.

Jürgen Habermas's concept of the emancipatory interest and self-knowledge and discourse theory of democracy provide a nuanced approach to how mindfulness applies to activism. In *The Past as Future*, Habermas (1994) describes emancipation as follows:

> Emancipation is very special kind of self-experience, because
> in it processes of self-understanding link up with an increase

of autonomy. In this way "ethical" and "moral" insights connect up with one another. If with "ethical" questions we
want to get clear on who we are and who we want to be, and
if with "moral" questions we want to know what is equally
good for all, then moral insights are linked with a new ethical
understanding in emancipatory consciousness. We learn
who we are by learning to see differently in relationships
with others. The expression "emancipation" thus has its
place in the realm of the subject's relation with itself: it refers
to discontinuous transformations in the practical self-
relations of persons. (pp. 103–104)

Habermas's conceptualization of emancipation views self-experience
as integral to social emancipation that is realized through the structures
of democracy and discursive deliberation. Habermas (1973) situates
self-reflection in praxis, or the integration of theory and practice, in the
sense that "self-reflection brings to consciousness those determinants
of a self-formative process of cultivation and spiritual formation which
ideologically determine a contemporary praxis of action and the conception of the world" (p. 22).

Habermas's dialectics is different from Marx's dialectical logic of history in that Habermas (1973) sees self-reflection as a dialectic task of
"reconstruct[ing] that which has been repressed from the historical
traces of repressed dialogues" (pp. 16–17). He posits that individuals
reach understandings with others through undistorted communication,
those repressed dialogues in history. In actualizing consensus, the com-
municator realizes a claim to authenticity and validity. According to a
Habermasian approach to dialectics, the activist exercise of self-
reflection is a means of engaging with the dialectical processes of history to achieve acts of undistorted communication free of repression.
Thus the activist works for mutual understanding that is legitimate on
the basis of its moral and ethical validity, rather than the historical replication of systematically distorted communication.

The activist chooses to position herself within the conflict of oppos-
ing claims at a particular point in history. The activist aims to get individuals who have power and influence to come to understand repressed
dialogues and to include them in decision-making processes. For example, Mahatma Gandhi chose to act for a united and independent India
on behalf of the members of all Indian religions and castes in the midst
of the conflicts of British colonialism. Wangari Maathai chooses to act
for environmental conservation and gender equality in developing
nations in the midst of the conflicts of globalized economic exploitation
and Kenyan political oppression. The fundamental difference between
an activist and a non-activist is the conscious choice to act for a truth

of inclusiveness for all individuals that is opposed by other forces. An activist is distinguished by her mindfulness in entering that conflict, but the quality of that mindfulness is fundamental to the ethical and moral dimensions of that social action.

From a societal perspective, history is replete with political and social movements that betrayed the original emancipatory intent behind their founding ideologies, as exemplified by the degeneration of the Enlightenment ideals of the French Revolution into the Reign of Terror (Andress, 2006), the Marxist-Leninist ideals of the Russian Communist Revolution into the Great Purge (Conquest, 1990), and the Straussian ideals of the neo-conservative movement into the war on terrorism in the twenty-first century (Fukuyama, 2006). The contribution of an individual's activism to a broader political and social movement has great historical significance.

Activism is value neutral in the sense that acting as a change agent to transform society might achieve either emancipatory or oppressive ends. Hence, how is one to know whether one's role is useful to the purpose of emancipation? Furthermore, if one wants to become a change agent, how does one realize one's own emancipatory potential when flummoxed by a professional role that enables an inequitable status quo?

If activism is to be founded upon emancipatory interests and democratic rights, moral consciousness and a corresponding ability to distinguish truth and knowledge from illegitimate claims are essential competencies that must be exercised by the activist. The activist exercises this competence in communication with herself. The activist also exercises this competence in communication with others via the media, literature, legal briefs, political campaigning, face-to-face-dialogue, and any other form of communication. The individual activist requires reason and understanding in engaging in tactics to establish norms of equality, freedom, justice, or environmental protection within the political, social, economic, or cultural fabric of the public sphere. However, the activist who practices without mindfulness, self-reflection, or self-awareness risks distorting the validity of her claims for justice, thus undermining her intended emancipatory ends and, at worst, replicating manipulative and oppressive practices.

Meehan (2000) views Habermas's notion of universality of moral engagement through a generalized other as problematic because some moral contexts require us to respond to a "unique person with a unique body, history, emotions and needs" (p. 49). Mahatma Gandhi's and Wangari Maathai's respective concepts of *satyagraha*, soul force, and *kwimenya*, self-knowledge, complement Habermas's emphasis on reason. As noted by Rudolph and Rudolph (2006), Gandhi's political activism democratized and realized Habermas's construction of the public sphere and participatory discourse.

Satyagraha and *Kwimenya*: Soul Force and Self-Knowledge

Though separated by historical time and space, parallels between Mahatma Gandhi and Wangari Maathai's lifeworks exemplify the praxis between mindfulness and their respective activist practices for social justice, which were realized through self-determination; sustainable development; and respect for human rights, peace, and democracy.

Gandhi's conceptualization of mindfulness—personal struggle and suffering in the pursuit of truth—was a cornerstone of his emancipatory practices. Through the force of righteousness, or *satyagraha,* that he exemplified in his activism, he sought to change others' awareness not by inflicting suffering, but through patient and sympathetic communication with his opponents. Truth is vindicated or legitimized through one's own selfless search for the truth. In this sense, Gandhi's practice of mindfulness in his personal suffering and in his experiments with truth was the very basis of his resistance against oppression, which was active rather than passive. As stated by Gandhi (2005) in 1919,

> The term *Satyagraha* was coined by me . . . in order to distinguish it from the movement then going on . . . under the name of Passive Resistance.
>
> Its root meaning is "holding on to truth," hence "force of righteousness." I have also called it love force or soul force. In the application of *Satyagraha,* I discovered in the earliest stages that pursuit of truth did not permit violence being inflicted on one's opponent, but that he must be weaned from error by patience and sympathy. For what appears truth to the one may appear to be error to the other. And patience means self-suffering. So the doctrine came to mean vindication of truth, not by the infliction of suffering on the opponent, but on one's self. (p. 84)

Walz and Ritchie (2000) note that the *satyagraha* ethic of practicing acts of moral courage in the face of violence and oppression is rarely addressed by social work in theory or practice. Wangari Maathai provides a contemporary example of how social work might practice *satyagraha* in theory and practice, and how the "force of righteousness" underlying Gandhi's political model of change reflects the mindfulness of one's personal truth. Maathai (2000) describes her state of mindfulness that propels her in her activist work thus:

> You know, when they attack me, I say this is violence against women. When they threaten me with female genital mutilation, this is violence against women. When they attack me, I

attack them back. A lot of people say, "They could kill you." And I say, "Yes, they could, but if you focus on the damage they could do, you cannot function. Don't visualize the danger you can get in. Your mind must be blank as far as danger is concerned." This helps you to go on. You look very courageous to people—and maybe you are courageous. But it is partly because you cannot see the fear they see. You are not projecting that you could be killed, that you could die. You are not projecting that they could cut your leg. If you do that, you stop. It's not like I see danger coming, and I feel danger. At this particular moment, I am only seeing one thing—that I am moving in the right direction.

Her mindfulness is willful blindness to the dangers that face her but is grounded within a broader awareness of the connections among gender inequities, environmental degradation, economic exploitation, political oppression, and the resulting distortion of individual consciousness. Maathai (2003) states that the overall goal at the beginning of the Green Belt movement "was to raise the consciousness of community members to a level that would drive them to do what was right for the environment because their hearts had been touched and their minds convinced—popular opinion notwithstanding" (p. 33). She describes *kwimenya*, or self-knowledge, as the foundational practice of her activism and the social justice movement. Like Gandhi's notion of *satyagraha*, Maathai's (2004) concept of *kwimenya* involves a powerful spiritual force that inspires social action with the goal of social justice by making mindfulness of the distortions in one's own mind created by colonialism:

By the end of the civic and environmental seminars organised by the Green Belt Movement, participants feel the time has come for them to hold up their own mirror and find out who they are. This is why we call the seminars kwimenya (self-knowledge). Until then, participants have looked through someone else's mirror—the mirror of the missionaries or their teachers or the colonial authorities who have told them who they are and who write and speak about them—at their own cracked reflections. They have seen only a distorted image, if they have seen themselves at all!

There is enormous relief and great anger and sadness when people realise that without a culture not only is one a slave, but one has actually collaborated with the slave trader, and that the consequences are long-lasting. Communities without their own culture, who are already disinherited, cannot protect their environment from immediate destruction or preserve it for future generations.

Maathai's *kwimenya* is consistent with Habermas's conceptualization of the importance of addressing distorted communication through self-reflection, such that the process of self-reflection translates into social action with the goal of undoing distorted communication and power relations in society. Maathai (2006) describes the distorted communication that *kwimenya* serves to undo in her people's struggle for social justice, and how *kwimenya* constructs an oppositional truth that addresses the relationship between an individual and nature:

> When European missionaries came to the central highlands at the end of the nineteenth century, they taught the local people that God did not dwell on Mount Kenya, but rather in heaven, a place above the clouds. The proper place to worship him was in church on Sundays, a concept that was unknown to Kikuyus. Nevertheless, many people accepted the missionaries' worldview, and within two generations they lost respect for their own beliefs and traditions. The missionaries were followed by traders and administrators who introduced new methods of exploiting our rich natural resources: logging, clear-cutting native forests, establishing plantations of imported trees, hunting wild-life, and undertaking expansive commercial agriculture. Hallowed landscapes lost their sacredness and were exploited as the local people became insensitive to the destruction, accepting it as a sign of progress. (p. 1)

The nature of the actualization of mindfulness in social action is not predetermined. Habermas's theoretical application of self-reflection is a means of identifying distorted communication in social processes, but his articulation of the significance of self-reflection does not provide specific insight into how the activist should adopt self-reflection. Wangari Maathai and Mahatma Gandhi exemplify the integration of mindfulness with activism. Maathai uses mindfulness in her activism in a manner that is consistent with her cultural and historical context and practices *kwimenya* to build her inner strength and courage for right action and for the movement's capacity for social justice activism. Gandhi described his process of translating *satyagraha*, the inner process of mindful reflection on truth, into social action as personal "experiments with truth":

But for the time being my error, if it be one, must sustain me. Is it not better that I satisfy my conscience though misguided, because not perfectly pure, than that I should listen to every voice, be it ever so friendly but by no means infallible? If I had a guru? and I am looking for one, I should surrender myself body and soul to him. But in this age of unbelief a true guru is hard to find. A substitute will be worse than useless, often positively harmful. I must, therefore, warn all against accepting imperfect ones as gurus. It is better to grope in the dark and wade through a million errors to Truth than to entrust oneself to one who "knows not that he knows not." Has a man ever learnt swimming by tying a stone to his neck?

And who shall lose by erroneous fasting? Of course, only myself. But I am public property, it is said. So be it. but I must be taken with all my faults. I am searcher after truth. My experiments I hold to be infinitely more important than the best-equipped Himalayan expeditions. And the results? If the search is scientific, surely there is no comparison between the two. Let me, therefore, go my way. I shall lose my usefulness the moment I stifle the still small voice within. (qtd. in Desai, 1972, p. 386)

Gandhi described with such humility and conviction the problem of mindfulness: that mindfulness does not necessarily provide light and guidance. Rather, mindfulness makes the activist even more aware of how she is groping in the dark to translate this inner truth into social justice, and that there are a million inaccuracies in those truths. I propose that we often have a false sense of certainty in communicating the righteousness of the activist's cause and that activism is defined by the historical context of its social consequences regardless of its emancipatory intent. As demonstrated by Habermas, self-reflection brings awareness of these distortions, but how does the activist proceed with *satyagraha* and force of righteousness with mindful clarity? Gandhi acknowledged his own propensity to err and falter even when being mindful and cautions against gurus and "false prophets" who offer easy paths to enlightenment. He reminds us that mindfulness in activism requires us to be mindful that our awareness might still be distorted and erroneous, and that we must listen to our still small voice in our experiments with truth. Mahatma Gandhi's and Wangari Maathai's praxis of mindfulness in activism demonstrates that the rationality of Habermas's self-reflection must be joined with Maathai's emotional strength of self-knowledge and with Gandhi's concept of soul force.

Personal Reflections on My Experiments with Truth

The writing of this chapter has been a personal journey that has allowed me, as an activist involved in human rights and environmental campaigns, to be mindful of my own commitments, and I have been struck by the existential complexity of the desire to contribute to the creation of a just world. As I contemplate how Habermas, Maathai, and Gandhi illuminate different aspects of mindfulness, I observe mystery and paradox. Habermas's critical theory on the significance of self-reflection in the actualization of the emancipatory interest involves a rational communicative process. However, reason is only a single element of mindfulness. There is wondrous mystery in the process of *kwimenya* that turns mindfulness into the divine source of leadership and courage for Wangari Maathai. There is a humble paradox in Gandhi's concept of *satyagraha* in that we hold a life force with the potential to create significant social change, yet there are few of us who actualize this potential because we are deaf to that small and still inner voice that would hold us true. Habermas's, Maathai's, and Gandhi's writings have contributed to my awareness that I have been afraid to surrender to my *kwimenya* and use this as a source of courage in my activism. I have also been afraid to let myself fail in my own experiments with truth, and to have confidence that I too hold the potential for *satyagraha* within me.

This chapter has also been a journey toward embracing the fact that everything that I could express about the connection between activism and mindfulness might be wrong, but like Wangari Maathai, I must see myself as moving in the right direction, and like Mahatma Gandhi, I will lose my usefulness if I do not listen to my still small voice. I am now mindful that, despite my accomplishments as an activist, I am trying to understand what my truth is, and that I must experiment from within rather than seek from without.

Conclusion

Engaging in self-reflective emancipatory practice in the fight for justice means that there is a unity within one's being as a change agent of oneself and of society. Habermas views this unity as a dynamic constellation of relationships between self-reflection and self-understanding, ethics and democracy. Gandhi views this unity as listening to one's own still small voice to realize *satyagraha,* or soul force, for moral and political transformation. Wangari views this unity as movements for equality and sustainability built through *kwimenya,* self-knowledge of how one's consciousness is colonized through oppression and exploitation. It is incumbent on us, as activists, to engage in our own Gandhian experiments with truth to realize the unity between ourselves and our social work practice.

There are many paths to practicing mindfulness and activism. However, Gandhi's "talisman" offers a way for activists to focus on which path to take. I take guidance from Gandhi's talisman on how to be mindful so that one's activism is truthful:

> I will give you a talisman. Whenever you are in doubt, or when the self becomes too much with you, apply the following test. Recall the face of the poorest and the weakest man whom you may have seen, and ask yourself, if the step you contemplate is going to be of any use to him. Will he gain anything by it? Will it restore him to a control over his own life and destiny? In other words, will it lead to swaraj [freedom] for the hungry and spiritually starving millions?
>
> Then you will find your doubts and your self melt away. (qtd. in Nayyar, 1958, p. 65)

Fellow activists, listen to that "still small voice within." Have the courage to listen to your doubts regarding whether your steps in life and work will restore respect and dignity to others, and then find your strength and inner freedom to act with focus and determination.

References

Abramovitz, M. (1998). Social work and social reform: An arena of struggle. *Social Work, 43*(6), 512–526.

Andress, D. (2006). *The merciless war for freedom in revolutionary France.* New York: Farrar, Straus and Giroux.

Conquest, R. (1990). *The Great Terror: A reassessment.* New York: Oxford University Press.

Desai, M. H. (1972). *Day-to-day with Gandhi* (Vol. 7). Varanasi, India: Sarva Seva Sangh Prakashan.

Fukuyama, F. (2006). *America at the crossroads: Democracy, power, and the neoconservative legacy.* New Haven, CT: Yale University Press.

Gandhi, M. K. (1925, December 3). The latest fast. *Young India*, p. 422.

Gandhi, M. K. (1993). *An autobiography: The story of my experiments with truth.* Boston: Beacon Press.

Gandhi, M. K. (2005). *All men are brothers: Autobiographical reflections.* New York: Continuum International.

Habermas, J. (1971). *Knowledge and human interests.* Boston: Beacon Press.

Habermas, J. (1973). *Theory and practice.* Boston: Beacon Press.

Habermas, J. (1994). *The past as future.* Lincoln: University of Nebraska Press.

Habermas, J. (1996). *Between facts and norms: Contributions to a discourse theory of law and democracy.* Cambridge, MA: MIT Press.

Howe, D. (1994). Modernity, postmodernity, and social work. *British Journal of Social Work, 24,* 513–532.

Maathai, W. (2000, May 4). *Speak truth to power.* Retrieved November 9, 2007, from http://wangari-maathai.org/a.php?id = 53

Maathai, W. (2003). *The Green Belt movement: Sharing the approach and the experience.* New York: Lantern Books.

Maathai, W. (2004). The cracked mirror. *Resurgence, 227.* Retrieved November 9, 2007, from http://www.resurgence.org/resurgence/issues/maathai227.htm

Maathai, W. (2006). *Unbowed: A memoir.* New York: Knopf.

Meehan, J. (2000). Feminism and Habermas' discourse ethics. *Philosophy & Social Criticism, 26*(3), 39–52.

Nayyar, P. (1958). *Mahatma Gandhi: The last phase.* Ahmebadad, India: Navajivan.

Polack, R. J. (2004). Social justice and the global economy: New challenges for social work in the 21st century. *Social Work, 49*(2), 281–290.

Reeser, L. C., & Epstein, I. (1990). *Professionalization and activism in social work: The sixties, the eighties and the future.* New York: Columbia University Press.

Rudolph, S. H., & Rudolph, L. I. (2006). The coffee house and the ashram revisited: How Gandhi democratized Habermas' public sphere. In L. I. Rudolph & S. H. Rudolph (Eds.), *Postmodern Gandhi and other essays: Gandhi in the world and at home* (pp. 140–176). Chicago: University of Chicago Press.

Schneider, R. L., & Netting, F. E. (1999). Influencing social policy in a time of devolution: Upholding social work's great tradition. *Social Work, 44*(4), 349–357.

Smith, D. E. (2006). George Smith: Political activist as ethnographer and sociology for people. In C. Frampton, G. Kinsman, A. K. Thompson, & K. Tilleczek (Eds.), *Sociology for changing the world* (pp. 18–26). Halifax, Nova Scotia: Fernwood.

Walz, T., & Ritchie, H. (2000). Gandhian principles in social work practice: Ethics revisited. *Social Work, 45*(3), 213–222.

CHAPTER THIRTEEN

From Environmental Despair to the Ecological Self: Mindfulness and Community Action

Mishka Lysack

For one species to mourn the death of another is a new thing under the sun.

—Aldo Leopold, 1970

One evening in February of 2007, I was watching a CBC documentary report on the dramatic increase in the slaughter of African elephants for ivory. The journalist reported that in 2006 alone, 26,000 elephants—5 percent of the entire population on earth—had been ruthlessly poached, despite the presence of laws and the efforts of sanctuary officers to protect the elephants. Research on elephant populations in the Congo and Zambia shows that unless dramatic action is taken immediately, human activity may soon drive elephants into extinction. As I watched, I felt a profound sense of sadness and anger.

My experience was not an isolated event. Browsing at a newsstand two days later, I noticed the latest issue of *National Geographic,* which showed a picture of elephants bathing in a river. The headline read, "Last Stand: Defending a Forgotten Herd." The article featured pictures of elephant families protecting each other, and of dead elephants mutilated for their tusks. Contemplating the sheer waste and cruelty, I experienced wave upon wave of rage and disgust, shot through with streaks of denial and numbness. The article went on to reveal the plight of this species: "About half of Africa's elephants—600,000 animals—died

I wish to thank Suzanne Nussey, Ruth Morrow, Laura Beres, and Steven Hick for their comments on this text.

between 1979 and 1990. Most were slaughtered for their tusks" (Fay, 2007, p. 34). Sadness and grief swept over me. As I returned to work, I had difficulty breathing and walking. After nearly being hit by a car, I finally reached my office, where I closed my door, sat down, and wept, truly an environmental dark night of the soul.

As my grief welled up, I remembered the Breathing Through exercises developed by Joanna Macy (Macy, 2006; Macy & Brown, 1998). At this point, I focused on my breath moving in and out, slowly enveloping and encompassing my sorrow. I began to experience my breath as something relational, as a cosmological pattern of healing, connecting me to the web of life, to the breath of the earth and animals, even the breath of the endangered elephants fighting for their survival. Though my grief remained, it had been recast as a renewed determination to bear witness to the plight of all endangered species in whatever way I can.

Using my own experience of grief and despair resulting from environmental losses as a starting point, this chapter is a reflective essay that traces the journey from environmental despair through the process of politicizing and contextualizing the experience of ecological loss by linking the personal and the environmental. I suggest that the process of politicizing environmental despair contributes to the "greening" or the emergence of an ecological self, a foundation for environmental activism and community action. After a brief review of Macy's theoretical resources of linking the personal, political, and ecological in her notion of the "Great Turning," I provide an overview of her despair/empowerment work, highlighting the mindfulness practices that are related to the healing of ecological despair and their relevance to sustained environmental activism. At the conclusion of the chapter, I return to my own reflective journey in making connections between the personal and the environmental by drawing on Macy's image of the Shambhala warrior as a metaphor for understanding how mindfulness and community action belong together as inner and outer dimensions of one journey.

The New Pivotal Psychological Reality

Until the late twentieth century, every generation throughout history lived with the tacit certainty that there would be generations to follow. Each assumed, without questioning, that its children and children's children would walk the same Earth, under the same sky. Hardships, failures, and personal death were encompassed in that vaster assurance of continuity. That certainty is now lost to us, whatever our politics.

> That loss, unmeasured and immeasurable, is the pivotal psy-
> chological reality of our time. (Macy, 1995, p. 241)

What happened to me that week is part of an undulating river of experience as I become more aware of the plight of the earth and how we are
destroying it in myriad ways: global warming and climate change, an
unprecedented rate of extinction of species, air pollution, toxic waste
in the earth and water, environmentally related illnesses such as
asthma, the increasing loss of fertile earth and agricultural land through
erosion and desertification, the clear-cutting and ongoing destruction
of the rainforests. The Stern Report in the United Kingdom in 2006 and
the latest series of reports from the International Panel on Climate
Change have stressed the importance of the global community making
significant and timely changes in moving to a post-carbon and sustainable society, arguing that failure to do so will lead to serious consequences for humanity and all species on the earth.

There is growing evidence that the actual rate and breadth of
changes are exceeding those predicted in the Stern Report and earlier
scientific projections (de Costa, 2007). Even the language used to
describe climate change is shifting in an effort to mobilize our society
to decisive action. Images of catastrophe and war abound. For instance,
the former environment minister in the United Kingdom, Michael
Meacher (2007), has written that what "we, and the government, need
to get our minds round is that we are at war: at war against climate
catastrophe, presenting us with a far greater threat towards our survival
than 1939; and that the measures adopted must rise to this unprecedented challenge" (p. 22). This perspective is not the expression of a
deluded or misguided apocalypticism but is an increasingly visible and
recurring theme in contemporary social discourse. The incisive analysis
and research of scientists and activists alike have yielded disturbing and
detailed explorations of the environmental crisis that we face (McKibben, 2006; Monbiot, 2006). Indeed, it was reading Flannery's (2005)
book on global warming that precipitated a radical shift in my own personal sense of vocation and galvanized me to focus my attention on
forging partnerships between social work practice and ecological
activism.

A small group of social work educators (Coates, 2003a), psychologists
(Kidner, 1994), and family therapists (Lysack, 2007) have discussed environmental concerns. Berger and Kelly (1993) view the environmental
crisis as an area urgently in need of consideration in social work, while
Soine (1987) urged social workers to include environmental hazards
assessments as part of their initial engagement with clients. Hoff and
McNutt (1994) trace the implications of the global ecological crisis for
social welfare and social work, and Park (1996) encourages social work

practitioners to make linkages between the personal and ecological. In describing his work, psychiatric social worker O'Connor (1995) poses the poignant question as to what it means to practice therapy on a dying planet.

Reconfiguring the social work field so that it acquires a greater environmental sensibility continues to be a pressing concern. Coates (2003a, 2003b) focuses on the cultural roots of the environmental crisis and sees great opportunity for developing a less anthropocentric and more eco-centric paradigm for social work. Ungar (2003) sees potential in using the conceptual resources of deep ecology in rethinking outdoor programs for at-risk youths, while Zapf (2005) is intrigued by the exploration of connections between place and people in terms of social work and spirituality. Reorienting social work toward an environmental emphasis is also the mission of Muldoon (2006), whereas Besthorn (2003) plumbs the depths of deep ecology and ecofeminism for theoretical resources that would enrich social work's approach to education, particularly in assisting students to make connections between ecological activism and social justice approaches. Pyles (2005) is fascinated by the potential of mindfulness practices in the engaged Buddhist movement to enhance social development practice in social work.

The Politicizing of Ecological Loss

As environmental issues move into the foreground of our collective consciousness, accompanied by the sobering projections of an earth on a collision course with our excessive consumer lifestyle, a new context has emerged for how we orient ourselves in the world. It is not simply the enormity of the challenge of climate change and ecological crisis that is so paralyzing. As a human species, we have always oriented ourselves in the world within a horizon of temporal and historical continuity, believing that even if I as an individual cease to exist, the human species and culture would nonetheless continue. However, with the growing awareness of the accelerating destruction of the environment, we are suffering from a loss of certainty with respect to the very continuation of the human race. With disarming and disconcerting accuracy, Macy (1990) calls this experience the "pivotal psychological reality of our time" (p. 56).

Macy and other environmentalists have provided a context for individuals to make sense of their sense of loss and grief over the devastation of the earth, and the threats that such an environmental degradation poses for our survival as a species. For instance, Windle (1995), who is both an environmentalist and a helping professional in palliative care, describes her own grief responses to endangered and extinct species in the biosphere. Rather than internalizing and repressing this profound loss, she finds solace in the voicing of this sadness in the writings of other ecologists. Windle writes that ecologists "are both blessed and cursed in seeing natural systems clearly. We see what is there and also know what is gone" (p. 140). Another activist, McKibben (2006), reflects on the loss of a forest system, suggesting that the "end of nature probably also makes us reluctant to attach ourselves to its remnants, for the same reason that we usually don't choose friends from among the terminally ill. I love the mountain outside my back door. . . . But I know that some part of me resists getting to know it better—for fear, weak-kneed as it sounds, of getting hurt" (p. 21). We internalize and individualize our grief, separating it from the political and ecological contexts in which it is embedded, thus incapacitating ourselves to take action on behalf of the earth to challenge and confront those structures and beliefs that contribute to its ongoing destruction.

These accounts of ecological loss resonated powerfully with my own lived experience. My personal responses to the destruction of the elephant herds in Africa need not be dismissed as a merely personal grief, or pathologized as a dysfunctional deficit within me as an individual. Macy (1990) experienced the power of contemporary discourses in the helping professions as well as in society at large in internalizing and pathologizing her own grief and anger in the Vietnam protests and the anti-nuclear movement, and the strong pull of society to incapacitate her and depoliticize her feelings. Similarly, social worker and activist Michael White (1997) has critiqued this tendency in factions of social work and psychology to decontextualize our lived experience and anger over injustice, arguing that such experience can restrain our commitment to justice-oriented forms of community practice. Macy is open in her exhortations regarding environmental despair and sadness: "Don't ever apologize for crying for the trees burning in the Amazon or over the waters polluted from mines in the Rockies. Don't apologize for the sorrow, grief, and rage that you feel. It is a measure of your humanity and your maturity. It is a measure of your open heart, and as your heart breaks open there will be room for the world to heal" (p. 57).

For Macy (1990), the sense of grief over environmental degradation is a healthy response. It is a "signal of our own evolution, a measure of our humanity. We are capable of suffering with our world, and that is the true measure of compassion. It enables us to recognize our profound interconnectedness with all beings" (p. 57). If we trace the source of this anger and grief back to the social and environmental contexts, my experience of sadness and loss becomes understandable. Indeed, Windle (1995) proposes that in order for "an environmental ethic to succeed, nature would need to be meaningful to us on a variety of levels, including the emotional. Here again it is the ecologists' deep attachment to organisms and systems that is our strength" (p. 145).

Social workers have also perceived that there is a need for practitioners to provide support for those experiencing grief or fear regarding the changes taking place in the environment and society. Coates
(2003a) proposes a reorientation of current social work practice so that
social workers may assist others in society with their own sense of anxiety and despair. He writes that one "task of social work and counselling
professions will be to help people deal with their sense of anxiety and
loss. While people may not be aware of the cause of these feelings, for
many the distress will be rooted in trepidation about the present and
the future" (p. 131). For others, the struggles may be related to their
sense of loss (including anger, depression, and guilt) regarding their
material security and wealth in a world where the environmental
demands of the consumerism of developed nations far exceeds the carrying capacity of the earth. Others will experience a deepening sense
of trauma as they become aware of the "many tragedies that humans
experience and so often inflict on each other and the Earth" (p. 131).
Still others, "when made aware of the severity and the implications of
pollution, extinctions, poverty and hunger, have withdrawn into denial,
become angry or despaired of their ability to 'make a difference' against
such enormous problems" (p. 98). In her account of how environmental impacts pose a challenge for social work, Muldoon (2006) suggests
that there are "few other professions capable of coping with fear and
illness, while simultaneously possessing the ability to listen, empathize,
analyze, and organize" (p. 1).

Equally important is the need for social work practitioners to devote
attention to their own sense of environmental despair by making links
to the social and political contexts in which they work, thereby providing a foundation for the emergence of their own sense of an ecological
self. Coates (2003a) envisions self-care for social workers as necessarily
entailing the experiencing of environmental loss and a willingness to
engage in the despair/empowerment work of figures like Macy, given
that many "social workers and students will encounter, each in their
own way, a sense of anguished awareness . . . as they deal with the
painful anxiety that so often accompanies an understanding of the great
dangers posed by the current global environmental crisis" (p. 157).

The Greening of the Ecological Self

It is obvious to me that the forests cannot be saved one at a
time, nor can the planet be saved one issue at a time: without
a profound revolution in human consciousness, all the forests will soon disappear. Psychologists in service to the earth
helping ecologists to gain deeper understanding of how to

> facilitate deeper change in the human heart and mind
> seems to be *the* key at this point. (personal correspondence
> between Seed and Roszak, Roszak, Gomes, & Kanner, 1995,
> p. 3)

While there are authors who allude to the necessity of grounding environmental activism in mindfulness practices, Joanna Macy is one of the activists who explores this in the greatest detail, fusing her knowledge of open systems thinking (Macy, 1991a), deep ecology (Macy, 1991b; Naess, 1989), and engaged Buddhism (Macy, 2004) with her meditation practice and her experience of forty years of political and environmental activism. Far from being naive about social action or romanticizing the activist lifestyle, Macy bears eloquent testimony to the social demands and psychological suffering incumbent in seeking social justice and environmental sustainability in a culture that coalesces much of its collective life around global structures of social injustice and environmental exploitation.

In her autobiography, *Widening Circles,* Macy (2000) chronicles the rigors and suffering that have accompanied her lifelong career of teaching and activism, detailing the exacting toll that such a way of life has taken on the activists she has encountered in her lifelong pilgrimage. For many in the activist movements, burnout and despair frequently gain the upper hand and circumscribe the range of their creative and empowering action, limiting the effectiveness of groups. In his book, *An Inconvenient Truth* (2006), Al Gore similarly highlights how many individuals move directly from denial to despair as they become acquainted with the magnitude of the problems of global warming and environmental degradation, thus failing to take decisive action to protect the earth. Similarly, Canadian activist and educator David Suzuki (2006) has also expressed concern that environmentalists must not become demoralized but must focus on finding solutions to the pressing ecological problems facing our society and engage in environmental activism. Although it is true that such psychological forces do not completely incapacitate individuals, there can be little doubt that ecological despair is a potent force.

Macy (2006) points to the key theoretical idea that underlies her community activism: the notion of the "greening" of the "ecological self." In place of the contemporary Western notion of the self as an isolated individual delimited by skin and ecologically separated from the world, Macy (1990) advances an alternative way of conceptualizing the self, where the ego-centered self "is replaced by wider constructs of identity and self-interest—by what you might call the ecological self or the eco-self, co-extensive with other beings and the life of our planet" (p. 53). She argues that the epistemological differentiation between an

"I" and the world as seemingly biologically distinct and unrelated entities is erroneous and fraught with misunderstanding. For Macy, this
absolute distinction between the self and the world is misleading
because "as open, self-organizing systems, our very breathing, acting
and thinking arise in interaction with our shared world through the
currents of matter, energy, and information that move through us and
sustain us. In the web of relationships that sustain these activities there
is no clear line demarcating a separate, continuous self" (p. 58).

The notion of the ego-self not only is idiosyncratic to Western culture
but also functions as a heuristic lens through which our interactions
with others and nature are shaped and informed, providing the basis
for our dysfunctional relationships, both socially and environmentally.
Macy (1990) succinctly draws together the psychological, social, and
ecological dimensions of this pathologized sense of the self as she proposes that it is a "delusion that the self is so separate and fragile that
we must delineate and defend its boundaries, that it is so small and so
needy that we must endlessly acquire and endlessly consume, and that
it is so aloof that as individuals, corporations, nations-states, or species,
we can be immune to what we do to other beings" (p. 57). Similarly,
Ungar (2003) suggests that one objective of outdoors-based programs
for youths at risk is the facilitation of the emergence of an expanded
notion of self: "there is much to be gained from transcending the individual 'self' in preference for the more universal and actualized 'Self'
which transcends the distinctions between humans and nature" (p. 3).

The greening of the ecological self is grounded in a keen awareness
of the interconnectedness of all existence, an attitudinal perspective
that is foundational to mindfulness practices. In her description of
mindfulness in relational psychotherapy, Surrey (2005) suggests that
"openness to relationship in our daily life expands to a felt connection
with the global community. Healing our personal wounds becomes the
first step in a process that gradually widens to include compassion for
the suffering of everyone and everything, potentially to include the
intent, described in ecopsychology, to heal planetary wounds" (p. 96).
Drawing on Thich Nhat Hanh's notion of "interbeing," Surrey muses
that the "uncommon experience of this level of interdependence is
regarded as direct insight into our original concordance with all of
nature" (p. 96).

In a similar manner, social work educators suggest that "social
empathy could be expanded to become global empathy, where the reality that a person experiences can be seen not only in the context of their
immediate situation (such as abuse or poverty) but also in the context
of global poverty and ecological destruction" (Coates, 2003a, p. 101).
Over the last decade, ecopsychologists (Conn, 1995, 1997; Roszak et al.,
1995) and eco-social workers (O'Connor, 1995) have explored in detail

the particularities of clinical practices that help people situate their personal distress within a larger context of globalized trauma and exploitation.

The political impact of such a reorientation is considerable, as it reconstitutes the way in which people position themselves in relation to the world. More specifically, such a shift contributes immeasurably to a renewal of a sense of empowerment, reshaping despair into an experience of compassion and connectedness by grounding the self in ever-widening circles of identification with the larger web of life on earth. Simultaneously, this shift also mobilizes and galvanizes personal and collective energies for taking action and challenging the social and political forces that undermine and threaten the health of the biotic community of the planet. These energies evoke the qualities needed for ongoing resilience in the face of social inertia and political opposition: humility and commitment (McKibben, 2006), courage, compassion, and patience (Macy, 1995). These attributes are so crucial for mindfulness-based environmental activism that Macy (1990) is "convinced that this expanded sense of self is the *only* basis for adequate and effective action" (p. 55).

Macy relates a conversation with the environmental activist John Seed that illustrates the potential of the greening of the self as a sustaining foundation for activism. Walking through the Australian rainforest in New South Wales, Macy asked Seed how he copes with the discouragement and despair that so frequently accompany environmental activism. In an evocative manner, John Seed answered, "I try to remember that it's not me, John Seed, trying to protect the rainforest. Rather I'm part of the rainforest trying to protect myself. I am that part of the rainforest recently emerged into human thinking" (Macy, 1990, p. 55). Likewise, in her account of how the engaged Buddhist movement can contribute to social development practice in social work, Pyles (2005) identifies that notion of the "interconnected self" as crucial for a shift of individuals in the movement to embrace a more relational sense of the universe as the ground for their community-based practice and activism.

The Great Turning: Moving from an Industrial Society to Sustainable Earth

The multicontextual approach to healing society on different levels— environmental, social, and personal—represents a broad conceptual framework for integrating mindfulness practices with activism. In addition to the notion of the ecological self, Macy has developed other theoretical resources that provide a foundation for her educational programs for activists and communities, such as her distinction between an "industrial growth society" and a "life-sustaining society" (Macy,

2006; Macy & Brown, 1998). Similar to Berry's (1990, 1999) incisive analysis of a "non-renewable, extractive economy and terminal society," Macy describes how the industrial growth society coalesces its economic, social, and cultural life around the growth imperative of ever-increasing consumption of the resources of the earth, where the earth is objectified as both a supply house of raw materials and a sewer and dumping ground for toxic waste. "The planet's body is not only dug up and turned into goods to sell, it is also a 'sink' for the poisonous by-products of our industries" (2000, p. 16). In contrast, Macy (2000) draws on the work of social critics (such as Lester Brown of the Worldwatch Institute) to define a life-sustaining society as one that "satisfies its own needs without jeopardizing the prospects of future generations" (Macy & Brown, 1998, p. 16) by staying within the carrying capacity of the earth in terms of both the materials it consumes and the waste it discharges. In her despair/empowerment work with communities, Macy's distinction between an industrial growth society and a life-sustaining society acts as a learning heuristic that enables people to focus their social analysis and to highlight the differences between the two ways in which society could position itself within the biosphere in the natural world.

The second conceptual resource that Macy (Macy & Brown, 1998) and other environmental activists (Kaza, 2002) have developed is the three-fold notion of the Great Turning as a framework for understanding individual and community response to the environmental crisis. The first element is holding actions of resistance in defense of life on earth, which entails all political, legal, and legislative initiatives as well as all forms of direct action/protest to prevent or minimize the destruction of the biosphere (animal and plant life) and ecosphere (rivers, wetlands, oceans, air). The second element is an analysis of structural causes (through a critique of societal dynamics, tacit cultural agreements, and interlocking economic forces), and the creation of alternative societal and economic institutions. The third element of the Great Turning is a shift in perceptions of reality, both cognitive and spiritual, and the accompanying cultural transformation. Similar to Berry's (1999) four wisdoms, Macy suggests that this perceptual shift and cultural transformation arise from three realms: (1) a move from ecological despair to the ecological self, (2) breakthroughs in scientific thought, and (3) resources in the wisdom writings and spiritual voices of religious traditions.

Despair/Empowerment Work, Mindfulness, and Environmental Activism

The accelerating barrage of disturbing ecological images in the media takes its toll on us as citizens both psychologically and socially. While the psychological effects of environmental devastation are internalized by citizens, little attention has been devoted to how environmentalists might respond to this impact as healing agents. Thomashow (1996) notes that when he looks through the children's section of a bookstore that has a proliferating number of books on endangered species, toxic waste, pollution, or environmental degradation, "few of these books seemed to acknowledge the feelings that a child has when confronted with the bleak outlook contained in their messages" (p. 147).

Environmentalists need to develop ways of assisting people to reflect on the impact of these discouraging and dispiriting images, drawing on these perceptions and experiences to explore the interior dimensions of the struggle for environmental justice and healing and to galvanize commitment to action. Thomashow (1996) highlights the example of the conjoint efforts of both engaged Buddhists and environmentalists to draw on the skills of mindfulness teachers such as Thich Nhat Hanh to enable eco-activists to "look more deeply into their work and to provide a reflective perspective on environmental action" (p. 160). Interestingly, he begins his own classes in environmental studies with mindfulness practices, suggesting that by "bringing mindfulness to a learning experience you focus all of your energy and attention on the task of the moment, applying concentration and reflection" (p. 191).

There is relatively little discussion of how mindfulness practices may play a role in the resourcing of social workers for practice in this new context of environmental crisis and its accompanying fears and anxieties. Like Pyles (2005), Coates (2003a) proposes that social workers "must be first firmly grounded in what Mische . . . calls a 'right ordering of spirit, mind, heart and will.' Such grounding involves cultivating a capacity for inner knowing, for a deeply felt resonance with the rest of nature" (p. 95). Moreover, Coates maintains, this "personal connectedness emerges from the depths of our spirit, which is beyond attachments and social status, where one realizes that one is deeply connected to all beings" (p. 95). Unfortunately, to my knowledge, there are virtually no detailed explorations in social work literature of the actual practices that would facilitate the emergence of such a consciousness.

Mindfulness practices form a crucial dimension of these despair/ empowerment processes. Pyles (2005), a social work educator, suggests that meditation contributes to community-building processes by facilitating learning about the self and its entangled relationships with delusions and mental events such as despair, anger, and fear. Ungar (2003) also senses the place that "breathing rhythm and rhythm in nature" as well as "focusing on breathing and release and breathing out" (p. 6) could have in contributing to the development of resilience among at-risk youths in outdoor programs. Macy (1991a) acknowledges the centrality of meditative practice: "Skillful meditation, that journey into the wilderness where we confront our own tricks and delusions, can empower social action, freeing us to respond in simplicity and immediacy to our fellow beings" (p. 217). Macy also maintains that the "grip of ego is weakened not only in meditation, but also in acting on behalf of others. The risk-taking and courage which moral action often requires can catapult us beyond constructs of individual self-interest. We are shot into a larger space where the old boundaries of self dissolve and the interdependence of all life-forms is brought into vivid focus" (p. 217). Meditation is one of the skillful means of cultivating the relational eco-centric rather than individually oriented ego-centric awareness. In this way, mindfulness contributes to the process of the greening of the ecological self.

The practices that Macy has developed for her despair/empowerment work that specifically focus on the breath may be found in her discussion on "Affirmation: Coming from Gratitude" (Macy & Brown, 1998, pp. 83–85), but these breath practices are also core exercises that are infused throughout the educational process as one of the "exercises for coming back to life" (Macy & Brown, 1998, pp. 190–191; see also Macy, 2006, disc 1, section 9). The meditative practice for loving-kindness is also one of the exercises in Macy's foundational cluster (Macy & Brown, 1998, pp. 188–190), although she has extended it into other meditation practices, such as the Web of Life, which helps individuals strengthen their awareness of being embedded in the ecological network of sustaining relationships in the natural world, and the Gaia Meditation, which fosters a deeper identification with the four ancient elements that make up earth's life history. Macy encourages practitioners of the breathing exercises to allow their awareness of the breath to connect their interior with the "outside, the mind and body, lending attention to the ever-flowing stream of air, stilling the chatter and evasions, and making us more present to life" (Macy & Brown, 1998, p. 83). However, Macy's approach to mindful breathing or sitting meditation is explicitly environmental in its language and its horizon of vision, where individuals are invited to deepen their awareness of how their breathing is embedded "in a vast exchange of energy with the living body of our planet, with seas and plants" (Macy & Brown, 1998, p. 83). Macy invites participants in her empowerment workshops to notice how "everyone in this room . . . on this planet now, is being breathed by life, sustained in a vast living breathing web" (Macy & Brown, 1998, p. 190). Finally, participants in the training programs are invited to "open your awareness to the suffering that is present in the world. . . . Let it pass through your heart. . . . Be sure that stream flows through and out again; don't hang on to the pain. . . . Surrender it for now to the healing resources of life's vast web" (Macy & Brown, 1998, pp. 190–191).

Macy has also developed a variety of body-centered exercises that make use of movement, dance, and physical objects and artwork to help participants reorient themselves in a more mindfully eco-centric relationship with the world. Macy and Brown (1998) write,

> All of the threats facing us in this planet-time—be they toxic wastes, world hunger, or global warming—come down in the final analysis to threats to our body. Our bodies pick up signals that our minds refuse to register. Our unexpressed and unacknowledged dreads are locked into our very tissues along with known and unknown toxins—in our muscles, in our throats and guts, in our ovaries and gonads. Essential joys come through the body as well: the tastes, sights, sounds, textures, and movement which connect us tangibly to our world. (pp. 83–84)

It is these mindfulness practices that provide a critical and supportive foundation for the other despair and empowerment exercises that Macy has developed in her mentoring work with activists.

Acting for the Future of Our Earth: The Shambhala Warrior

> We could say that the world is literally and metaphorically dying for us as a species to come to our senses, and now is the time. Now is the time for us to wake up to the fullness of our beauty, to get on with and amplify the work of healing ourselves, our societies, and the planet, building on everything worthy that has come before and that is flowering now. (Kabat-Zinn, 2005, p. 16)

For Kabat-Zinn (2005), mindfulness practices cannot be a pretext for failure to work tirelessly "for greater ecological balance and for a more peaceful world for all sentient beings" (p. 239). For both Kabat-Zinn and Macy, mindfulness is the ground out of which focused commitment and deepened compassion for the earth may emerge and be sustained. But unlike Kabat-Zinn, who has not developed a robust critique of the social structures that maintain environmental degradation, Macy makes environmental activism nurtured by mindfulness her center of gravity, rather than simply relying on a change in consciousness in order to usher in social transformation.

Social workers and ecopsychologists would also insist that practice on behalf of the environment needs to be extended into community and political realms. Coates (2003b) would advocate that social workers need to discover practices that "nurture an understanding and appreciation of the connectedness of all things, and the hope and direction that can flow from this" (p. 6; see also pp. 4, 7). In their ecological credo for social workers, Berger and Kelly (1993) insist that social work acknowledge "the obligation of its professionals to speak out when they have knowledge of damage to the environment that will adversely affect the quality or sustainability of life for current or future generations of living systems" (qtd. in Coates, 2003a, p. 105). Environmental activism and advocacy on behalf of species that are unable to defend themselves against the destructive activities of humankind are both expressions of the compassion and commitment that are born out of the practice of mindfulness.

One image that has captured my own imagination is a metaphor that Macy (2000; see also Macy & Brown, 1998) learned from one of her teachers, Choegyal Rinpoche, while visiting the Tashi Jong community in northern India: the Shambhala warrior. While I feel uncomfortable with the word *warrior* and the military discourse that it represents, I find that Macy's image of the Shambhala warrior resonates powerfully with my own sense of how my mindfulness practices and environmental activism are linked together. Macy relates how a time comes when all life on earth is threatened by the barbarian powers that have consumed all their wealth in preparing to annihilate each other. The weapons developed by the barbarian powers possess incredible destructive powers, and their technologies poison and lay waste to the earth.

It is when the "future of sentient life hangs by the frailest of threads, that the kingdom of Shambhala emerges" (Macy, 2000, p. 161). It is not a physical place where one can go, as it exists in the minds and hearts of the Shambhala warriors, who themselves are unrecognizable, as they wear no uniform. Having no land of their own, they move invisibly, guided by wisdom on the terrain of the barbarians. Great courage is demanded of the Shambhala warriors, "for they must go into the very heart of the barbarian power, into the pits and pockets and citadels where the weapons are kept, to dismantle them. To dismantle them . . . they must go into the corridors of power where decisions are made" (Macy & Brown, 1998, p. 61). In training, the Shambhala warriors develop two "weapons" of compassion and insight, each of which is needed to balance the other. Compassion emerges out of our recognition of our pain as the heart of our pathos for the world. Insight is the "recognition and experience of our radical, empowering interconnectedness with all life" (Macy & Brown, 1998, p. 61).

I first read this narrative of the Shambhala warrior after I had been deeply affected by Flannery's (2005) *The Weather Makers,* and as I was preparing to move to a full-time teaching position at the University of

Calgary. Macy's description of the citadels and corridors of power in the Shambhala story evoked images of the Alberta government and the oil industry, which is fuelling the explosive growth of the province and feeding the wealth, comfort, and apathy (and the unspoken guilt of knowing that we depend on that which is wrong) of Alberta's citizens. Other images surfaced of the tar-sands industry, which emits huge amounts of greenhouse gases while consuming land, water, and natural gas, and laying waste to the landscape and the animal/plant life of northern Alberta.

In my current context of teaching and activism in Calgary—the city that surely represents a "ground zero" of the clash between wealth/consumerism and ethical demands to protect the environment—I find both comfort and a sustaining vision in Macy's story of the Shambhala warrior, a participant in the Great Turning, that process of transforming our terminal civilization into an environmentally sustainable society. With all that I am and do, I persevere and work in the radical hope that that is true.

References

Berger, R., & Kelly, J. (1993). Social work in the ecological crisis. *Social Work, 38*(5), 521–526.

Berry, T. (1990). *The dream of the earth.* San Francisco: Sierra Club Books.

Berry, T. (1999). *The great work: Our way into the future.* New York: Bell Tower.

Besthorn, F. (2003). Radical ecologisms: Insights for educating social workers in ecological activism and social justice. *Critical Social Work, 4*(1). Retrieved March 19, 2007, from http://www.uwindsor.ca/units/socialwork/critical.nsf/982foe5fo6b5c9a285256d6eoo6cff78/832ef6e6559c5f4285256fo40062c71d!OpenDocument

Coates, J. (2003a). *Ecology and social work.* Halifax, Nova Scotia: Fernwood.

Coates, J. (2003b). Exploring the roots of the environmental crisis: Opportunity for social transformation. *Critical Social Work, 4*(1), Retrieved March 19, 2007, from http://cronus.uwindsor.ca/units/socialwork/critical.nsf/982foe5fo6b5c9a285256d6eoo6cff78/d8b8aao70b431afb85256fo400513e74!OpenDocument

Conn, S. (1995). When the earth hurts, who responds? In T. Roszak, M. Gomes, & T. Kanner, (Eds.), *Ecopsychology: Restoring the earth, healing the mind* (pp. 156–171). San Francisco: Sierra Club Books.

Conn, S. (1997). *What aileth thee? Ecopsychological principles and practices for activists.* Retrieved November 7, 2006 from http://ecopsychology.athabascau.ca/0197/intro.htm

de Costa, A. (2007). The science of climate change. *Ecologist, 37*(0), 10–16.

Fay, J. M. (2007). Ivory wars. *National Geographic, 211*(3), 34–65.

Flannery, T. (2005). *The weather makers: How we are changing the climate and what it means for life on earth.* Toronto: HarperCollins.

Gore, A. (2006). *An inconvenient truth.* Emmaus, PA: Rodale.

Hoff, M., & McNutt, J. (1994). *The global environmental crisis: Implications for social welfare and social work.* Brookefield, VT: Avebury.

Kabat-Zinn, J. (2005). *Coming to our senses: Healing ourselves and the world through mindfulness.* New York: Hyperion.

Kaza, S. (2002). Green Buddhism. In C. Matthews, M. Tucker, & P. Kefner (Eds.), *When worlds converge: What science and religion tell us about the story of the universe and our place in it* (pp. 293–309). Chicago: Open Court.

Kidner, D. (1994). Why psychology is mute about the environmental crisis. *Environmental Ethics, 16,* 359–376.

Lysack, M. (2007). Family therapy, the ecological self, and global warming. *Context, 91,* 9–11.

Macy, J. (1990). The greening of the self. In A. Badiner (Ed.), *Dharma Gaia: A harvest of essays in Buddhism and ecology* (pp. 53–63). Berkeley, CA: Parallax Press.

Macy, J. (1991a). *Mutual causality in Buddhism and general systems theory: The dharma of natural systems.* Albany: SUNY Press.

Macy, J. (1991b). *World as lover, world as self.* Berkeley, CA: Parallax Press.

Macy, J. (1995). Working through environmental despair. In T. Roszak, M. Gomes, & T. Kanner (Eds.), *Ecopsychology: Restoring the earth, healing the mind* (pp. 240–259). San Francisco: Sierra Club Books.

Macy, J. (2000). *Widening circles: A memoir.* Gabriola Island, Canada: New Society Publishers.

Macy, J. (2004). Buddhist resources for despair. In S. Moon (Ed.), *Not turning away: The practice of engaged Buddhism* (pp. 162–167). Boston: Shambhala.

Macy, J. (2006). *The work that reconnects* [DVD]. Berkeley, CA: Joanna Macy Intensives.

Macy, J., & Brown, M. Y. (1998). *Coming back to life: Practices to reconnect our lives, our world.* Gabriola Island, Canada: New Society Publishers.

McKibben, B. (2006). *The end of nature.* New York: Random House.

Meacher, M. (2007). I would turn the lights out. *Ecologist, 37*(1), 22–23.

Monbiot, G. (2006). *Heat: How to stop the planet from burning.* Toronto: Doubleday Canada.

Muldoon, A. (2006). Environmental efforts: The next challenge for social work. *Critical Social Work, 7*(2). Retrieved from http://cronus.uwindsor.ca/units/socialwork/critical.nsf/982f0e5f06b5c9a285256d6e006cff78/5882c9990dfda1e185257277002bd457!OpenDocument

Naess, A. (1989). *Ecology, community, and lifestyle.* New York: Cambridge University Press.

O'Connor, T. (1995). Therapy for a dying planet. In T. Roszak, M. Gomes, & T. Kanner (Eds.), *Ecopsychology: Restoring the earth, healing the mind* (pp. 149–155). San Francisco: Sierra Club Books.

Park, K. (1996). The personal is ecological: Environmentalism of social work. *Social Work, 41*(3), 320–323.

Pyles, L. (2005). Understanding the engaged Buddhist movement: Implications for social development practice. *Critical Social Work, 6*(1). Retrieved March 19, 2007, from http://cronus.uwindsor.ca/units/socialwork/critical.nsf/8c20dad9f1c4be3a85256d6e006d1089/3e9b18c1f86ebce385256fd700634820!OpenDocument

Roszak, T., Gomes, M., & Kanner, T. (Eds.). (1995). *Ecopsychology: Restoring the earth, healing the mind.* San Francisco: Sierra Club Books.

Soine, L. (1987). Expanding the environment in social work: The case for including environmental hazards content. *Journal of Social Work Education, 23*(2), 40–46.

Surrey, J. (2005). Relational psychotherapy, relational mindfulness. In C. Germer, R. Diegal, & P. Fulton (Eds.), *Mindfulness and psychotherapy* (pp. 91–110). New York: Guilford Press.

Suzuki, D. (2006). *David Suzuki: The autobiography.* Vancouver, Canada: Greystone Books.

Thomashow, M. (1996). *Ecological identity: Becoming a reflective environmentalist.* Cambridge, MA: MIT Press.

Ungar, M. (2003). Deep ecology and the roots of resilience: The importance of setting in outdoor experience-based programming for at-risk children. *Critical Social Work, 4*(1), Retrieved March 19, 2007, from http://cronus.uwind sor.ca/units/socialwork/critical.nsf/982foe5fo6b5c9a285256d6eoo6cff78/ob cd7e76cc12b74885256fo2004f3dfi!OpenDocument

White, M. (1997). *Narratives of therapists' lives.* Adelaide, Australia: Dulwich Centre Publications.

Windle, P. (1995). The ecology of grief. In T. Roszak, M. Gomes, & T. Kanner (Eds.), *Ecopsychology: Restoring the earth, healing the mind* (pp. 136–145). San Francisco: Sierra Club Books.

Zapf, M. K. (2005). Profound connections between person and place: Exploring spirituality, location, and social work. *Critical Social Work, 6*(2), Retrieved March 19, 2007, from http://units/socialwork/critical.nsf/EditDoNotShow InTOC/62C3Co75C4133F288525701900280CFB

Contributors

Laura G. Béres, PhD, RSW, is assistant professor in the School of Social Work at King's University College at the University of Western Ontario. She also has a small private practice, where she primarily works with individuals and couples. She is influenced by postmodern thinking and incorporates narrative and feminist approaches into her direct practice, research, and teaching. She first became interested in mindfulness while working in a Catholic family service association in Toronto and completing her doctoral work. During this time she attended a Buddhist silent retreat and also was a guest at an Anglican convent during the final stages of her dissertation work. She has been incorporating approaches to mindfulness and contemplative prayer with reflective practice since that time.

Liora Birnbaum, PhD, is a certified family therapist and a teacher who uses mindfulness regularly with her clients and students. She was the vice-chairperson of the social work department in the College of Judea and Samaria, Israel, where she developed and implemented mindfulness-based projects with her students. She was the first teacher to offer a master's-level course on spirituality and social work in Israel and conducted a national survey of social work students regarding the integration of spirituality into social work education in Israel. She is interested in altered states of consciousness and researches the transformative nature of mindfulness. She publishes and presents her work internationally. Among her publications are *Connecting to Inner Guidance: Mindfulness Meditation and Transformation of Professional Self-Concept in Social Work Students* (2005), *In Search of Inner Wisdom: Guided Mindfulness Meditation in the Context of Suicide* (2005), *Adolescent Aggression and Differentiation of the Self: Guided Mindfulness Meditation in the Service of Individuation* (2005), and *The Use of Mindfulness Training to Create an "Accompanying Place"* (2007). She is on the editorial board of the *International Journal for Transpersonal Studies* and the human development domain of the *Scientific World Journal.* Currently she is in private practice in Kfar Yona, Israel.

Diana Coholic, PhD, RSW, is associate professor in Laurentian University's School of Social Work in northeastern Ontario, Canada. Her research program is currently investigating the usefulness of spiritually influenced arts-based/experiential group practice in assisting participants to develop their self-awareness and self-esteem. Her research program is funded by the Social Sciences and Humanities Research Council of Canada and the Sick Kids Foundation. She is also a practicing clinical social worker.

Miriam George, MSW, RSW, MA, is a social worker at the Centre for Addiction and Mental Health and a doctoral student at the University of Toronto's Faculty of Social Work. She practiced as a social worker in India for four years before joining CAMH seven years ago. She obtained master's degrees in social work from both Mahatma Gandhi University in India and the University of Toronto. She also completed an MA in theory and policy studies at the University of Toronto, with a research focus on continuing professional education for health care professionals. She practices social work from an anti-oppressive framework. She has extensive experience and a specific interest in working with mentally ill, immigrant, and refugee populations. Her research interests include health education, health promotion, immigration and refugees, postcolonialism, mental health, and women's issues. Her doctoral research will focus on the impact of settlement experiences on refugee women's trauma, from the perspective of a postcolonial epistemology that seeks to elevate marginalized voices through an analysis of power, place, and resistance.

John R. Graham, PhD, RSW, is Murray Fraser Professor of Community Economic Development in the Faculty of Social Work, University of Calgary, Canada. The author of over fifty journal articles and forty book chapters, and the holder of over $1.1 million in research funds, Professor Graham has worked on various mindfulness-related social work research projects for fifteen years. This includes publications on the religious origins of Canadian social work, and the significance of traditional healing and other ways of knowing to Bedouin Arab indigenous communities in the Middle East. His latest book, *Helping Professional Practice with Indigenous Peoples: The Bedouin-Arab Case,* coauthored with Alean Al-Krenawi, was released in 2007. A co-founding member of the Canadian Society for Spirituality and Social Work, Professor Graham was one of two keynote speakers at the First North American Conference on Spirituality and Social Work (2006), a joint international conference of the Canadian Society for Spirituality and Social Work and the Society for Spirituality and Social Work.

Susan M. Graham, MEd, is a doctoral student at the Faculty of Education, University of Calgary, Canada. She has over twenty years' experience teaching at the primary, secondary, and postsecondary levels; is currently an educational administrator with the Calgary Board of Education; and is working on a dissertation on subjective well-being and educational leadership.

Ellen Katz, MSW, has a BA in anthropology from McGill University and an MSW from the University of Toronto and is currently a PhD student at the University of Toronto, where she studies the ability of mindfulness meditation to enhance affect regulation in families seen in family therapy. Prior to becoming a social worker, she studied childbirth education, taught childbirth education classes for ten years, and also wrote health information for distribution to the non-Western world. She has been practicing social work for the last fifteen years in both children's mental health and hospital settings. Currently she teaches and supervises family therapy and carries her own caseload of families at a children's mental health center in Toronto, where she coordinates social work education. She is also adjunct professor at the Faculty of Social Work, University of Toronto. She maintains her own practice of meditation in the Zen tradition at the Toronto Zen Centre.

Christine Kessen, DSW, LCSW, is a licensed clinical social worker with over twenty years of social work practice experience in health, mental health, and school settings. She has been a practitioner and teacher of meditation practices for the past fifteen years and currently facilitates a weekly meditation group. As associate professor of social work at Marywood University in Scranton, Pennsylvania, Professor Kessen teaches graduate social work courses in practice, ethics, psychopathology, and spirituality. She has presented widely at professional conferences on topics related to ethics, meditation, and social work practice. Professor Kessen is the author of a chapter in *Decision Cases for Christians in Social Work,* edited by Terry A. Wolfer, entitled "Sister's Keeper," which details a case of a social worker's conflict between faith and ethics in social work practice. She is a member of the provisional board of the Society for Spirituality and Social Work.

Julie LeBreton, BSW, RSW, is a clinical social worker practicing in the area of sexual assault. She is also a research assistant on Diana Coholic's research team.

Tracy London, JD, MSW, is an environmental activist with Markets Initiative, and a member of the Business and Human Rights Steering Committee of Amnesty International Canada (English Speaking). She is a doctoral student at the University of British Columbia School of Social Work and Family Studies, where she examines activist strategies to realize corporate accountability for international human rights and environmental norms. She received her JD and MSW from the University of Toronto.

Mishka Lysack, PhD, is a family therapist and a certified clinical supervisor and educator in family therapy. He teaches in the areas of family therapy, individual and group counseling, and clinical social work practice. Professor Lysack developed a two-year post-master's certificate program in family therapy with the University of Calgary and the Calgary Family Therapy Centre. Professor Lysack has published his work in peer-reviewed journals such as the *Journal of Systemic Therapies,* the *Canadian Social Work Review,* the *Canadian Journal of Counselling,* and *Sciences pastorale/Pastoral Science.* His clinical work with multi-stressed youths and their families in a maximum-security prison has been profiled in a book by David Denborough, *Beyond the Prison: Gathering Dreams of Freedom* (1996). He has also published his research on therapy with high-risk youths in publications such as *Forum on Corrections Research, Psychologica,* and *Omni Newsletter.* Professor Lysack is a clinical member and approved supervisor of the American Association for Marriage and Family Therapy, and a registered marriage/family therapist on the registry of MFTs in Canada. He has been also designated a clinical teaching member of the American Academy of Family Therapy. He has presented his clinical work internationally in Canada, England, Australia, and Finland.

David A. Paré, PhD, is a psychologist and counselor educator at the University of Ottawa. For the past fifteen years his work has focused on the "postmodern turn" in family therapy and psychotherapy. In addition to writing and presenting widely on that topic, he offers training and supervision to practitioners interested in developing collaborative therapeutic practices. He is currently conducting research on the formation of therapist communities of practice organized around teamwork. For many years, Professor Paré has practiced Vipassana meditation.

Richard Potter, MSW, has taught social work at Dana College in Nebraska for twenty-two years. He served as social work program director from 2001 until 2005. He has also practiced social work in child welfare and mental health settings since 1967. From 2001 to 2003, he served as president of the Nebraska chapter of the National Association of Social Workers. He has been a lifelong student of religion and spirituality. Having studied most deeply within a universalist form of Sufism, he has experienced the depth of the exploration of a specific spiritual path and the breadth of working with spiritual practices from many traditions. He has authored two books on spirituality for the general public: *Authentic Spirituality: The Direct Path to Consciousness* (2004) and *Spiritual Development for Beginners* (with Jan Potter, 2006). In addition to teaching at Dana College, he and his wife, Jan, travel and conduct workshops on spirituality and spirituality and social work.

Brian Richardson, MEd, works as a counselor and consultant. His academic interests focus on the philosophy of psychology, particularly existentialism and Eastern approaches to the field. His work on flow theory and mindfulness form a significant part of this pursuit.

Margarita Tarragona, PhD, is a therapist and teacher in Mexico City. She is a co-founder of Grupo Campos Elíseos and is on the faculty of the Universidad Iberoamericana and ILEF in Mexico City and of the Houston Galveston Institute in Texas. In her practice, she is especially interested in collaborative and narrative therapies, the therapeutic use of writing, and the implications of positive psychology for therapy and consultation. Her research interests include clients' and therapists' experiences of therapeutic processes and the development of psychotherapists.

Sarah Todd, EdD, is assistant professor in the School of Social Work at Carleton University. Her research and teaching interests are community development, sexuality, spirituality, and pedagogy. She teaches at both the graduate and undergraduate levels in the areas of sexuality, HIV/AIDS, counseling skills, and community practice. She is currently on the executive editorial board of *Studies in Political Economy* and the board of Somerset West Community Health Centre, where she is involved in the advocacy committee. Professor Todd has a book co-edited with Bill Lee entitled *A Casebook of Community Practice: Problems and Strategies* (2006) and has recently published articles and chapters on domestic violence, anti-oppressive pedagogy, feminist community organizing, spirituality and community practice, and sexual and gender diversity. Most recently, she has become involved in a project in the Dominican Republic involving the development of a school of social work by a team of Canadians at the Autonomous University of Santo Domingo.

Index

Page numbers followed by *n* refer to notes.